Thomas Leslie Papillon

Terence Claims

P. Terentii Afri Comoediae

Thomas Leslie Papillon

Terence Claims
P. Terentii Afri Comoediae

ISBN/EAN: 9783742848963

Manufactured in Europe, USA, Canada, Australia, Japa

Cover: Foto ©Thomas Meinert / pixelio.de

Manufactured and distributed by brebook publishing software
(www.brebook.com)

Thomas Leslie Papillon

Terence Claims

CATENA CLASSICORUM

EDITED BY

THE REV.

ARTHUR HOLMES M.A.

FELLOW OF CLARE COLLEGE CAMBRIDGE AND LATE FELLOW OF ST JOHN'S
PREACHER AT THE CHAPEL ROYAL WHITEHALL

AND

THE REV.

CHARLES BIGG M.A.

LATE SENIOR STUDENT AND TUTOR OF CHRIST CHURCH OXFORD
SECOND CLASSICAL MASTER OF CHELTENHAM COLLEGE

RIVINGTONS

London ...   .   *Waterloo Place*

Oxford ...   .   *High Street*

Cambridge   ...   .   *Trinity Street*

P. TERENTII AFRI
COMOEDIAE

EDITED BY

T. L. PAPILLON M.A.
FELLOW OF NEW COLLEGE, OXFORD, AND LATE FELLOW OF MERTON

ANDRIA
EUNUCHUS

RIVINGTONS
London, Oxford, and Cambridge
1870

Cambridge:

PRINTED BY C. J. CLAY, M.A.

AT THE UNIVERSITY PRESS.

GEORGIO GRANVILLE BRADLEY

COLLEGII MARLBURIENSIS PRAESIDI

PRIMITIAS DEDICO

DISCIPULUS MAGISTRO

AMICO AMICUS.

PREFACE.

THE present edition of Terence claims no merit of critical research or independent collation of MSS. ; its aim being to assist the ordinary students in the higher forms of schools and at the Universities in the study of an author whose writings offer so admirable a model of Latinity. One great want, no doubt, in Terentian criticism is a thoroughly good "apparatus criticus:" a want which but few English scholars are qualified to supply, and which even the learning and industry of Germany has not fully met; Fleckeisen's larger edition, promised in 1857, not having yet appeared.

The text followed is mainly that of Zeune (1774; reproduced by Giles, London 1837). This edition contains most of what is useful in early commentators, especially Aelius Donatus (4th century), whose pithy remarks often throw more light than pages of more diffuse commentary, and are best conveyed by simple quotation. Bentley's edition (1726), as the first attempt at methodical examination of the text, was an era

in Terentian criticism and a valuable contribution to
philology, though marked by all that great scholar's
love of arbitrary emendation and many strange vagaries
of scholarship. He errs, too, in many cases by at-
taching too much weight to later MSS. in preference
to the Codex Bembinus (now in the Vatican Library)
which is our only trustworthy guide, all other MSS.
representing the text as settled by the grammarian
Calliopius (e. g. Codex Ambrosianus, C. Vaticanus,
C. Basilicanus, all of 9th century). The best critical
edition of late years is that of Fleckeisen, in the
Teubner series.

The commentaries by which the present editor has
profited are (besides those of Donatus and others
quoted in Zeunc's edition) Stallbaum's (1830), Parry's
(in the "Bibliotheca Classica"), and latterly Wagner's
(1869). The two latter of these have dealt instruc-
tively with the metres and prosody of Terence; a difficult but necessary portion of the subject, which the
present editor is compelled to defer till the completion
of his work. His obligations to them are, it is hoped,
sufficiently acknowledged in the course of the Introduction and Notes. He has endeavoured also, by
illustration and quotation from those ancient writers
whose works have been best edited in modern times
to direct the student to the most abundant fountains
of scholarship. If, for example, references to Lucretius and Vergil help to keep the student of Terence
familiar with such storehouses of Latin scholarship as

Lachmann's or Munro's *Lucretius*, Forbiger's or Conington's *Vergil*, more real good will be done than by the most elaborate explanation of particular passages. Readers of the following pages should keep such commentaries at their side and turn to them at every reference to the authors in question.

The grammars to which reference has been made are Madvig's Latin Grammar and Greek Syntax, as in other editions of this Series. Donaldson's *Varronianus* and *New Cratylus* are referred to for the same reason. Roby's smaller Latin Grammar (a larger one is in progress) and Curtius' Greek Grammar (translated into English and published as *The Student's Greek Grammar*) will be found serviceable : while Farrar's *Greek Syntax* is a useful and suggestive compilation.

Besides the ordinary numbering of lines in each scene, there will be found (in brackets) a continuous numbering from beginning to end of each play. This is often employed by editors of other books in their references to Terence.

The editor desires to express his best thanks to the Reverend John Wordsworth, Fellow and Tutor of Brasenose College, for assistance rendered in correction for the press, and many valuable suggestions.

INTRODUCTION.

I. *Life and Writings of Terence.*

OF the personal history of Terence but little is known, and that on the doubtful authority of a *Vita Terentii* ascribed to Suetonius: according to which he was in his 35th year (nondum quintum atque tricesimum[1] egressus annum) at the performance of his last play (*Adelphi*) in B.C. 160. His *cognomen* Afer bears out the common story that he was brought from Africa to Rome, if not actually of Carthaginian blood[2]. At Rome he became the slave of P. Terentius Lucanus, a senator, who had him well educated and at last gave him his freedom : when according to custom he assumed his patron's *nomen* Terentius. He at once devoted himself to the only literary occupation of that time, the reproduction in Latin of the works of Greek authors. His first piece (*Andria*) was referred by the curule aediles to Caecilius Statius, one of the most popular play-wrights at Rome ; to whom, as the story goes, Terence recited the opening scene and was at once welcomed as a poet. This interview, if historically true, must have taken place B.C. 168[3], two years before the production of the play. Its success introduced him to the most intellectual society of Rome, especially that literary circle which gathered round Scipio Aemilianus, comprising such men as C. Laelius (consul 140), Sp. Mummius (brother of the destroyer of Corinth), Lucilius the satirist, Polybius the historian, and Panaetius the philosopher. His intimacy with these men provoked reports that he was assisted by them in the composition of his plays; or further, that they were in fact the real authors, who made him their playmate and butt and left him to starve.

In the years 166—160 he produced the six extant plays:

---

[1] The last critical research would read *vicesimum;* this would place Terence's birth 10 years later.

[2] His physical characteristics, as described to us, are not those of the Punic race. See *Dict. Biogr.* "Terentius."

[3] See Introduction to *Andria*, page 1.

Andria, 166; *Hecyra*, 165; *Heauton timorumenos*, 163; *Eunuchus, Phormio*, 161; *Adelphi*, 160. These are probably all that were put upon the stage: but we are told that while residing and travelling in Greece he translated 108 comedies of Menander[1].

The time and place of his death were variously reported, the general rumour being that he died of grief for the loss at sea of his translations from Menander. Whatever be the truth of this or other stories of his death, it seems certain that he left Rome after the production of the *Adelphi* and never returned. His death is generally assigned to the year 159 B.C.; by some to the year following.

The story of his poverty and the assistance rendered by his friends in composition was believed by Cicero (*Att.* VII. 3) and is noticed by Quinctilian (*Inst. Or.* X. 1): while Nepos (*Frag. Incert.* 6) ascribes the *Heautontimorumenos* to Laelius. Terence's poverty seems unlikely, if we are to believe that he travelled for some time in Greece: and the tone of his Prologues is sufficiently independent. As to the assistance he is said to have received, we may perhaps believe it with certain limitations. Terence himself does not deny it *in toto*, but seems even to take pride in it (*Adelphi*, Prol. 15—21)[2]: and a foreigner and freedman might well find difficulties of idiom, for which he might avail himself of the help of friends, without discredit to himself. From the purity of his idiom we should in any case infer a close intimacy with the best society of Rome. There is too *a priori* probability that Terence would be the object of calumny. Roman prejudices were always strong against freedmen and foreigners; even Horace in the Augustan period was exposed to taunts on this score[3]: and if we consider the literary position of Terence as the representative at a period of transition of an innovating party, we shall

[1] This number however seems open to doubt. Ritschl ingeniously suggests that CVIII is only a dittography of CUM—that is a mistaken repetition of a word by the scribe.
[2] Suetonius (or whoever was the author of the *Vita Terentii* before referred to) says on this; "Videtur se levius defendisse, quia sciebat Laelio et Scipioni non ingratam esse hanc opinionem." *Vit. Ter.* ch. II.
[3] Hor. *Sat.* I. vi. 46, "Quem rodunt omnes libertino patre natum."

see how likely it was that he should be obnoxious to the more conservative spirit of those who followed Cato and the Fabii.

The period at which he wrote was a period of transition and reaction in literature. An extended study of the masterpieces of Greek literature had produced in the minds of the educated 'literati' of Rome a keener appreciation for beauty and elegance of style and a proportionate dissatisfaction with the literary efforts of the previous age. The homely Roman savour of the *Plautini sales* and the clumsy attempts of earlier dramatists to give a Roman colouring to their Greek models jarred upon more refined ears. Men could not help contrasting with the perfection of Greek art the very slight artistic merits of their own new-born literature. The attempt to create a national Roman literature seemed to them hopeless: and as, on their view, the object of literature was the cultivation of taste and refinement in thought and language, that object seemed more likely to be attained by the mere copying and reproducing Greek models of undoubted taste and beauty, than by attempts at creating a national literature to which such qualities had hitherto been wanting. Reproduction therefore, not creation, was to be the aim of Roman literature; imitation rather than originality the test of literary merit.

The centre from which these doctrines proceeded was the famous "Scipionic circle," with which as we have seen Terence was intimately connected: a connection to which are due the features that gave Terence his peculiar position in Roman literature, distinguishing him from the earlier dramatists, e.g. from Plautus. Plautus had aimed at giving a Roman colouring to Greek models, and by distinctively Roman allusions and broad, often coarse humour, had attracted the masses: Terence wrote rather for the educated few, for so many at least as could appreciate purity of language and artistic skill. He was content with the praise of a successful copyist; and yet in process of his work tried to impart to his own language something of the purity and elegance of Greek. He was thus the representative of a new school of literature and of a reactionary party, at a time when not only

literature but social life and manners and religious faith were
being subjected to the newly discovered influences of Greek
thought and feeling; when, in the happy phrase of Horace,
the conquered country was beginning the conquest of her con-
queror. It is easy therefore to understand how patriots and
conservatives of the school of Cato and the Fabii, jealous
for the old Roman manners and hating innovation, would
disapprove of one who made deliberate professions of Grae-
cism in the department of literature. They desired no refinement in language any more than in manners; and to
them Terence and his friends must have appeared as re-
presentatives of all the abominations of reform.

The position of Terence in the history of Roman literature
and the contrast in which he stands to Plautus are admirably
treated by Mommsen [*Hist. of Rome*, Book IV. ch. xiii; see
also earlier chapters on Literature and Art]. To this and the
articles "Plautus" and "Terentius" in Smith's *Dictionary of
Biography* the student is referred for the details upon which
the foregoing remarks are based.

II. *Style and Literary merits of Terence.*

To take first the criticisms of ancient writers:

CICERO (*De Opt. Gen. Orat.* I. 3) states that Terence
differs 'genere' from Attius, and praises him as an interpreter of
Menander, "Quicquid come loquens atque omnia dulcia dicens."

HORACE (*Epp.* II. i. 59) praises his artistic skill:

"Dicitur...vincere Caecilius gravitate, Terentius *arte.*"

OVID (*Trist.* II. 357) praises his festive humour:

"Nec liber indicium est animi, sed honesta voluptas,
    Plurima mulcendis auribus apta ferens.
Accius esset atrox: conviva Terentius esset:
    Essent pugnaces, qui fera bella canunt."

QUINCTILIAN (*Inst. Or.* X. 1) depreciates Roman comedy generally: "In comoedia maxime claudicamus." Terence, he thinks,
was wrong in deserting the senarian measure of his originals;

"Terentii scripta...quae tamen sunt in hoc genere elegantissima et plus adhuc habitura gratiae si inter versus trimetros stetissent."

SERVIUS the commentator on Vergil (A.D. 400) says in a note to *Aen.* I. 414, "Sciendum est Terentium propter solam proprietatem (apposite neatness of language) omnibus comicis esse praepositum."

CAESAR's famous epigram is the best summary of ancient criticism upon Terence:

"Tu quoque tu in summis, O dimidiate Menander,
Poneris et merito, puri sermonis amator ;
Lenibus atque utinam scriptis adjuncta foret vis
Comica, ut aequato virtus polleret honore
Cum Graecis, neque in hac despectus parte jaceres.
Unum hoc maceror et doleo tibi deesse, Terenti."

Ancient critics of Terence we see were struck by (1) the elegance and grace of his language, (2) a want of "vis comica." On the first point their judgment has received the sanction of later times: but many have asked what is meant by the want of "vis comica" ascribed to Terence. "Comic power" in one sense will hardly be denied to him by those who appreciate refined and delicate humour, or artistic skill in working out comic incidents and play of character. But the "vis comica" present to the mind of his Roman critics is probably that which distinguishes Plautus, the "Plautini sales," whose homely wit indicates a spring of genuine comic humour, coarser perhaps than that of Terence but more original and more popular. This kind of "vis comica" Terence had not. He represents a reaction against the broad humour and uncouth style of earlier dramatists and professedly departs from their standard : but in the artistic skill and delicate humour, which all recognise in him, rests a true "vis comica ;" the spirit not of broad farce but of the more polished comedy of life and manners, which Terence introduced upon the Roman stage.

If from style we turn to matter, there is less to be said. His plots are marked by tiresome uniformity; in each play the same stock characters play out the same stock rôles of immoral intrigue and unfilial deceit which in the end are triumphant: so that however elegant the language, however artistic the by-play of character, the story has but little interest or profit. The cause of these defects lies in the source from which Terence drew, the literature of the New Attic Comedy; which reflected the degeneracy of a society whose political, social, religious and domestic life had alike become demoralised and decayed. This literature, repugnant in tone to Roman ideas, was yet the only available fountain of inspiration for a Roman dramatist. He must imitate Greek models: he must reproduce them as nearly as possible. But he could not reproduce the works of the Old Comedy, with its personal and political allusions. The plays of Aristophanes, if directly translated, would have no meaning to Roman ears; and a similar treatment of contemporary politics and persons would have incurred the censure of the Roman authorities, already suspicious of dramatic exhibitions and disinclined to show too much favour to dramatic writers. The police regulations of Rome no doubt contributed indirectly to keeping Roman drama in the groove along which it had first started, as a simple reproduction of Greek manners, Greek characters, Greek scenery, dress and names. This being the case, Roman dramatists naturally imitated those Greek dramas which could most easily be produced on a Roman stage, those which had no political or personal interest, but were, so to speak, cosmopolitan, the comedies of Menander and his school. Unfortunately the life and manners they portrayed were those of a depraved society; and Roman comedy at its outset incurred the stigma of immorality, and was looked upon with suspicion by all who prided themselves upon the simplicity of old Roman manners. Nor can we fairly say that this suspicion was undeserved. To us far more than to Romans of the 2nd century B. C. the morality of the extant remains of Latin Comedy must appear simply objectionable: and they can only have a literary and historical value. But to the student of a great language and a great literature Terence must always have charms. His morality is that of an age long past: his language is a κτῆμα ἐς ἀεί, a treasure for all time.

INTRODUCTION TO THE ANDRIA.

THE original title of this play "*Andria Terentii*" bears out the received opinion that it was the first exhibited by Terence: if by an author already known, "Terentii Andria" would have been the title. It was produced B.C. 166, and if we accept the story of its previous recitation to Caecilius who died B.C. 168, must have circulated in MS. for at least two years previous to its exhibition: during which period it was subject to the adverse criticism of some literary men, jealous perhaps of the promise of the young poet, and among them Lavinius, the '*malevolus vetus poeta*' alluded to in the Prologue (cf. also the Prologues to the "Heautontimorumenos" and "Phormio"), which we may conclude was written, or at any rate retouched, shortly before exhibition.

The plot turns upon the previous history of Glycerium, the "Andrian." Chremes, an Athenian citizen, when sailing for Asia, left his daughter Pasibula with his brother Phania, who, following Chremes in order to escape a war, was shipwrecked with Pasibula upon the island of Andros, where he became the client of an Andrian citizen. This man, upon Phania's death, adopted Pasibula, changing her name to Glycerium, and brought her up with his daughter Chrysis: and on his death the two girls removed to Athens, where Chrysis took up the profession of an ἑταίρα, or courtezan. Among those who frequented her house, Pamphilus the son of Simo fell in love with Glycerium, and promised her marriage; and Chrysis on her death-bed commended Glycerium to his charge. Simo meanwhile had betrothed his son, without the latter's knowledge, to Philumena, the second daughter of Chremes, born since the loss of Pasibula. His first suspicion of opposition on his son's part was roused by observing at Chrysis' funeral the behaviour of Pamphilus to her young sister : while Chremes, learning the whole story, broke off the match.

At this point begins the action of the play. Simo announces to Pamphilus that he must marry Philumena at once, hoping that if his son's consent can be extorted, Chremes may be reconciled, and the match take place after all. Pamphilus, at his wits' end, is met by Mysis, Glycerium's servant, who revives his old affections. Davus meantime ferrets out the whole matter, and advises Pamphilus to humour his father by pretending consent, while keeping up the suspicions of Chremes by his intimacy with Glycerium. Meanwhile Charinus a friend of Pamphilus, in love with Philumena, hears with dismay that she is to be married to Pamphilus and urges him to put off the marriage. While matters are in this state Glycerium gives birth to a son. Simo hears of it, but is encouraged by Davus to believe it an artifice to prevent Pamphilus' marriage, to which he extracts Chremes' reluctant consent. Charinus is now angry at the supposed treachery of Pamphilus : while Davus is abused by Pamphilus for the advice which has turned out so ill, and to get himself out of the scrape, lays the child before Simo's door and contrives that Simo shall hear its history from Mysis. This causes a fresh quarrel between Chremes and Simo : at which juncture arrives Crito, a native of Andros, and next of kin to Chrysis, who clears up Glycerium's history. She is recognized as Chremes' daughter, and all ends happily.

The 'Andria' has been imitated by Baron the celebrated French actor in his 'Andrienne;' and by Sir Richard Steele in his 'Conscious Lovers.' It has also suggested certain scenes in Moore's 'Foundling.'

P. TERENTII ANDRIA

FABULAE INTERLOCUTORES.

SIMO, senex.
SOSIA, libertus.
DAVUS, servus.
MYSIS, ancilla.
PAMPHILUS, adolescens.
CHARINUS, adolescens.
BYRRIA, servus.
LESBIA, obstetrix.
GLYCERIUM, adolescentula.
CHREMES, senex.
CRITO, hospes.
DROMO, lorarius.

Acta ludis Megalensib. M. Fulvio et M' Glabrione Aedilib. curulib. Ege-
runt L. Ambivius Turpio et L. Atilius Praenestinus. Modos fecit
Flaccus Claudi F. Tibiis Parib. Dextris et Sinistris. Et est tota
Graeca. Edita M. Marcello Cn. Sulpicio Coss.

Ludi Megalenses] or Megalesia, in honour of Cybele (μεγάλη θεός), were held in April. The first ludi scenici at Rome were introduced at this festival (see *Dict. Ant.* "Megalesia"). Cicero (*De Har. Resp.*) calls them *maxime casti, sollemnes, religiosi.* In Juvenal's time the chariot races were the principal feature; cf. *Sat.* XI. 193 sqq.

Egerunt] "Managers and Actors, L. Ambivius Turpio and L. Atilius Praenestinus." They contracted with the Aediles for the performance of the play; the Aediles having settled in the first instance with the poet. Ambivius Turpio is mentioned by Cicero (*Sen.* 14), and in the dialogue *De Oratoribus* ascribed to Tacitus (ch. 20), as a firstrate actor in connection with Roscius.

Modos fecit] "Conductor, Flaccus." He arranged the musical accompaniment, so that each part of the dialogue should have proper emphasis. Parry quotes Cicero, *De Or.* III. 26.

Tibiis Paribus Dextris et Sinistris] *Tibia dextra* was the higher or treble note, *sinistra* the lower or bass. Herodotus calls them male and female. The former was used to begin (*incentiva*); the latter afterwards as an accompaniment (*succentiva*). *Paribus*, in the same mode, Dorian, Lydian, or Phrygian: cf. *Dict. Ant.* "Musica," "Tibia."

Tota Graeca] i. e. a *Comoedia Palliata*, in which the characters and scene were Greek. See *Dict. Ant.* "Comoedia."

PROLOGUS.

POETA quum primum animum ad scribendum adpulit,
id sibi negoti credidit solum dari,
populo ut placerent, quas fecisset fabulas:
verum aliter evenire multo intellegit.
Nam in prologis scribundis operam abutitur,   5
non qui argumentum narret, sed qui malevoli
veteris poetae maledictis respondeat.
Nunc, quam rem vitio dent, quaeso animum advortite.
Menander fecit Andriam et Perinthiam.
Qui utramvis recte norit, ambas noverit.   10
Non ita dissimili sunt argumento, sed tamen

3 quas...fabulas] This absorption of a subst. into the relative proposition by which it is defined is one of the frequent instances of attraction in Latin: v. Madvig, *Gr.* 319.

fecisset] does not imply that they had been already written at the time indicated by *credidit*: it = "any that he might hereafter have written" (or "write"), and answers to the fut. perf. following a primary tense. *Quas fecerit* after a pres. tense becomes, according to Latin usage, *quas fecisset* after a past tense : v. Madvig, *Gr.* 379.

5 operam abutitur] "Expends all his labour."

6 qui] not for *ut*, or *quippe qui*, as some explain, but the "ablativus modi" = *quo* with a comparative adj. or adv., and used with the subjunctive mood to express a purpose. In Greek this might be expressed by ὅπως in fut. ind.; but in Latin

the use of the subjunctive mood (expressing the supposition or conception of a fact as opposed to the assertion of it) is strictly adhered to. "Design" is the expression of a fact or action as intended; "wish" of a fact as desired, &c. [Roby's *Gr.* 232].

8 vitio dent] The explanation of this and similar constructions (*laudi, crimini, dare*, &c.) must be sought in the primitive function of the dative case, viz. *place at which*, and the widest meaning of *dare* = to present, exhibit, place. It means literally "to place or set down at (in the category of) fault." Cf. *appone lucro*, Hor.

11 argumento] must be pronounced as trisyll. *arg'mento*, a licence quite conceivable in rapid conversation; and the elision of a long syllable is paralleled by *quaestor* from *quaesitor*, *mala* from *maxilla*; cf. French "serment" from *sacra-*

dissimili oratione sunt factae ac stilo.

Quae convenere, in Andriam ex Perinthia hic
fatetur transtulisse, atque usum pro suis.

Id isti vituperant factum, atque in eo disputant,   15
contaminari non decere fabulas.

Faciunt nae intellegendo, ut nihil intellegant:
qui quum hunc accusant, Naevium, Plautum, Ennium
accusant, quos hic noster auctores habet:

quorum aemulari exoptat negligentiam   20
potius, quam istorum obscuram diligentiam.

Dehinc, ut quiescant porro, moneo, et desinant
maledicere, malefacta ne noscant sua.

Favete, adeste aequo animo, et rem cognoscite,
ut pernoscatis, ecquid spei sit reliqüum,   25
posthac quas faciet de integro comoedias,
spectandae an exigendae sint vobis prius.

---

mentum. This is more satisfactory than omitting *sunt,* or (with Bentley) reading *et tamen.*

12 **oratione ao stilo**] "Style of thought and diction." Donatus, "*Oratio*" *in sensu est,* "*stilus*" *in verbis.* Aristotle's διάνοια and λέξις might be quoted as a parallel distinction (*Poet.* VI.).

16 **contaminari**] (*con-tag-imen, contămen*) = "mingle together." So *Heaut. Prol.* 17; *Eun.* III. 5. 4; Lucr. III. 883, Sensuque suo *contaminat* astans, "impregnates."

17 **nae**] Bentley reads *ně* (interrogative); but *nae* is often written *ně;* cf. *ναί, νή.* Others take *nā = non*

(or rather *ne* is the original negative from which *non* is derived, *ne unum:* v. Andrews, *Dict.* s.v.).

18 **N. P. E.**] Respecting the chronological order of these poets, v. *Dict. Biog.* Art. "Plautus."

19 **auctores**] "Models:" Hor. *Sat.* I. 4. 122.

25 **reliqüum**] or *relicuum,* always four syllables in Lucr. and older writers. The first syllable only long by metrical necessity; for it is short where metre admits, and was never lengthened after the word became trisyllabic. See Lachmann, *ad Lucr.* V. 679.

ACTUS I. SCENA I.

SIMO. SOSIA.

SI. Vos istaec intro auferte : abite.—Sosia,
adesdum : paucis te volo. So. Dictum puta :
nempe ut curentur recte haec. SI. Immo aliud. So. Quid
      est,   (30)
quod tibi mea ars efficere hoc possit amplius?
SI. Nihil istac opus est arte ad hanc rem, quam paro ;   5
sed iis, quas semper in te intellexi sitas,
fide et taciturnitate. So. Exspecto, quid velis.
SI. Ego postquam te emi, a parvulo ut semper tibi
apud me iusta et clemens fuerit servitus,

Sc. I.] The art of this scene has been much praised, especially by Cicero, *De Or.* II. 80. It unfolds the argument of the play in such a manner that it appears to be part of the action; and there is no employment of a *deus ex machina*, no bald piece of narration in the form of a prologue, to make the audience comprehend the "situation" at the point where the real action begins, viz. the attempt of Simo to ascertain the feelings of his son Pamphilus and to bring about the match with Philumena, which her father, Chremes, had just broken off on hearing of the affair with Glycerium. Cicero also praises the narrative of Simo, especially the description of Chrysis' funeral, vv. 80—109: "Mores adolescentis ipsius et servilis perconta-tio, mors Chrysidis, vultus et forma et lamentatio sororis, reliqua pervarie iucundeque narrantur," &c. (*De Or.* II. 80, 327). Diderot, in his *Essai sur la Poesie Dramatique*, praises the narrations of Terence as "a pure and transparent stream flowing evenly and taking neither swiftness nor noise but that which it derives from its course and the ground over which it runs...When he generalizes a maxim, it is in so simple and popular a manner, that you believe it to be a common proverb: nothing is there but what belongs to the subject."

2 **paucis**] Supply *colloqui verbis*.

3 **haec**] Sosia's cooking utensils ; the others having withdrawn with theirs (*istaec*).

9 **iusta**] "moderate" or "reasonable."

clemens] We need not suppose a "transfer of the idea of 'clemency' from the imposer of service to the service itself." This view regards only the ordinary classical meaning of the word, whereas its original application seems to have been to

scis. Feci, ex servo ut esses libertus mihi,   10
propterea quod servibas liberaliter.
Quod habui summum pretium, persolvi tibi.
So. In memoria habeo. Si. Haud muto factum. So. Gaudeo,
si tibi quid feci aut facio quod placeat, Simo,   (41)
et id gratum fuisse advorsum te habeo gratiam.   15
Sed hoc mihi molestumst: nam istaec commemoratio
quasi exprobratio est immemoris benefici.
Quin tu uno verbo dic, quid est, quod me velis.
Si. Ita faciam. Hoc primum in hac re praedico tibi:
quas credis esse has, non sunt verae nuptiae.   20
So. Cur simulas igitur? Si. Rem omnem a principio audies:
eo pacto et gnati vitam et consilium meum
cognosces, et quid facere in hac re te velim.   (50)
Nam is postquam excessit ex ephebis, Sosia,
liberius vivendi fuit potestas;—nam antea   25

the quiet, placid state of the wind
or air (*clementi flamine pulsae*, Catullus); so here = "mild," "easy."
   10] ἐγώ σ᾽ ἔθηκα δοῦλον ὄντ᾽ ἐλεύ-
θερον, Menander.
   11 **liberaliter**] "So as to deserve
freedom." So *illiberalis*, Ad. V. 5. 5.
   13 **Haud muto factum**] "I don't
wish it changed." Cf. *nil mutat
tragici comis Lucilius Acci?* Hor.
Donatus and the older edd. retain
this arrangement. Bentley altered
it to *Haud muto*. So, *factum Gaudeo*, regarding *muto* as absolute,
=repent. Cf. Plaut. *Rud.* III. 6.
27; V. 4. 46, of this play; where,
however, the active force is equally
admissible. *Muto* absol. has two
meanings: (a) = "mutari;" *quantum
mores mutaverint*, Livy XXXIX. 51;
(b) in late writers = "to differ;"
*mutare a Menandro Caecilius visus
est*, Gellius.
   17] Parry quotes in illustration
of this sentiment from Dem. *Cor.
81, and Cicero, *de Am.* 19.
   18 **Quin...dic**] "Why don't you

say." This use of *quin* illustrates
the growth of familiar expressions
without regard to their original construction. *Quin* (*qui non*) *agis?* conveyed a polite command: hence
quin becomes an emphatic particle,
used with an imperative mood, *quin
age!* then without such connection.
= "moreover."
   quid est] The direct form of the
question is retained.
   24 **postquam excessit**] "After he
had passed." Note the tendency of
Latin writers always to employ the
perfect tense with *postquam*, even
where, as here, the sense would
seem to require a pluperfect.
   excessit ex ephebis]=ἐξῆλθεν
ἐξ ἐφηβῶν. A Greek expression
which has really no meaning in
Latin. ἔφηβοι at Athens were the
youths from 18 to 20 employed as
περίπολοι, on home service.
   25 **vivendi**] is dissyllabic. Bentley to avoid this read *libera*,
which alters the meaning. Cf.
Eun. V. 8. 1.

qui scire posses, aut ingenium noscere,
dum aetas, metus, magister prohibebant? So. Ita est.—
SI. Quod plerique omnes faciunt adulescentuli,
ut animum ad aliquod studium adiungant, aut equos
alere, aut canes ad venandum, aut ad philosophos: 30
horum ille nihil egregie praeter cetera
studebat; et tamen omnia haec mediocriter.
Gaudebam. So. Non iniuria: nam id arbitror   (60)
adprime in vita esse utile, ut ne quid nimis.
SI. Sic vita erat: facile omnes perferre ac pati: 35
cum quibus erat cunque una, iis sese dedere:
eorum obsequi studiis: advorsus nemini:
numquam praeponens se illis: ita facillume
sine invidia laudem invenias, et amicos pares.
So. Sapienter vitam instituit: namque hoc tempore   40
obsequium amicos, veritas odium parit.
SI. Interea mulier quaedam abhinc triennium
ex Andro commigravit huc viciniae,   (70)

---

30 **alere equos**] in apposition to *studium*. Such apposition of the infinitive mood to a substantive is not common; the descriptive genitive of the gerund is more usual. See Madvig, *L. Gr.* 286 b, obs.

ad philosophos] Another Greek allusion applicable to Athens, but not to Rome.

33 **Gaudebam**] "I began to feel happy."

iniuria] is of course ablative.

34 **adprime**] A curious formation from the adverbial expression *ad prima*, "in the highest degree." Virg. *G.* II. 134 (where some MSS. read *apprimĕ*), cf. *ad plenum.* So *comprime* and even an adj. *apprimus* (probably a later formation than the adverb), and from *cum maximis*, *cum maxime.* On the other hand *imprimis* preserves its unmutilated form.

ne quid nimis] may be as it were one word = the μηδὲν ἄγαν of Greek philosophy, so that *ne* has no part in the construction. But *ut...ne* is employed instead of the simple *ne*, *ut* signifying the general purpose, *ne* the negation (v. Madvig, *Gr.* 456), and especially where a precaution or restriction is indicated. Cf. Cic. *Verr.* II. 30, V. 3. 31, *dum ne ita rem augere ut ne quid de libertate deperderet:* cf. II. I. 35, *qui ne detur.* So *ut non* (especially after *facio, efficio,* &c.). This helps to shew the original equivalency of *ne non,* and to account for the use (by Virgil and others) of *non* to convey a direct prohibition; e.g. *Georg.* I. 456.

38 **illis**] is not much to the point. Bentley's *aliis* is adopted by Wagner.

42 **abhinc**] always of past time. Plaut. and Ter. use *dehinc* (*Eun.* II. 3. 5; V. 2. 33) for future time; v. Hand, *Turs.* I. 63—6.

inopia et cognatorum negligentia

coacta, egregia forma atque aetate integra. 45

So. Hei, vereor ne quid Andria adportet mali.

Si. Primum haec pudice vitam, parce ac duriter

agebat, lana ac tela victum quaeritans.

Sed postquam amans accessit, pretium pollicens,

unus et item alter: ita ut ingenium est omnium 50

hominum ab labore proclive ad lubidinem,

accepit condicionem; dein quaestum occipit.

Qui tum illam amabant, forte, ita ut fit, filium (80)

perduxere illuc, secum ut una esset, meum.

Egomet continuo mecum: Certe captus est; 55

---

44 **cognatorum negligentia**] i. e. in not providing her with a dower, as was the duty of the ἀγχιστεύς of an orphan girl (*Phorm.* L 2. 75): v. *Dict. Ant.* "Matrimonium." *Cognatus* is used as a translation of ἀγχιστεύς, not in the strict sense attached to it by Roman law, viz. descendants of one pair. The ἀγχιστεύς, or heir-at-law, might be an *Agnatus*, which term included, besides all *Cognati* descended from males, all persons admitted to a family by adoption. On the family relationship of ancient society see Maine's *Ancient Law*, ch. v.; Grote's *Hist. of Greece*, Part II. ch. x. (Athens before Solon); Mommsen's *Hist. of Rome* (translated by Dickson), Book 1. ch. v. (Original Constitution of Rome).

47 **duriter**] "Rigorously." "Est duriter, sive sensu laboris, dure autem, crudeliter." Donatus. *Dure* is not used in this sense before late writers, but we have *duriter* = "harshly," *Ad.* IV. 5. 28. Ennius, Afranius, and Caecilius quoted by Non. 512.

48 **victum**] of the mere necessaries of life. Donatus quotes *Aen.* III. 649 to shew its special application to coarse and meagre fare. The jurists of the empire used the word to denote all necessaries, clothing

included.

52 **condicionem**] "Terms." That this is the correct orthography is shewn by Cic. *Leg. Agr.* II. 39, where he puts together *dicioni, iudicio*, and implies that *dicere : dicio :: iudicare : iudicium*. The "conventional spelling" of the 15th century scholars is in this case wrong. See Munro's *Lucretius*, Vol. II. p. 23 sqq. on the general subject of Latin orthography. "*Condicio* est pactio, certam legem in se continens." Don. "A compact" is the earliest meaning of the word, and the derivation from *dicere* carries us back to the *spoken* formulae which marked the earliest stage of contract. The later application of the word to "a marriage" (*Phorm.* IV. 1. 13) is appropriate: the ceremonial formulae being retained in the marriage contract after they had been dispensed with in the transaction of ordinary business. Cf. Maine's *Ancient Law*, ch. IX. and *Dict. Ant.* "Matrimonium."

accepit] "Was content with." So we speak of "accepting terms." Cf. Hor. *Sat.* I. 5. 58.

55 **captus**, &c.] "He's in the toils: he has caught it!" But whether *captus* contains a gladiatorial allusion (to the *retiarius'* net), as some suppose, is uncertain: the allu-

habet ! Observabam mane illorum servolos
venientes aut abeuntes : rogitabam, Heus puer,
dic sodes, quis heri Chrysidem habuit ? Nam Andriae
illi id erat nomen. So. Teneo. Si. Phraedrum aut Cliniam aut
Niceratum dicebant. Nam hi tres tum simul   60
amabant. Eho, quid Pamphilus ? Quid ? symbolam
dedit, coenavit. Gaudebam.   Item alio die
quaerebam : comperiebam nihil ad Pamphilum   (90)
quicquam adtinere.   Enimvero spectatum satis
putabam, et magnum exemplum continentiae :   65
nam qui cum ingeniis conflictatur eiusmodi,
neque commovetur animus in ea re tamen,
scias posse habere iam ipsum suae vitae modum.
Quum id mihi placebat, tum uno ore omnes omnia
bona dicere, et laudare fortunas meas,   70
qui gnatum haberem tali ingenio praeditum.

sion of *habet* is familiar. Cf. Virg.
Æn. XII. 295.

58] Note the skilful introduction
of the name "Chrysis" which has
not yet occurred.

61 **symbolam**] See Liddell and
Scott, s. v. συμβόλη. Cic. *Or.* II. 57.
233 uses *collecta* in same sense, cf. *Eun.*
III. 42 : *asymbolus, Phorm.* II. 2. 25.

64 **quicquam**] is surely adverbial
acc. here, and not in agreement with
nihil. Nemo quisquam, Eun. II.
1. 21, is referred to in support of
Donatus' view that *nihil quidquam*
is a redundant expression = *nihil* or
non quicquam; but see note *ad loc.*
On orthography of *quicquam,* cf.
Ad. IV. 2. 51.

spectatum] met. from testing me-
tals. Ov. *Tr.* I. 5. 25 ; cf. *spectator,
Eun.* III. 5. 18. *Spectatio pecuniae,*
Cic. *Verr.* II. 3. 78.

66 **qui**] is personal, not agreeing
with *animus.*

conflictatur] may suggest the rubbing together of metals as a test
(Aesch. *Ag.*390, Hdt. VII. 10): but the

passages quoted of its use point rather
to violent collision. Our "rubs shoul-
ders with" has somewhat of the
same metaphor.

69 **Quum...placebat**] Trans. "I
was pleased, and at the same time,"
&c.   *Quum* with imp. indic. expresses mere coincidence in time :
e.g. in this passage *quum...tum*
might have been *tum...et tum.* The
frequent use of the subjunctive mood
with imp. and plup. in historical relation arises from the idea that in
the order and sequence of historical
events there is more than a mere
temporal relation of antecedence or
coincidence ; i. e. that an element of
cause enters into such relation :
quum temporale borders upon *quum
causale.*

70] Cf. Manoah in *Samson Ago-
nistes:*

     "I gained a son,
And such a son, as all men hailed
   me happy ;
Who now would be a father in my
   stead?"

Quid verbis opus est? hac fama impulsus Chremes,

ultro ad me venit, unicam gnatam suam   (100)

cum dote summa filio uxorem ut daret.

Placuit: despondi: hic nuptiis dictust dies.   75

So. Quid obstat, cur non verae fiant? Sī. Audies.

Fere in diebus paucis, quibus haec acta sunt,

Chrysis vicina haec moritur. So. O factum bene!

beasti: hei, metui a Chryside. Sī. Ibi tum filius

cum illis, qui amabant Chrysidem, una aderat frequens: 80

curabat una funus: tristis interim;

nonnumquam collacrumabat. Placuit tum id mihi.

Sic cogitabam: Hic parvae consuetudinis   (110)

---

73 **ultro**] "Actually came to me:" i. e. not only, as was natural, was willing to give his daughter, but took the initiative. Servius on *Aen.* II. 145 *his lacrimis vitam damus et miserescimus ultro* hits the true meaning. "Non est 'sponte,' nam rogaverat Sinon, sed 'insuper.' Et venit ab eo, quod est '*ultra*,' quia plusquam rogarat praestitissent." Cf. Conington, *ad loc.* A few quotations from Virgil, who often uses the word, will shew how the meaning "over and above" (*insuper*) underlies the various uses of *ultro*.

Nunc et oves *ultro* fugiat lupus, *Ecl.* VIII. 52 (beyond what is usual, "actually").

Ultro hortantem, *G.* IV. 265 (beyond what is necessary).

*Ultro*que animam sub fasce dedere, *G.* IV. 264 ("with a strange devotion").

Ultro animis tollit dictis, *Aen.* IX. 127 (beyond what could be expected under the circumstances, "with strange confidence").

So *petere ultro*, i. e. not only act on the defensive, but assume the offensive: *compellare ultro* not only to answer, but to take the initiative, as in our present passage. The old distinction "ultro, non rogatus;

sponte, non coactus," defines but imperfectly the force of *ultro*, which as we have seen always expresses something unnecessary, unusual, or unexpected. See Donaldson, *Varron.* ch. X. § 3.

77 **in diebus paucis**] "Within the few days." *Diebus paucis*=in, or *at*, the period of a few days: the preposition is added to bring out more clearly what is already implied, that it was *within* this period of time. The force of the preposition is almost adverbial; and it is determined by, rather than "governs," the case to which it is attached.

78 **O factum bene!**] "Good business!" (modern slang), is perhaps admissible.

79 **a Chryside**] Locative, from the direction of Chrysis. Livy has *metuens ab Hannibale.*

83] Cf. *Twelfth Night*, I. 1. 32. "O she that hath a heart of that fine frame
To pay this debt of love but to a brother,
How will she love, when the rich golden shaft
Hath killed the flock of all affections else
That live in her?"

causa huius mortem tam fert familiariter:
quid si ipse amasset? quid hic mihi faciet patri? 85
Haec ego putabam esse omnia humani ingeni
mansuetique animi officia. Quid multis moror?
Egomet quoque eius causa in funus prodeo,
nihil suspicans etiam mali. So. Hem, quid id est? Si.
    Scies.

Effertur. Imus. Interea inter mulieres, 90
quae ibi aderant, forte unam aspicio adulescentulam,
forma... So. bona fortasse. Si. et voltu, Sosia,
adeo modesto, adeo venusto, ut nil supra. (120)
Quae quum mihi lamentari praeter ceteras
visa est, et quia erat forma praeter ceteras 95
honesta et liberali, accedo ad pedisequas:
quae sit, rogo. Sororem esse aiunt Chrysidis.
Percussit illico animum. Atat, hoc illud est,

84 **tam...familiariter**] With so much friendly feeling (of sorrow).

85]. Bentley's transposition of the words *hic mihi* relieves a difficulty as to the metre, though how the sense is improved (see Parry's note) is not so clear, unless *mihi* is to be taken as "dat. ethicus"="What, I ask;" which is unnecessary.

86 **putabam**] as often, gives the notion of *mistaken* thoughts. "I thought in my ignorance that all these attentions were those of ordinary feeling and civility."

88 **eius causa**] i.e. *hum. et mans. animi.*

89 **etiam**] (*et iam*) "Even now," so "still," "as yet." Cf. Virg. *G.* III. 189; *Aen.*VI. 485; *Eun.*IV. 4. 1.

id] Qu. the *malum* at which Simo's words hint, or those words generally, "What is that you say?" Perhaps the former is better: "H'm, 'mischief' say you, what's that?"

91 **unam...adulescentulam**] *U-nam* has the force of an *indefinite*, as the pronouns (*ille, is,* &c.), in all pro-

bability had the force of a *definite* article in colloquial Latin—"an instinct of clearness anticipating grammatical development." The French *un* (*unus*), and *le* (*il-le*) prove this usage in the provincial Latin, from which the modern Romance languages have been developed. "Noster sermo articulos non desiderat," says Quinctilian (*Inst. Or.* I. 4. 19): but this and similar uses shew that a Latin speaking people both felt and endeavoured to supply the want. This use of pronouns is parallel to the development in Greek of the article ὁ from the originally demonstrative form ὅς, demonstrative, article, and relative being one and the same form. (Donaldson's *New Cratylus,* § 148). So in German *der* is article, relative, demonstrative.

98 **Percussit...animum**] Almost proverbial. Cic. *Att.* IV. 8. 3, "audivi Romae esse hominem—percussit animum." Also Lucr. II. 886.

hoc illud] "δεικτικὸν eius rei est quam in animo conceperamus," hinc illae lacrumae, haec illast misericordia.

So. Quam timeo, quorsum evadas.   Si. Funus interim 100
procedit.   Sequimur: ad sepulcrum venimus:
in ignem impositast: fletur.   Interea haec soror,
quam dixi, ad flammam accessit imprudentius,   (130)
satis cum periclo.   Ibi tum exanimatus Pamphilus
bene dissimulatum amorem et celatum indicat: 105
adcurrit: mediam mulierem complectitur:
mea Glycerium, inquit, quid agis? cur te is perditum?
Tum illa, ut consuetum facile amorem cerneres,
reiecit se in eum flens quam familiariter.
So. Quid ais?   Si. Redeo inde iratus atque aegre ferens. 110
Nec satis ad obiurgandum causae.   Diceret:
quid feci? quid commerui aut peccavi, pater?
Quae sese in ignem iniicere voluit, prohibui: (140)
servavi.   Honesta oratio est.   So. Recte putas:

Donatus, who compares Virg., *Hoc illud germana fuit.*   So τοῦτ᾽ ἐκεῖνο frequently in Gk. Trag.

99 **hinc illae lacrumae**] A familiar proverb, cf. Hor. *Epp.* I. 19. 41.

101 **sepulcrum**] in the widest sense includes the place where the body was burnt. The whole passage is a translation from the Greek: some think that the practice of burning the dead was not introduced at Rome before the death of Sulla: but cf. Cic. *Legg.* II. 23, and *Dict. Ant.* "Sepulcrum."

104 **Ibi**] (temporal) pleonastically with *tum.* Cf. Cic. *Caec.* X. 27: or perhaps *ibi* is local = "then and there."

109 **quam familiariter**] This use of *quam* with a positive adj. or adverb may be explained on the same principle as the more familiar use with superlative; viz. as an elliptical construction: in full, *tam familiariter quam potuit.* Cf. *vino quam possit excellenti,* Pliny. Then, the original construction being lost

sight of, comes in the use of *quam* as a mere intensitive; *admodum quam, valde quam.* Under this some quote the present passage: but it has been shewn that we can go further back in the history of the word for its explanation.

111 **Diceret**] "He might have said." When the subj. mood is used potentially of something possible in past time, the imperfect tense is generally employed: e.g. *vellem, nollem,* &c., "I could have wished." The imperfect indic. expresses action continuing in past time: the supposition of such action is naturally expressed by imp. subj. Cf. Virg. *Aen.* III. 187, *crederet;* VIII. 643, *at tu dictis, Albane, maneres.*

114 **Recte putas**, &c.] Sosia is a simple and stupid character, whose unintelligent questions and remarks serve to bring out Simo's feelings. He disappears after this first scene, being only a πρόσωπον προτακτικὸν, who appears at the beginning (πρό-τασις), for unfolding the argument.

nam si illum obiurges, vitae qui auxilium tulit;　　115
quid facias illi, qui dederit damnum aut malum?
Si. Venit Chremes postridie ad me, clamitans,
indignum facinus: comperisse, Pamphilum
pro uxore habere hanc peregrinam. Ego illud sedulo
negare factum. Ille instat factum. Denique　　120
ita tum discedo ab illo, ut qui se filiam
neget daturum. So. Non tu ibi gnatum...? Si. Ne haec
　　　quidem
satis vehemens causa ab obiurgandum. So. Qui, cedo? (150)
Si. Tute ipse his rebus finem praescripsti, pater.
Prope adest, quum alieno more vivendumst mihi:　　125
sine nunc meo me vivere interea modo.
So. Qui igitur relictus est obiurgandi locus?
Si. Si propter amorem uxorem nolit ducere,
ea primum ab illo animadvertenda iniuriast.

---

121 **ut qui neget**] Under the impression that he declines. Greek ὡς with participle, Soph. *O. T.* 11. *et saep.*

122 **gnatum**] sc. *obiurgasti.*

123 **ad obiurgandum**] The more usual construction is the objective genitive, *obiurgandi.* The use of the case that expresses motion towards, perhaps brings out more clearly the object or design.

124] Supply *diceret* [v. 111]. Simo imagines his son's reply.

125 **alieno more**] "At another's whim." Cf. *morem gerere alicui.*

129] "That is the first offence on his part for punishment," *ab illo*, lit. "from his direction," cf. *a dextra*, &c., Lucr. II. 51 and Munro's note. From this to abl. of agent *ab illo factum* is a short step; illustrating the way in which all the various meanings of the cases are expansions of their first locative signification.

animadvertenda] "Nota participium a passivo," says Donatus: a view of the participle in *-dus* now almost exploded (cf. Donaldson, *Varron.* ch. XI. § 13). On the other hand, the conclusion that it is an *active* participle is not certain. The similarity of form, and interchange of letters, *volven-t-s, volven-d-us* cannot be safely relied upon: while its ordinary usage often partakes of a passive, or at any rate middle character, though *volvenda dies* (Virg. *Aen.* IX. 7), and *oriundus, secundus* = *oriens, sequens*, are more decidedly active. In the gerundial sense of the oblique cases of the neut. sing. the active force is generally retained: yet here we are met by *urit videndo* (Virg. *G.* III. 215), *annulus subter-tenuatur habendo*, &c.; which at first sight appear passive. The truth is, that in these cases the part. in *-dus* is neither active nor passive, but simply indefinite, expressing the verbal notion as an abstract subst. Greek would use either τῷ ἔχειν or τῷ ἔχεσθαι; and this leads us to a corresponding ambiguity in the usage of the Latin

Et nunc id operam do, ut per falsas nuptias   130
vera obiurgandi causa sit, si deneget : .
simul sceleratus Davos si quid consili
habet, ut consumat nunc, quum nihil obsint doli :   (160)
quem ego credo manibus pedibusque obnixe omnia
facturum : magis id adeo, mihi ut incommodet,   135
quam ut obsequatur gnato.   So. Quapropter ?   Sı. Rogas ?
Mala mens, malus animus.   Quem quidem ego si sensero,—
Sed quid opust verbis ?   Sin eveniat, quod volo,
in Pamphilo ut nihil sit morae, restat Chremes,
qui mi exorandus est : et spero confore.   140
Nunc tuumst officium, has bene ut adsimules nuptias,
perterrefacias Davom, observes filium,
quid agat, quid cum illo consili captet.   So. Sat est: (170)
curabo : eamus iam nunc intro.   Sı. I prae, sequar.

infin., *facilis videre* or *videri :* cf. also *dat habere,* Virg. *Aen.* IX. 362, &c. =*dat habenda* with *tradam portare* =*tradam portanda,* in either of which expressions the infin. pass. might occur; cf. English, "He is the man to see." As, then, the part. in -*dus* cannot be certainly identified with either the active or passive voice in *form,* so in *usage* it fluctuates between the two, approximating on the whole to the active in its gerundial, to the passive in its gerundival use.

130 **id**] may be explained as in apposition to *ut...sit,* but more correctly as an adverbial accusative, defining the *manner* of the verbal notion *operam do,* than itself expanded by the clause *ut...sit,* which is adverbial, not substantival. On the other view it should be in dat. *ei:* the instance quoted from II. 1. 7 is not

conclusive, for there *id loqui* is naturally accus. after *loqui.* A passage, however, in II. 1. 7. 8, where both these expressions occur, perhaps makes against the view here taken.

132 **consili**] The contracted form of the genitive in -*ii* is used by all earlier writers. Horace and Virgil contract in subst. not in adj. *egregii altique silenti:* Cicero, Caesar, Ovid, and Livy, use the uncontracted form. *Fluvii* occurs in Virgil but may be considered as an adj. (*fluvia* is quoted by Nonius): so also *Latii.* See Lachm. *ad Lucr.* V. 1006.

137 **Mala mens, malus animus**] δόλιαι ψυχαί, δόλιαι φρένες, Ar. *Pax,* 1068.

140 **confore**] Only tense in use. Cf. Plaut. *Mil. Glor.* III. 3. 66. *Confio* used in similar sense, *Ad.* V. 8. 23 (see note).

ACTUS I. SCENA II.

SIMO. DAVUS.

SI. Non dubiumst, quin uxorem nolit filius:
ita Davom modo timere sensi, ubi nuptias
futuras esse audivit. Sed ipse exit foras.

DA. Mirabar, hoc si sic abiret, et heri semper lenitas
verebar quorsum evaderet: 5
qui postquam audierat non datum iri filio uxorem suo,
numquam cuiquam nostrum verbum fecit, neque id aegre tulit.

SI. At nunc faciet; neque, ut opinor, sine tuo magno malo.

DA. Id voluit, nos sic nec opinantes duci falso gaudio, (180)
sperantes, iam amoto metu, interea oscitantes opprimi,   10

Sc. II.]ˈ Simo and Davus appear, each soliloquising; at v. 13 the dialogue commences, S. expostulating on his son's marriage, D. feigning stupidity. Metre: iamb. trim. (1—4, 25—27); iamb. dimeter (5); iamb. tetram. (6, 9—24, 28—34); troch. tetr. cat. (7, 8).

4 sic] Sometimes gathers up, as it were, and resumes an expression in earlier clauses of a sentence; cf. especially Virg. *Aen.* II. 225, VII. 668, VIII. 488; and Lucr. v. 970, where Munro quotes Donatus on this passage for the other meaning into which this readily passes, viz. *sic temere*, ["Pro *leviter* et *negligenter* quod Graeci οὕτως dicunt,"] and compares the *positum sic* of Horace; *sicut erat*, Ov. *Fasti*, VI. 331; Seneca, *Hipp.* 394, *Sic temere iactae comae;* Persius, *sic poeta prodirem;* and mimetic οὕτως in Greek. Its meaning in this and similar places was probably enforced by an imitative gesture, cf. Plaut. *Amphitr.* 117, *Ego huc processi sic cum servili schema.* Tr. "I was wondering if it would turn out like this, and I was always

afraid of what would be the end of my master's forbearance." *Abiret* cf. *Phorm.* III. 2. 5; Cat. 14. 16. *Lenitas* opposed to *difficultas* = offering no obstacles; *semper* better with *verebar* than with *lenitas* = ἡ ἀεὶ ἡσυχία. A purely adjectival use of the adverb cannot be shewn in Latin, which has not the article necessary for such a construction.

8 faciet] *sc. verbum.* "He'll have something to say *now.*"

9 nec opinantes] Sometimes written *ne opinantes:* the *e* was doubtless inserted to avoid the hiatus. This and similar compounds (*nefandus, nimirum*) illustrate the true relation of *ne* and *non; ne* being the original negative particle, cf. note to I. 1. 34 *supra.*

10 oscitantes] "Off our guard;" "gaping," "listless." *interea* Bentley's correction for *inter*, which, as he says, "turbat sensum," since there is no point in supposing Davus and Phormio among other idlers; but hardly "nocet metro," for the fifth foot is then iambus, instead of anapaest as with *interea.*

TER.

2

ne esset spatium cogitandi ad disturbandas nuptias.

Astute! Sɪ. Carnufex quae loquitur? Dᴀ. Herus est, neque provideram.

Sɪ. Dave. Dᴀ. Hem, quid est? Sɪ. Ehodum ad me! Dᴀ.
Quid hic volt? Sɪ. Quid ais? Dᴀ. Qua de re?
Sɪ. Rogas?

Meum gnatum rumor est amare.   Dᴀ. Id populus curat
scilicet.

Sɪ. Hoccine agis, an non? Dᴀ. Ego vero istuc. Sɪ. Sed
nunc ea me exquirere,   15

iniqui patris est.   Nam, quod antehac fecit, nihil ad me
adtinet.

Dum tempus ad eam rem tulit, sivi animum ut expleret suum:
nunc hic dies aliam vitam adfert, alios mores postulat.

Dehinc postulo, sive aequumst, te oro, Dave, ut redeat iam
in viam.   (190)

Dᴀ. Hoc quid sit? Sɪ. Omnes, qui amant, graviter sibi dari
uxorem ferunt.   20

---

14 scilicet] Ironical. "O, I suppose the whole town is interested in
that." Davus ridicules the notion
of Pamphilus' love being important
enough to be the subject of a general "rumor."

15 Hoccine agis] "Do you hear
me, or not?" The formula "hoc
age" was used to bespeak silence at
religious rites: cf. II. 5. 4; Hor. Sat.
II. 3. 152. Hence followed by ut=
"to attend to" (in Cicero, id agere,
ut...): cf. alias res agere, like alia
curare="to be inattentive." Eun.
I. 2. 50, "Hoc agite, amabo."

17 ad eam rem] may be taken
with tempus on comparison of Eun.
IV. I. 6; but more probably with
tulit. "So long as his time allowed
him to do so, I permitted him, &c."

tulit] Donatus and the older commentators understand an ellipse of

se: but the absolute use of fero=
"allow" is common enough in
Cicero, ratio fert, &c.: cf. Greek ὁ
λόγος αἱρεῖ.

18] Cicero quotes this verse,
Epist. ad Div. XII. 25. A Greek
proverb, ἄλλος βίος ἄλλη δίαιτα, is
quoted from Zenobius.

19 sive aequumst] A sarcastic
ἐπανόρθωσις of his expression postulo: "Or if I may venture so far,
I entreat you."

20 Hoc quid sit?] "What can
this be?" (i.e. this returning to the
right way, &c.). sit potential. Davus
still feigns to misunderstand S.
Donatus understands quaeris: in that
case he must have referred the words
to Simo, on seeing Davus's expression of puzzled wonder, for S. has
asked no question.

DA. Ita aiunt. SI. Tum si quis magistrum cepit ad eam
   rem improbum,

ipsum animum aegrotum ad deteriorem partem plerumque
   adplicat.

DA. Non hercle intellego. SI. Non? hem! DA. Non:
   Davos sum, non Oedipus.

SI. Nempe ergo aperte vis, quae restant, me loqui. DA.
   Sane quidem.

SI. Si sensero hodie quicquam in his te nuptiis   25
fallaciae conari, quo fiant minus,

aut velle in ea re ostendi, quam sis callidus;

verberibus caesum te, Dave, in pistrinum dedam usque ad
   necem,

ea lege atque omine, ut, si te inde exemerim, ego pro te
   molam.   (200)

---

21 **magistrum**] "an *adviser*,"
"instigator." Cf. Cic. *Ep. ad Div.*
III. 22 and *Verr.* II. 5. 21, quoted
by Parry.

22 **adplicat ad det. part.**] Perhaps in allusion to the phrase *ad-
plicare navem* (Virg. *Aen.* I. 616)
= "'lands' his mind in something
worse." Or perhaps, "influences
for the worse."

27 **ostendi**] has almost a middle
voice, "shew yourself," not uncommon in Virgil and others. "Lo-
ricam *induitur* fidoque *accingitur*
ense."

29 **ea lege atque omine**] "On
this condition, and with this assurance." So usually translated, but
this sense of *omen* is not elsewhere
found, and in the pass. of Virg. *Aen.*
VII. 174, quoted for the meaning of
a "solemn custom," the ordinary
meaning is equally suitable. The
idea of "prognostic" may of course
pass into that of "warning."

si ... exemerim] corresponds in
construction to *si sensero*, v. 25. So
transierim (*G.* II. 110, *Aen.* VII.

186) and *crediderim* are used by
Virgil where the second fut. would
be expected. From these instances
and the similarity of form between
the two tenses it has been argued
that they are but *one*, and that the
second fut. has no place in the scheme
of the indic. mood (Donaldson,
Varron. ch. XI. sect. 15). But (i) the
similarity in form is paralleled by that
between fut. ind. and pres. subj. in
third and fourth conjug., and that
of usage by the frequent confusion
between the same tenses, and between the ind. and subj. mood generally in Latin; e.g. (to indicate one
point only) the Latin subj. differs
modally from the ind. only in being
used in dependent sentences; and
in these Greek generally requires
the indicative. (ii) An analysis of
the scheme of tenses speaks in favour
of a tense to express *completed action*
in future time; for both incomplete
and complete action are expressed
in past (by imp. and plup.), and in
present time (by pres. and perf.):
it is therefore probable à *priori* and

2—2

Quid, hoc intellextin? an nondum etiam ne hoc quidem?
DA. Immo callide;   30
ita aperte ipsam rem modo locutus, nihil circuitione usus es.
SI. Ubivis facilius passus sim, quam in hac re, me deludier.
DA. Bona verba, quaeso. SI. Inrides: nihil me fallis. Edico
    tibi,
ne temere facias. Neque tu †hau̯d† dicas tibi non prae-
    dictum. Cave.

ACTUS I. SCENA III.

DAVUS.

Enimvero, Davo, nihil loci est segnitiae neque socordiae,
quantum intellexi modo senis sententiam de nuptiis;

only consistent that there should be
the same provision in future time;
viz. first and second future. Such
prevision exists in the passive voice
in Greek (paulo post. fut.), and in
the active voice it can be supplied
by a future tense of the auxiliary
verb with a past partic. (πεποιηκὼς
ἔσομαι). But this expedient is only
available in the Latin passive (ama-
tus ero), which makes a distinct form
in the active voice the more necessary. Lindemann on Plaut. Capt.
II. 2. 64 enumerates four principal
senses of this futurum exactum:
1. past action in future time: 2. momentary action in present time: 3.
instantaneous action: 4. expressing
an opinion or expectation.

32] I can stand (as I often have)
being cheated in anything rather
than in this. Passus sim potential:
the perf. tense is used apparently to
refer to past deceptions, though the
strict sense requires patiar.

33 Bona verba] A sacrificial formula, like Greek εὐφημεῖτε: cf. Tib.

II. 2. 1.

34 Neque haud] v.l. hoc, but with
less MS. authority. The repetition
of the negative, common in Greek,
is unusual in Latin. It occurs where
a general negation is afterwards distributed (cf. Virg. Ecl. IV. 55, and
passages from Cicero quoted by
Madvig, Gr. 460, obs. 2), and a
single idea is brought forward by
ne quidem. Cf. Cic. Verr. I. 60,
"Non enim praetereundum est ne
id quidem."

Sc. III.] Davus deliberates on his
line of conduct, mentioning as in-
credible the story of Glycerium.
Thus a hint at the ultimate solution
is given.

Metre: 1—9, 20—22, iambic tetram.; 10—19, iamb. trim.

1 Enimvero] "Significationem
habet nimium permoti atque irritati
animi," Donatus. It rather con-
veys a strong asseveration resulting
from a conviction, Germ. denn wahr-
lich: so an old gloss ὁμολογουμένως
ἀσφαλῶς. Cf. Heaut. II. 3. 79; V.

quae si non astu providentur, me aut herum pessum dabunt.
Nec quid agam certumst: Pamphilumne adiutem, an auscultem
seni.

Si illum relinquo, eius vitae timeo: sin opitulor, huius minas;
cui verba dare difficilest. Primum iam de amore hoc comperit: (211)
me infensus servat, ne quam faciam in nuptiis fallaciam.

Si senserit, perii; aut si lubitum fuerit, causam ceperit:
quo iure quaque iniuria praecipitem in pistrinum dabit.

Ad haec mala hoc mi accedit etiam: haec Andria, 10
sive ista uxor sive amicast, gravida e Pamphilo est.

Audireque eorum est operae pretium audaciam:
nam inceptiost amentium, haud amantium:
quicquid peperisset, decreverunt tollere:
et fingunt quandam inter se nunc fallaciam, (220) 15

1. So often when a definite time and circumstance is indicated; *enimvero nunc*, Plaut.; *tum enimvero eorum ira admonuit*, Livy, II. 36.

3 **pessum**] is probably accus. of a subst. *pessus* used adverbially: *pessum in altum*, Plaut. *Rud.* II. 3. 64. *Pessum ire* is like Greek κακῶς ἥκειν: cf. *venum, nuptum dare*, which are "supines," i.e. accus. cases of verbal nouns.

6 **verba dare**] = *decipere*: explained by Donatus on *Eun. prol.* 24, "Quia qui rem exspectat et nihil praeter verba invenit deceptus est."

Primum] No *deinde* or other particle follows; a use not uncommon in later writers: cf. Virg. *Geor.* III. 384.

7 **in nuptiis**] is read by two MSS. and the older editions, and is preferred by Bentley.

8 **senserit**, &c.] The employment of the tense which represents *completed* action in future time makes the narration more vivid than the simple fut.

9] This is the reading of all MSS.

and old edd. Bentley reads *qua jure qua me injuria*, καὶ δικαίως κἀδίκως, Ar. *Plut.* 233: *qua...qua = tum...tum* in Plaut. *Trin.* IV. 4. 38, also in Cicero. This no doubt makes better sense; but Donatus read the other, and "potior lectio difficillima." It is a proverb expressed like *fas nefas, nolis velis*, &c.

The relatives are in sense adverbial, though in agreement with *jure injuria* = "How, rightly or wrongly," &c.: cf. Virg. *Aen.* I. 8, quo numine laeso, and frequent use of *primus*, &c.

13 **inceptio**] "'Tis the way fools set to work, not lovers." The force of the abstract *inceptio*, as distinguished from *inceptum*, should be kept.

14 **peperisset**] cf. Prol. 3, and note.

tollere] The father acknowledged his child by the symbolical action of raising it from the ground. So *suscipere*, II. 3. 27: Greek ἀναιρεῖν. Virg. *Aen.* IV. 327; Hor. *Sat.* II. 5. 45.

civem Atticam esse hanc. Fuit olim quidam senex,
mercator: navem is fregit apud Andrum insulam:
is obiit mortem. Ibi tum hanc eiectam Chrysidis
patrem recepisse orbam, parvam.—Fabulae.
Mihi quidem non fit verisimile; atque ipsis commentum
      placet.   20
Sed Mysis ab ea egreditur. At ego hinc me ad forum, ut
conveniam Pamphilum, ne de hac re pater imprudentem op-
      primat.

ACTUS I. SCENA IV.

MYSIS.

Audivi, Archylis, iamdudum: Lesbiam adduci iubes.
Sane pol illa temulenta est mulier et temeraria,
nec satis\digna, cui committas primo partu mulierem; (230)
tamen eam adducam.—Importunitatem spectate aniculae.
Quia compotrix ejus est.—Di, date facultatem obsecro   5
huic·pariundi, atque illi in aliis potius peccandi locum.
Sed quidnam Pamphilum exanimatum video? Vereor, quid
      siet.
Opperiar, ut sciam, numquidnam haec turba tristitiae adferat.

16 **civem Atticam**] If so, Pamphilus must marry her (IV. 4. 41). Cf. V. 3. 8. 9 and *Dict. Ant.* "Civitas."

20 **atque**] MSS.: Bentley *at:* "Atque pro tamen," Donatus. Rather, *atque, ac* often introduce an adversative clause especially in connection with *tamen:* cf. II. 2. 33; *Ad.* I. I. 15.

21 **ad forum**] The lounging-place of idle young men: cf. Plaut. *Capt.* III. I. 18, "accessi ad adolescentes in foro."

Sc. IV.] Metre: 1—6 trochaic tetrameter catal.; 7, 8 iambic tetra-meter.

1 **iamdudum**] "Just now:" cf. *Eun.* III. I. 58 note; IV. 5. 8.

8 **numquidnam**] II. I. 25.

haec turba] "This confusion," i.e. exhibited by Pamphilus. It seems here = *turbatio, commotio,* of which I can find no other instance: and it is rarely used of a disturbance raised by a few or a single person: v. Plaut. *Aul.* II. 9. 9; *Amph.* I. 2. 14. Bentley read *turbae tristitia,* which Parry adopts; *tristitia* then refers to the appearance of Pamphilus, and *turbae* to the impending trouble it betokens.

ACTUS I. SCENA V.

PAMPHILUS. MYSIS.

PA. Hocinest humanum factum aut inceptum? hocinest officium patris?

My. Quid est?   PA. Pro deum atque hominum fidem, quid
est, si haec non contumeliast?

Uxorem decrerat dare sese mi hodie: nonne oportuit
praescisse me ante? nonne prius communicatum oportuit?

My. Miseram me, quod verbum audio?   (240) 5

PA. Quid Chremes? qui denegarat se commissurum mihi
gnatam suam uxorem: id mutavit, quia me inmutatum videt.

Itane obstinate operam dat, ut me a Glycerio miserum abs-
trahat?

Quod si fit, pereo funditus.

Adeon' hominem esse invenustum aut infelicem quemquam, ut
ego sum?   10

Sc. V.] Mysis overhears Pamphilus debating with himself whether
to obey his father, or adhere to Glycerium; and by her appearance
turns the scale.

Metre: 1—4, 8, 18, 26—35, 64,
65 iambic tetrameter; 5, 9, 17 iambic dimeter; 6, 7 trochaic tetram.
cat.; 11 trochaic dimeter catalectic;
10, 12—16, 19—25, trochaic tetrameter.

3 decrerat] The pluperfect is emphatic. His resolution had been
taken some time ago, which makes
its concealment so much the worse.

4 communicatum oportuit] The
omission of the auxiliary verb is
common with this partic. constr.:
cf. *Ad.* II. 3—6, and Parry, *on Heaut.*
I. 2. 26.

5 Miseram me] "accusativus exclamantis;" see Madvig's *Lat. Gr.*
§ 236, and note on v. 10 below.

8] Bentley reads *ita...abstrahat*, on
the ground that the following words

quod...funditus point to v. 8 as an
affirmative statement, not doubtfully
and negatively. But *itane?* does not
imply denial any more than affirma-
tion: it is an exclamation of surprise
at something wonderful, but true;
Greek ἄληθες; our "Really?": and
may of course be used ironically, so
as to imply disbelief. Cicero always
prefixes it as a separate interrogation, and so Hand (*Turs.* III. p. 496)
would read here "Itane? obstinate
...trahat."

10 Adeone esse hominem] cf.
Eun. II. I. 19. The addition of
the interrogative particle *ne* to the
accus. and infin. *indignantis* intro-
duces a further element of doubt
into the expression, originally analogous to the accus. in exclamations
[*me miserum !*] as being the object
to a verb understood. Though we
call such expressions "elliptical,"
we cannot say that there is grammatical deficiency; for the speaker

Pro deum atque hominum fidem!

Nullon' ego Chremetis pacto adfinitatem effugere potero?

Quot modis contemptus, spretus?   Facta, transacta omnia.
    Hem.

repudiatus repetor: quamobrem? nisi si id est, quod sus-
        picor:

aliquid monstri alunt: ea quoniam nemini obtrudi potest, 15

itur ad me.   My. Oratio haec me miseram exanimavit metu.

PA. Nam quid ego nunc dicam de patre? Ah,   (252)

tantamne rem tam negligenter agere?   Praeteriens modo

mi apud forum, uxor tibi ducenda est, Pamphile, hodie, in-
        quit: para:

abi domum.   Id mihi visust dicere, abi cito, et suspende te.

Obstipui: censen' me verbum potuisse ullum proloqui?   21

aut ullam causam, ineptam saltem, falsam, iniquam?   Ob-
        mutui.

expresses his meaning sufficiently. They are rather a convenient method of calling attention to some object or action, sufficient to convey a meaning, if not logically correct. Greek exhibits more purely "elliptical" uses—e.g. in *commands* (sub. θέλε), or *wish* (sub. δός).

invenustum] "Unblest by love," ἀναφρόδιτος. Cf. *Hec.* v. 4. 8. It is very doubtful whether there is any allusion to the Venus of dice (Macleane, *ad Hor.* II. 7. 25).

13 **Facta transacta omnia]** a legal phrase like our "signed and sealed." Cf. Cic. *Cat.* III. 6. 15.

14 **repudiatus repetor]** Plautus and the comic poets generally employ alliteration and assonance of words to produce a comic effect (v. *Captivi*, IV. 3. 3 for a good instance) as puns are used in our farces: while others employ it for poetical effect. The usage was transmitted from most ancient times, and is common to the earliest poetical efforts in all languages. Cf. the alliterative poetry of the middle

ages, e.g. the Romance writers and the "Vision of Piers Plowman," vid. Milman, *Latin Christianity*, Bk. XIV. ch. 7. It becomes less frequent in Latin poetry after Virgil's time. Cf. Munro, *Lucr.* Notes II. Introd.

15 **aliquid monstri]** "Some deformity." *Monstrum hominis, Eun.* IV. 4. 29.

17 **nunc]** occurs in most MSS. and must therefore be retained, though undoubtedly injurious to the metre (which is iambic dim.) and unnecessary for the sense. Bentley rejected it without scruple.

19 **ducenda]** "There is a wife for you to marry." Cf. note to sc. I. v. 129.

21 **Obstipui]** So the best MSS. of Terence and Plautus, and one of the three principal MSS. of Virgil, the Roman.

22 **saltem]** "Be it ever so inappropriate." *Saltem = salutem = salva re*, and points out what remains or holds good in spite of something opposed to it—implied here in the word *ineptam*.

Quodsi ego rescissem id prius,—quid facerem, si quis me
    roget:
Aliquid facerem, ut hoc ne facerem.   Sed nunc quid pri-
    mum exsequar?
Tot me impediunt curae, quae meum animum divorse tra-
    hunt;   (260) 25
amor, misericordia huius, nuptiarum sollicitatio,
tum patris pudor, qui me tam leni passus est animo usque
    adhuc,
quae meo cunque animo lubitumst, facere.   Eine ego ut ad-
    vorser? Hei mihi,
incertumst, quid agam.   My. Misera timeo, incertum hoc
    quorsum accidat.
Sed nunc peropust, aut hunc cum ipsa, aut me aliquid de
    illa adversum hunc loqui.   30
Dum in dubio est animus, paulo momento huc vel illuc im-
    pellitur.
Pa. Quis hic loquitur? Mysis, salve.   My. O salve, Pam-
    phile.   Pa. Quid agit?   My. Rogas?
Laborat e dolore; atque ex hoc misera sollicita est, diem

23] This punctuation seems preferable to the? which most editors
place at the end of the line. *Si quis
me roget* is of course a supposition:
quid facerem an interrogation explained by delib. subj. A break
or colon after *prius* is best. He
first puts a general supposition,
"Supposing I had known it beforehand"—then breaks off to suggest
and answer an imaginary question.
This seems better than to include
quod si…facerem in the supposed
question. Bentley reads, *Quod si ego
scissem…interroget* "metri gratiâ."

24 facerem] takes up and answers
quid facerem: but the repetition
cannot well be kept up in translation. "What was I to do?"…
"I might have done something to
avoid holding my tongue." Cf. on

I. I. 34: and for *ut ne* I. I. 34.

26 nuptiarum] The source from
which comes the *sollicitatio.* So
animi dubius, Virg., *sanus mentis,*
Plaut. The first meaning of gen.
is "place from which:" hence the
most general idea is that of *origin,*
which is retained in the ordinary
objective gen. in Lat. though the
local has been merged in that of the
ablative.

27 patris pudor] "Respect for
my father," *i.e.* a feeling of shame
at disobeying him after his forbearance (cf. sc. I. 134; 2. 3 sq.).

28 Eine ego] sc. *faciam.*

29 quorsum] altered to *quorsus*
by Bentley to avoid the hiatus after
timeo, but without MS. authority.

33 Laborat e dolore] "She is
weighed down with grief."

quia olim in hunc sunt constitutae nuptiae.　Tum autem hoc
　　timet,

ne deseras se.　PA. Hem, egone istuc conari queam?　35
Ego propter me illam decipi miseram sinam　　　　　(271)
quae mihi suum animum atque omnem vitam credidit,
quam ego animo egregie caram pro uxore habuerim,
bene et pudice eius doctum atque eductum sinam
coactum egestate ingenium inmutarier?　　　　　　　40
Non faciam.　MY. Haud vereor, si in te solo sit situm:
sed vim ut queas ferre.　PA. Adeon' me ignavom putas,
adeon' porro ingratum aut inhumanum aut ferum,
ut neque me consuetudo, neque amor, neque pudor
commoveat, neque commoneat, ut servem fidem?　(280) 45
MY. Unum hoc scio, hanc meritam esse, ut memor esses sui.
PA. Memor essem?　O Mysis Mysis, etiam nunc mihi
scripta illa dicta sunt in animo Chrysidis
de Glycerio.　Iam ferme moriens me vocat:
accessi: vos semotae: nos soli: incipit:　　　　　　50

---

35 **queam**] "Can I bear to,"...
potential; less probably deliberative subj. "Am I to."

38 **habuerim**] The change from
indic. *credidit* causes difficulty. According to one explanation, *credidit*
expresses an action *external* to himself, *habuerim* his own feelings:
but this, though a convenient formula for grouping this and parallel
passages (*And.* IV. 1. 25, 26: *Eun.*
II. 3. 11), does not throw much
light. The key to the apparent
difficulty is that *quae...credidit, quam
...habuerim* are not two *parallel*
relative clauses. *Quae...credidit* belongs merely to *illam*, and might be
expressed in Greek by a participle,
τὴν ἐπιτρέψασαν: *quam...habuerim*
belongs to the whole sentence *ego...
sinam*, and would have to be explained in Greek by a relative
clause. On the first mention of
Philumena (*illam*) her devotion to

him is expressed as a *simple fact*
by an adjectival sentence (*quae...
credidit*): his own feelings are then
given, in strong antithesis to the
possibility of his deserting her (v. 36),
and in the construction which both
qui and *quum* take when the action
is conceived as the cause or circumstance *under* or *notwithstanding*
which other events take place—*i.e.*
when they = "because" or "although." Translate *quam...habue-
rim* "*though* I have held her...."

44 **consuetudo**] "Common feeling," i.e. the customary manners
&c. of society: "contra morem
consuetudinemque civilem," frequent in Cicero. It is antithetical
to *ferum; amor* to *inhumanum;
pudor* to *ingratum.*

47 sqq.] Colman quotes a passage from Otway's *Orphan*, apparently imitated from this speech of
Pamphilus.

Mi Pamphile, huius formam atque aetatem vides :

nec clam te est, quam illi nunc utraeque inutiles

et ad pudicitiam et ad rem tutandam sient.

Ego te per hanc dextram oro et ingenium tuum,

per tuam fidem, perque huius solitudinem   (290) 55

te obtestor, ne abs te hanc segreges, neu deseras :

si te in germani fratris dilexi loco,

sive haёc te solum semper fecit maxumi,

seu tibi morigera fuit in rebus omnibus.

Te isti virum do, amicum, tutorem, patrem.   60

Bona nostra haec tibi permitto, et tuae mando fidei.

Hanc mi in manum dat: mors continuo ipsam occupat.

Accepi: acceptam servabo.   My. Ita spero quidem.

Pa. Sed cur tu abis ab illa ?   My. Obstetricem adcerso.   Pa.

    Propera.   Atque audin ?

Verbum unum cave de nuptiis; ne ad morbum hoc etiam.

    My. Teneo.   (300) 65

---

52 clam te est] cf. *Ad.* I. 1. 46, *te* after *clam est=fallit* is a construction κατὰ σύνεσιν.

54] Most edd. read *Quod ego te*, &c.: but this makes great metrical difficulty, and it is a question whether it may not have been inserted to square this passage with Hor. *Epp.* I. 7. 9, *Quod te per genium dextramque deosque Penates*, &c. Bentley also read *per genium* for *ingenium*. But similar invocations are frequent, e. g. in Virgil, *Aen.* IV. 314. With *quod, ego te* must be transposed if the line is to scan at all.

56] Donatus put a stop at *solitudinem*, and drew a distinction between *oro* and *obtestor;* "Obtestatio dicitur, quando eum adjuramus quem rogamus: oramus per eas res, propter quas rogamus:" but this is unnecessary.

60 isti] "To her, as your own."

Note the transition from the pronoun *hujus*, by which Chrysis at first speaks of Pasibula as belonging to her. In v. 52, speaking of her as absent when misfortune is hinted at, Chrysis employs the pronoun *illi*.

62 in manum] Donatus supposes that marriage "per conventionem in manum" (the general term including *usus confarreatio coemptio;* cf. *Dict. Ant.* MATRIMONIUM) is here intended. But more probably it = "into my charge," with no technical meaning, cf *Phor.* IV. 3. 29: legal allusions in Terence being generally Greek; e. g. I. 3. 16: I. 1. 44.

64 adcerso] This form of the causative *ar-cesso* from *accedo* has been repudiated (cf. Parry's note here): but apparently without justice. It can hardly be said to "violate all analogy:" the form *ar-* in *ar-cesso*, though it can be paralleled (*ar meadvenias*, Plaut. *Truc.* II. 2. 17,

ACTUS II. SCENA I.

CHARINUS. BYRRIA. PAMPHILUS.

CH. Quid ais Byrria? daturne illa Pamphilo hodie nuptum?
BY. Sic est.

CH. Qui scis? BY. Apud forum modo e Davo audii. CH.
Vae misero mihi.

Ut animus in spe atque in timore usque antehac adtentus fuit,

ita postquam adempta spes est, lassus, cura confectus stupet.

BY. Quaeso edepol, Charine, quoniam non potest id fieri,
quod vis,   5

id velis, quod possit. CH. Nil volo aliud nisi Philumenam.
BY. Ah,

quanto satiust te id dare operam, qui istum amorem ex
animo amoveas,

quam id loqui, quo magis lubido frustra incendatur tua.

CH. Facile omnes, quum valemus, recta consilia aegrotis
damus.

Tu si hic sis, aliter sentias.   BY. Age, age, ut lubet. CH.
Sed Pamphilum   (310) 10

---

ar-fuerunt, &c. in inscrr., *ar-biter*), is more exceptional: and for the change of one *s* into *r* we may compare the forms *rursus, prorsum, quorsum* with the Plautine forms *russus, prossum, quossum*.

65] "Don't say a word about the marriage, for fear even this might make her ill" (*ad morbum sit*).

Act. II. Sc. I.] Charinus, in love with Philumena, has been informed by Byrria of her approaching marriage with Pamphilus, whom he then urges to postpone it. Pamphilus explains that he is only too glad to do so.

Metre: 1, 5, 7 troch. tetram.; 2,

6, 8, 17, 19—97 troch. tetram. catal.; 3, 4, 9—16 iamb. tetram.; 18 iamb. trim.

1 **nuptum**] "In marriage." Cf. *Phormio*, V. I. 25, and note to *And.* I. 3. 3.

7 **id**] cf. I. I. 129.

9] Cf. Soph. *Trach.* 729:
τοιαῦτα δ᾽ ἂν λέξειεν οὐχ ὁ τοῦ κακοῦ
κοινωνός, ἀλλ᾽ ᾧ μηδέν ἐστ᾽ οἴκοις βαρύ.
vid. Shakespeare, *Much Ado about Nothing*, v. I. 27.

10 **hic**] "In my place." Cf. v. 3. 19.

video. Omnia experiri certumst prius quam ·pereo. BY.
    Quid hic agit?

CH. Ipsum hunc orabo: huic supplicabo: amorem huic nar-
    rabo meum:

credo impetrabo, ut aliquot saltem nuptiis prodat dies:

interea fiet aliquid, spero. BY. Id aliquid nihil est. CH.
    Byrria,

quid tibi videtur? Adeon' ad eum? BY. Quidni·? Si nihil
    impetres,   15

ut te arbitretur sibi paratum moechum, si illam duxerit.

CH. Abin' hinc in malam rem cum suspicione istac, scelus?

PA. Charinum video. Salve. CH. O salve, Pamphile.

Ad te advenio, spem, salutem, auxilium, consilium expetens.

PA. Neque pol consili locum habeo, neque auxili copiam. 20

Sed istuc quidnamst? CH. Hodie uxorem ducis? PA. Aiunt.

CH. Pamphile,   (321)

si id facis, hodie postremum me vides. PA. Quid·ita? CH.
    Hei mihi!

13 **prodat**] Acc. to Donatus =
"put off:" he quotes from Lucilius
An porro prodenda dies sit? Even
thus we should expect to have *prodere nuptias in aliquot dies:* we do
not talk of "postponing" the in-
terval of time granted, but the event
itself or a particular day, e.g. Hor.
Od. 15. 33. Might not the word
mean simply to "give" or "ap-
point"? *prodere exemplum, prodere
dictatorem*, etc., occur in Cicero
and Livy. A passage in III. 5. 9,
huic malo aliquam producam moram,
may throw some light: we may
perhaps take *prodat* here as = pro-
long, spin out a few days for the
marriage (*i.e.* to prevent it—a kind
of *dativus incommodi*).

15 **Adeone**] "Shall I go up to
him?" This emphatic use of the
present where the future would be
expected is not uncommon in questions; *imusne sessum?* Cic. *Or.* III.

5. Cf. Virg. *Aen.* II. 322.

16] supply *impetres* from *nihil
impetres*, v. 15.

17 **Abine in malam rem**] ἐς κό-
ρακας ἴθι.

20] The old edd. read *consilii* and
auxilii: on which cf. I. I. 132.
Bentley read *consili*, but *ad auxilium*, a construction unsupported by
examples, though we find *copia*
with infin. mood, and also with an
adverbial sentence expressing purpose. The text certainly involves
metrical difficulty, which is not
satisfactorily explained by the strong
assumption that the penultima of
auxili is lengthened by "ictus."
[Since this note was written,
Bentley's emendation has received
the sanction of Dr Wagner, who
thinks that Terence *may* have written something like *neque mi copia
auxilist.*]

νereor dicere : huic dic quaeso, Byrria. By. Ego dicam.
     Pa. Quid est?

By. Sponsam hic tuam amat. Pa. Nae iste haud mecum
     sentit. Ehodum dic mihi :

numquidnam amplius tibi cum illa fuit, Charine? Ch. Ah,
     Pamphile,   25

nihil. Pa. Quam vellem! Ch. Nunc te per amicitiam et
     per amorem obsecro,

principio, ut ne ducas. Pa. Dabo equidem operam. Ch.
     Sed si id non potest,

aut tibi nuptiae hae sunt cordi....Pa. Cordi? Ch. saltem
     aliquot dies

profer. dum proficiscor aliquo, ne videam. Pa. Audi nunc
     iam.

Ego Charine neutiquam officium liberi esse hominis puto,   30
quum is nihil promereat, postulare id gratiae adponi sibi. (331)
Nuptias effugere ego istas malo, quam tu adipiscier.

Ch. Reddidisti animum. Pa. Nunc si quid potes aut tu aut
     hic Byrria,

facite, fingite, invenite, efficite, qui detur tibi :

ego id agam, mihi qui ne detur. Ch. Sat habeo. Pa. Da-
     vom optume   35

video, cuius consilio fretus sum. Ch. At tu hercle haud
     quicquam mihi ;

---

29 **profer**] sc. *nuptias. Aliquot dies*, acc. of duration, not direct object of *profer*. *Iracunda diem proferet Ilio* quoted from Horace, *Od.* I. 15. 33, is not parallel; cf. note to v. 13.

dum proficiscor] "Until I set out," cf. *Eun.* I. 2. 126 (where see note). It might = simply "whilst," —"put off the marriage while I am going." As however *proficiscor* does not generally imply continuous action, the former is most agreeable. This idiomatic construction of *dum* with indic. = "until" is quite clas-

sical: cf. Virg. *Ecl.* IX. 23, Cic. *Att.* X. 3, *Ego in Arcano opperior, dum haec cognosco:*. Lucr. I. 949, &c. *Donec* in older writers takes past indic. in sense "until." In Lucr. this is the invariable constr. with but one exception, vid. Munro, *ad Lucr.* I. 222.

31 **gratiae**] Prol. 8 (note).

35 **id agam**] "I will do my best to prevent her being married to me." Cf. I. 2. 15 (note). *Qui* (how) seems almost superfluous: but cf. the constr. *ut ne*, and l. 1. 34 (note).

nisi ea, quae nil opus sunt sciri.   Fugin' hinc?   Bv. Ego
    vero, ac lubens.

ACTUS II.   SCENA II.

Davus.   Charinus.   Pamphilus.

Da. Di boni, boni quid porto!   Sed ubi inveniam Pam-
    philum,

ut metum, in quo nunc est, adimam, atque expleam animum
    gaudio?

Ch. Laetus est nescio quid.   Pa. Nihil est: nondum haec
    rescivit mala.   (340)

Da. quem ego nunc credo, si iam audierit sibi paratas nup-
    tias—

Ch. Audin' tu illum?   Da. toto me oppido exanimatum
    quaerere.   5

Sed ubi quaeram? aut quo nunc primum intendam?   Ch.
    Cessas adloqui?

Da. Abeo.   Pa. Dave, ades.   Resiste.   Da. Quis homo est,
    qui me?   O Pamphile,

te ipsum quaero.   Euge Charine: ambo opportune.   Vos
    volo.

Pa. Dave, perii.   Da. Quin tu hoc audi.   Pa. Interii.   Da.
    Quid timeas, scio.

---

37 **sciri**] So Bentley for vulg.
scire. "Legendum est aut *opus est
scire* aut *opus sunt sciri.*" *Opus* is the
predicate (as in Plaut. *Capt.* I. 2. 61,
maritimi milites opus sunt tibi.
Cic. *Fam.* II. 6, *dux nobis opus est*),
and *scire* is added epexegetically:
cf. Cic. *Att.* VII. 6, *Si quid forte sit
quod opus sit sciri.*

Sc. II.] Davus appears, and re-
lates his discovery that the marriage
was a pretence.

Metre, trochaic tetrameter catalectic.

5 **toto oppido**] "Over the whole
town." This is no exception to the
use of accusative case to express
space over which: for where *totus* is
used the whole space is conceived
as one place *at which*: cf. Virg.
Aen. II. 421.

7 **Abeo**] Some old MSS. and ·
edd. have *habeo* (for *abeo*; as *hostium,
holim* in MSS.), which Bentley retains.

9 **quin tu audi**] The origin of

CH. Mea quidem hercle certe in dubio vitast. DA. Et quid
tu, scio.   10

PA. Nuptiae mi.... DA. Etsi scio? PA. hodie.   DA. Ob-
tundis, tametsi intelligo?

Id paves, ne ducas tu illam: tu autem, ut ducas.   CH.
Rem tenes.

PA. Istuc ipsum.   DA. Atque istuc ipsum nil pericli est:
me vide.   (350)

PA. Obsecro te, quamprimum hoc me libera miserum metu.
DA. Hem,

libero; uxorem tibi non dat iam Chremes.   PA. Qui scis?
DA. Scies.   15

Tuus pater modo me prehendit: ait tibi uxorem dare sese
hodie; item alia multa, quae nunc non est narrandi locus.

Continuo ad te properans percurro ad forum, ut dicam tibi
haec.

Ubi te non invenio, ibi ascendo in quendam excelsum locum.

Circumspicio. Nusquam.   Forte ibi huius video Byrriam;
rogo : negat vidisse.   Mihi molestum.   Quid agam, cogito. 21

Redeunti interea ex ipsa re mi incidit suspicio: hem,
paululum obsoni: ipsus tristis : de improviso nuptiae : (360)
non cohaerent.   PA. Quorsumnam istuc?   DA. Ego me continuo ad Chremem.

Quum illo advenio, solitudo ante ostium : iam id gaudeo.

---

this use of *quin* is the phrase *quin tu narras?* [cf. below, sc. 3, v. 25, IV. 4. 15] for a gentle command, Greek τί οὐκ ἀπεκοιμήθημεν; (*quin* = *qui non*). This expression was then made imperative in form, the original construction being overlooked, *quin age*, &c.: and finally *quin* was used simply as an emphatic particle.

11 **Et scio?**] "Do you go on, though I know all?"

13 **me vide**] Common in Plautus and Terence, as confirmation of a promise, &c. *Phorm.* IV. 4. 30. Cf.

respicio of looking to a person for help, depending on, Hor. *Epp.* I. I. 105. Cf. *subsidia respicere*, Livy.

15 **iam**] is emphatic; "*now* there's no doubt."

22 **ex ipsa re**] goes with *incidit*, "from looking at the facts."

23 **ipsus**] "My master." So the Greek αὐτὸς ἔφα, *Ipse dixit*, Ar. *Nub.* 219, and Juv. V. 86.

25 **illo**] Bentley for *illoc*, which is found in Latin writers, as *hoc* = *huc*, Virg. *Aen.* VIII. 423, and in several passages of Plautus.

CH. Recte dicis.　PA. Perge.　DA. Maneo : interea introire
　　neminem　　　　　　　　　　　　　　　　　　　26
video, exire neminem : matronam nullam in aedibus,
nihil ornati, nihil tumulti : accessi : intro aspexi.　PA. Scio.
Magnum signum.　DA. Num videntur convenire haec nup-
　　tiis ?
PA. Non opinor, Dave.　DA. Opinor narras ?　Non recte
　　accipis.　　　　　　　　　　　　　　　　　　30
Certa res est.　Etiam puerum inde abiens conveni Chremi,
olera et pisciculos minutos ferre obolo in cenam seni.
CH. Liberatus sum hodie, Dave, tua opera.　DA. Ac nullus
　　quidem.　　　　　　　　　　　　　　　　　(370)
CH. Quid ita ?　Nempe huic prorsus illam non dat.　DA.
　　Ridiculum caput !
Quasi necesse sit, si huic non dat, te illam uxorem ducere :

27 matronam] i. e. as *pronuba*, to dress the bride : cf. Cat. 61. 186.

28 ornati...tumulti] Forms of gen. of fourth decl. Donatus quotes from a fragment of Sallust, "senati decreto serviendum ne sit." *Eun.* II. 2. 6, *ornati.* Ritschl (*Prooem. de titulo Aletrinatium*) gives a list of such forms from various Latin writers, among them *quaesti, tumulti, fructi, adventi, ornati,* from Terence.

30 Opinor narras] "*Think,*" do you say?

31 Chremi] So *Archonidi, Heaut.* v. 5. 21. The -ου of Greek second decl. in -ης is generally represented in Latin by *ae. Achilli, Ulixi,* which are quoted as examples, are probably due to taking the term -ευς as dissyllable and declining as nouns of second decl. in *-us, Achillēus, Achillei* (cf. Hor. *Laboriosi remiges Ulixei*).

32 ferre] The infin. must depend on some verb implied in *conveni.* Parry suggests that *conveni=venire vidi,* and that *ferre* depends on *vidi.*

Bentley reads *conspexi,* cutting the knot after his manner. [Wagner adopts Fleckeisen's punctuation, *Chremi: olera, &c.* making *ferre* historic infin.=*ferebat.*]

obolo] i. e. *exiguo pretio.* Greek ὀβόλου ἀγόρασαι.

33 Ac nullus quidem] "No, not at all." Cf. *Eun.* II. 1. 10; Plaut. *Trin.* III. 1. 5: also found in Cicero. It may be compared with the frequent transfer of an adverbial notion to agreement with the subject of the action qualified; e.g. especially with *primus,* &c.

ac] is MS. reading, altered by some editors to *at ;* but *ac atque* not unfrequently connect an adversative clause; hence often with *tamen :* cf. I. 3. 2o, *Ad.* I. 1. 15, and Greek use of καί="although." The placing two ideas or clauses side by side as co-ordinate may be conceived of as opposition no less than connection.

35 sit] The subj. marks what a mere supposition this idea is : *si... dat* expresses not a supposition but a fact, and might be translated, "now that," or "seeing that."

nisi vides, nisi senis amicos oras, ambis. CH. Bene mones.
Ibo : etsi hercle saepe iam me spes haec frustrata est. Vale.

ACTUS II. SCENA III.

PAMPHILUS. DAVUS.

PA. Quid igitur sibi volt pater? cur simulat? DA. Ego
dicam tibi.
Si id succenseat nunc, quia non dat tibi uxorem Chremes,
ipsus sibi esse iniurius videatur : neque id iniuria :
prius quam tuum ut sese habeat animum ad nuptias per-
spexerit.
Sed si tu negaris ducere, ibi culpam in te transferet :   5
tum illae turbae fient. PA. Quidvis patiar. DA. Pater est,
Pamphile.   (380)
Difficilest. Tum haec solast mulier. Dictum ac factum in-
venerit
aliquam causam, quamobrem eiiciat oppido. PA. Eiiciat?
DA. Cito.
PA. Cedo igitur quid faciam, Dave? DA. Dic te ducturum.
PA. Hem. DA. Quid est?
PA. Egon' dicam? DA. Cur non? PA. Numquam faciam.
DA. Ne nega.   10

---

36 nisi vides] Supply, "which
will come off, unless..."
Sc. III.] D. and P. agree that the
latter shall profess willingness to
marry Philumena.
Metre: 1—9 trochaic tetram. catal.; 10—19 iambic trimeter; 20—29
iamb. tetram.
3 sibi] with *videatur* not *injurius. Injurius...injuria:* the play
on words may be kept up. "He
will feel that he is in the wrong, and
he won't be far wrong in that."

4 prius...perspexerit] refers to
succenseat.
ut sese habeat ad nuptias] Greek
πῶς ἔχει πρὸς τοὺς γάμους. *habere
se,* of bodily or mental health (*Eun.*
IV. 2. 6; 7. 30): then *habeo,* neut.
like ἔχω, *Phorm.* II. 3. 82: cf. Cic.
Mur. VI. 14, *bene habet;* Hor. *Sat.*
I. 9. 53.
7 Dictum ac factum] "No sooner
said than done :" ἅμα ἔπος ἅμα
ἔργόν. Cf. *Heaut.* IV. 5. 12, and
Homer, *Il.* XIX. 242. So *dicto citius.*

PA. Suadere noli.   DA. Ex ea re quid fiat, vide.

PA. Ut ab illa excludar, huc concludar.   DA. Non itast.

Nempe hoc sic esse opinor: dicturum patrem,   .

ducas volo hodie uxorem: tu, ducam, inquies.

Cedo quid iurgabit tecum?   Hic reddes omnia,   15

quae nunc sunt certa ei consilia, incerta ut sient,   (390)

sine omni periclo: nam hocce haud dubiumst, quin·Chremes

tibi non det gnatam.   Nec tu ea causa minueris

haec quae facis, ne is mutet suam sententiam.

Patri dic velle: ut, quum velit, tibi iure irasci non queat. 20

Nam quod tu speres, propulsabo facile; uxorem his moribus

dabit nemo.   Inveniet inopem potius, quam te corrumpi sinat.

Sed si te aequo animo ferre accipiet, negligentem feceris:

aliam otiosus quaeret: interea aliquid acciderit boni.

PA. Ita credis?   DA. Haud dubium id quidemst.   PA. Vide

       quo me inducas.   DA. Quin taces?   25

---

12. **concludar**] as if into a cell, cf. *Phorm.* V. 1. 17: and III. 4. 23, in *nuptias coniici herilem filium.* It is doubtful however whether any special senses of *excludo, concludo* are here intended: similarity of sound is the object, v. Parry's note.

17. **sine omni per.**] An unusual form of expression (we should expect *ullo*) peculiar to Plautus and Terence. In Greek we find a somewhat similar use of τᾶς = "anyone" (τὸ μὲν ἐτιτιμᾶν φήσαι τις ἂν παντὸς εἶναι Dem.); but this cannot perhaps be distinguished from the sense "every one," ἄνευ παντός.

18 **minueris**] From the particular meaning "to lessen" comes the more general one "to alter," "change." m. *opinionem* = "refute," Cic.; m. *controversias* = "to put an end to," Caesar. Tr. "make no difference in your present conduct from a fear that he may change his mind;" cf. *Hec.* IV. 3. 10, *Haec quae facis,* i.e. the pretended acquiescence in his father's wishes: *sententiam,* Chremes' determination that the marriage is not to come off.

21, 22 **Uxorem...sinat**] These words, somewhat obscurely expressed by the abrupt disconnected language of Davus, may be thus paraphrased: "You may perhaps hope that, if you resist your father as to this marriage you are safe: for 'no one,' you think, 'will give his daughter to a man of my character.' But I tell you your father will find a girl without dowry and marry you to her, rather than let you be ruined by this connection with Glycerium."

his moribus] in *Hec.* IV. 4. 22 fuller, *uxorem his moratam moribus.*

23] "But if he finds that you take it quietly, you will have put him off his guard: he will take his time about finding another bride for you, and meanwhile something lucky may turn up."

25 **Quin taces?**] see above, sc. 2, v. 9 note.

3—2

PA. Dicam. Puerum autem ne resciscat mi esse ex illa, cau-
    tio est: (400)
nam pollicitus sum suscepturum. DA. O facinus audax! PA.
    Hanc fidem
sibi me obsecravit, qui se sciret non deserturum, ut darem.
DA. Curabitur. Sed pater adest. Cave, te esse tristem
    sentiat.

ACTUS II. SCENA IV.

SIMO. DAVUS. PAMPHILUS.

SI. Reviso quid agant, aut quid captent consili.
DA. Hic nunc non dubitat, quin te ducturum neges.
Venit meditatus alicunde ex solo loco:
orationem sperat invenisse se,
qui differat te: proin tu fac apud te ut sies.   5
PA. Modo ut possim, Dave. DA. Crede inquam hoc mihi,
    Pamphile,
numquam hodie tecum commutaturum patrem   (410)
unum esse verbum, si te dices ducere.

---

27 **suscepturum**] cf. I. 3. 14
note.

28 **deserturum**] Bentley reads
desertum iri on authority of one MS.

Sc. IV.] Simo comes up to see
how P. and D. are arranging matters.
Metre iambic trimeter. "Haec scena
nodum iniicit fabulae et periculum
comicum," Donatus.

3 **meditatus**] "with his speech
got up," "prepared in his part,"
cf. Plaut. *Trin.* III. 3. 89. Verg.
Ecl. I. 2. Hence *orationem* = a set
speech, "quod quasi ad plenum co-
gitari potuisset," Donatus.

5 **differat**] "distract:" Hor. *Epod.*
V. 99. *Ad.* III. 4. 40.

ACTUS II. SCENA V.

BYRRIA. SIMO. DAVUS. PAMPHILUS.

BY. Herus me relictis rebus iussit Pamphilum
hodie observare, ut quid ageret de nuptiis
scirem: id propterea nunc hunc venientem sequor.
Ipsum adeo praesto video cum Davo: hoc agam.
SI. Utrumque adesse video. DA. Hem, serva. SI. Pam-
   phile!   5
DA. Quasi de improviso respice ad eum. PA. Ehem, pater.
DA. Probe. SI. Hodie uxorem ducas, ut dixi, volo.
BY. Nunc nostrae timeo parti, quid hic respondeat.
PA. Neque istic, neque alibi tibi erit usquam in me mora.
   BY. Hem.   (420)
DA. Obmutuit. BY. Quid dixit? SI. Facis, ut te decet, 10
quum istuc, quod postulo impetro cum gratia.
DA. Sum verus? BY. Herus quantum audio, uxore excidit.
SI. I nunc iam intro; ne in mora quum opus sit sies.
PA. Eo. BY. Nullane in re esse homini cuiquam fidem?
Verum illud verbumst, volgo quod dici solet,   15

Sc. V.] Byrria, set by his master
Charinus to watch Pamphilus, over-
hears P. give his consent to marry
Philumena. Metre; iambic trimeter.

1 **rebus relictis**] "before everything else," a common phrase in
Plaut. and Ter. cf. Lucr. III. 1071.

3 **id propterea**] pleonastic, but the
oldest reading: *hunc* i. e. Simo now
coming on the stage (venientem):
not, as Bentley supposed, Pamphilus. B., on the ground that Pamphilus could not be said to be coming on the stage "now," read *ob-
servarem quid* in v. 2, and omitted
v. 3 altogether. *Ipsum* v. 4 naturally refers to Pamphilus.

4 **Ipsum adeo**] "The very
man," cf. IV. 4. 20 note.

5 **serva**] "remember," so *perdo* =
"forget," τοιγαροῦν σώ᾽ζου τόδε,
Soph. *El.* 1257: *O.T.* 318.

11 **cum gratia**] with a good grace,
cf. *Phorm.* IV. 3. 17 for the full
phrase.

12 **excidit**] "has lost his wife."
Perhaps in allusion to its technical
use in juridical language (Parry):
but more probably adapted from
Greek ἐκπίπτειν, cf. Soph. *Ai.* 1177,
ἐκπίπτειν χθονὸς ἄθαπτος: ἀπ᾽ ἐλπί-
δων, Thuc. VIII. 81: and more
commonly ἀρχῆς, πατρίδος, κ.τ.λ.

omnes sibi malle melius esse quam alteri.
Ego illam vidi virginem ; forma bona
memini videre: quo aequior sum Pamphilo,
si se illam in somnis, quam illum, amplecti maluit.   (430)
Renuntiabo, ut pro hoc malo mihi det malum.   20

ACTUS II. SCENA VI.

DAVUS. SIMO.

DA. Hic nunc me credit aliquam sibi fallaciam
portare, et ea me hic restitisse gratia.
SI. Quid Davos narrat? DA. Aeque quicquam nunc quidem.
SI. Nihilne? Hem. DA. Nihil prorsus. SI. Atqui expec-
     tabam quidem.
DA. Praeter spem evenit: sentio: hoc male habet virum. 5
SI. Potin' es mihi verum dicere? DA. Nihil facilius.
SI. Num illi molestae quippiam hae sunt nuptiae,
huiusce propter consuetudinem hospitae?
DA. Nihil hercle: aut, si adeo, bidui est aut tridui   (440)
haec sollicitudo: nosti: deinde desinet.   10
Etenim ipsus secum recta reputavit via.

16] cf. Eur. *Med.* 84, ὡς πᾶς τις αὑτὸν τοῦ πέλας μᾶλλον φιλεῖ, and Menander, φιλεῖ δ'ἑαυτοῦ πλεῖον οὐδεὶς οὐδένα.

Sc. VI.] Simo tries to ascertain from Davus whether Pamphilus still cares for Glycerium. Metre, iambic trimeter.

2 **ea gratia**] attraction from *eius gratia*, cf. *Eun.* I. 2. 19, Greek ταύτην χάριν.

3 **Aeque quicquam**, &c.] "Just as much now as ever," i.e. nothing; [though Madvig (Cic. *Fin.* III. 8) explains, He says something as good as you—for you say nothing]. Cf.

Eun. v. 2. 23. Simo does not quite understand; *nihilne?* = "nothing, do you mean?"

5 **hoc male habet virum**] "This is what annoys him."

8] The ordinary reading, *Propter huiusce hospitai consuetudinem*, involves the scansion prŏptĕr, and the archaic form of gen. *-ai*, which is not Terentian. Bentley has introduced it on his own authority in *Heaut.* III. 2. 4; v. I. 20; *Phor.* IV. 2. 7. Ritschl (Preface to Plautus, p. cccxxvii.) proposes the reading of our text.

11] Faernus read in cod. Vatic. "Etenim ipsus secum eam rem re-

Si. Laudo. Da. Dum licitum est ei, dumque aetas tulit,
amavit: tum id clam: cavit, ne umquam infamiae
ea res sibi esset, ut virum fortem decet:
nunc uxore opus est: animum ad uxorem adpulit.　　　15
Si. Subtristis visust esse aliquantulum mihi.
Da. Nihil propter hanc rem: sed est, quod succenset tibi.
Si. Quidnamst? Da. Puerilest. Si. Quid id est? Da.
　　　Nihil. Si. Quin dic, quid est?
Da. Ait nimium parce facere sumptum. Si. Mene? Da.
　　　Te.　　　　　　　　　　　　　　　　　　　(450)
Vix, inquit, drachmis est obsonatus decem:　　　20
num filio videtur uxorem dare?
Quem, inquit, vocabo ad cenam meorum aequalium
potissimum nunc? Et, quod dicendum hic siet,
tu quoque perparce nimium. Non laudo. Si. Tace.
Da. Commovi. Si. Ego istaec, recte ut fiant, videro.　　　25
Quidnam hoc rei est? Quid hic volt veterator sibi?
Nam si hic malist quicquam, hem illic est huic rei caput.

putavit via:" Bentley rejects *secum* and restores *recta* which Faernus saw in the MS.: but *eam rem* is more likely to have been inserted as a gloss, and is not noticed by Donatus. *Reputavit* intrans. So Tac. *Hist.* IV. 17, *vere reputantibus*. *recta via*, "straightforwardly," *Heaut.* IV. 3. 28.

20] Bentley reads *obsonatum* on authority of two MSS. and Plaut. *Bacch.* I. 2. 35: both *obsono* and *obsonor* are in use.

23 quod...siet] "as far as it can be said by one in my place"=if it can be said, so *quod sciam: quod meminerim.* The subjunctive is here potential, cf. Lucr. II. 248, *quod cernere possis*, and Munro's notes to I.

327; II. 350 (*quoad licet ac possis*). Cf. also *Eun.* II. 1. 9: *Hec.* V. 1. 34.

26 **veterator**] "old rogue," Lit. one who has grown old in anything: so "practised," "skilled," Cicero. In bad sense, as here, Cicero *Fin.* II. 16. 53; *Verr.* II. 1. 54. In the jurists opp. to *novitius* (*Eun.* III. 5. 34), cf. Greek τρίβων, ἐπίτριπτός.

27] "If there is anything wrong here (if Pamphilus does not do as I wish), there goes the head and front of it all." Simo, as they leave the stage, hints his suspicions of Davus. *caput*, cf. *Ad.* IV. 2. 29. Verg. *Aen.* XI. 361, *caput horum et causa malorum*. The metaphor is from the head or source of a river.

ACTUS III. SCENA I.

MYSIS. SIMO. DAVUS. LESBIA. GLYCERIUM.

MY. Ita pol quidem res est, ut dixti, Lesbia:
fidelem haud ferme mulieri invenias virum.
SI. Ab Andriast ancilla haec.   DA. Quid narras? SI.
     Itast.   (460)
MY. Sed hic Pamphilus.. SI. Quid dicit? MY. firmavit
     fidem. SI. Hem.
DA. Utinam aut hic surdus, aut haec muta facta sit.   5
MY. Nam quod peperisset, iussit tolli. SI. O Iuppiter!
quid ego audio? Actumst, siquidem haec vera praedicat.
LE. Bonum ingenium narras adulescentis. MY. Optumum.
Sed sequere me intro, ne in mora illi sis. LE. Sequor.
DA. Quod remedium nunc huic malo inveniam? SI. Quid
     hoc?   10
Adeone est demens? Ex peregrina? Iam scio; ah
vix tandem sensi stolidus. DA. Quid hic sensisse ait? (470)
SI. Haec primum adfertur iam mihi ab hoc fallacia:
hanc simulant parere, quo Chremetem absterreant.
GL. Iuno Lucina, fer opem: serva me, obsecro!   15
SI. Hui, tam cito? Ridiculum: postquam ante ostium

Sc. 1.] Simo overhears Mysis and Lesbia talking about the honourable conduct of Pamphilus towards Glycerium, and thinks he sees through a trick concocted to prevent the marriage with Philumena. Metre, iambic trimeter.

2 **haud ferme**] "scarcely ever." *ferme* extenuates a negative. According to Varro it is derived from *fero* (superl. suffix as in fini*timus* &c.), and signifies being brought near: hence a double signification as idea of coming near or nearness predominates, (i) "nearly," "almost:" (ii) "quite," "precisely." But it is

more prob. connected with *fir-m-us*, *fre-tus*, *fre-num*, and the *f*=Gk. θ as in θρᾶνος, θρόνος. Sense (i) would then follow from (ii), just as αὐτίκα= Eng. "presently" means "*not* immediately."

6 **peperisset**] Cf. Prol. 3 note. *tolli* I. 3. 14 note.

11 **Ex peregrina**] His children would be illegitimate in the eyes of the law. There is an aposiopesis— *ut suscipiat?*

13] Simo fancies that this conversation is all a trick to impose upon him.

me audivit stare, adproperat. Non sat commode
divisa sunt temporibus tibi, Dave, haec. DA. Mihin'?
SI. Num immemor es discipuli? DA. Ego, quid narres,
          nescio.
SI. Hiccine me si imparatum in veris nuptiis   20
adortus esset, quos mihi ludos redderet?
Nunc huius periclo fit; ego in portu navigo.   (480)

ACTUS III. SCENA II.

LESBIA. SIMO. DAVUS.

LE. Adhuc Archylis, quae adsolent quaeque oportet
signa esse ad salutem, omnia huic esse video.
Nunc primum fac istaec lavet: post deinde,
quod iussi ei dari bibere, et quantum imperavi,
date: mox ego huc revertor.   5

17 **Non sat commode**, &c.] "Your
incidents are ill timed, Davus," a
theatrical metaphor.

19 **Num immemor es dis.**]
"What! have you forgotten your
scholar?" i.e. Pamphilus: another
reading *immemores* would be the "Have
your pupils forgotten their parts?"
This Donatus and most of the commentators take. The objection to
it is that *nonne* would then be more
appropriate than *num*, for it is implied that they *have* forgotten.

20] Cf. I. 1. 132, where Simo
hopes that Davus may play any
tricks he has in view while they can
do no harm.

21 **quos...redderet**] "What a game
he would be playing me!" distinct
from *ludos aliquem* (or *alicui*) *facere*
= to make a joke of one, common
in Plaut.: *ludos praebere* = to make
oneself ridiculous, *Eun.* v. 6. 9:
and *ludum dare alicui* = to humour

or indulge.

si adortus esset...redderet] in
Greek *εἰ* with aorist ind. followed by
imperfect indic. with ἄν, *εἰ τότε
ἐβοηθήσαμεν, οὐκ ἂν ἠνώχλει νῦν ὁ
Φίλιππος.* Cic. *Rosc. Am.* 6, *Si
Roscius inimicitias cavere potuisset
viveret.*

22 **in portu navigo**] Cf. Verg.
Aen. VII. 598, *Nunc mihi parta
quies, omnisque in limine portus*, cf.
omnis res in vado est, V. 2. 4.
Greek *ἐν λιμένι πλέω.*

Sc. II.] Simo fancies his suspicions confirmed, and is encouraged
by Davus, who at the same time
persuades him that Pamphilus has
abandoned Glycerium. Metre: 1—4,
bacchiac tetrameter: 5, iamb. dim.
catal.: 6, 17, 18, 44—5, 20, iamb.
trim.: 7—16, 19—25, 27—29, iambic
tetrameter: 26, iambic tetram. catal.:
30—36, 38—43, trochaic tetram.
catal.: 37, troch. dimeter catal.

Per ecastor scitus puer est natus Pamphilo.

Deos quaeso, ut sit superstes, quandoquidem ipsest ingenio
      bono ;

quumque huic est veritus optumae adulescenti facere in-
      iuriam.

SI. Vel hoc quis non credat, qui te norit, abs te esse or-
      tum? DA. Quidnam id est?

SL. Non imperabat coram, quid opus facto esset puer-
      perae :   (490) 10

sed postquam egressast, illis, quae sunt intus, clamat de via.

O Dave, itan' contemnor abs te? aut itane tandem idoneus

tibi videor esse, quem tam aperte fallere incipias dolis?

Saltem accurate : ut metui videar certe, si resciverim.

DA. Certe hercle nunc hic se ipsus fallit, haud ego.   SI.
      Edixin' tibi,   15

interminatus sum, ne faceres? Num veritus? Quid retulit?

Credon' tibi hoc nunc, peperisse hanc e Pamphilo?

DA. Teneo, quid erret, et quid agam habeo.   SI. Quid
      taces?

---

6 **Per...scitus**] separated by tmesis
—so Cic. *Or.* II. 67, *per mihi scitum
videtur:* cf. *Hec.* I. I. I, and in Cicero
with other compounds, v. dictt. s. v.
per. scitus (part. of *scisco* with middle
sense) "shrewd," "knowing." Then
of things "suitable," "witty :" and
transf. "beautiful," "elegant" in
Plautus and post-class. writers. Here
= "a very fine boy." Gellius has
scitamenta = niceties (of speech),
ὁμοιοτέλευτα καὶ ὁμοιόπτωτα *caetera-
que huiusmodi scitamenta.*

8 **huic est veritus**] So Bentley
on auth. of a MS. at Cambridge for
the common reading *huic veritus est.*
Some edd. in order to write *veritust*
(the orthography of Plaut. and Ter.)
read *huiic*, a form unsupported in
Plaut. and Ter. [Wagner reads
huice veritust].

10 **quid opus facto**] Instead of
the constr. *opus facere* the past participle is used, apparently conveying
in an indefinite sense the abstract
notion of the verb, as is more usually done by the participle in *-dus :* and
(like that part. in its *gerundial* use)
it seems to be followed by the case
which the verb governs : thus *quid*
is here apparently governed by *facto*
of v. 43, *quod parato.* But it seems
better to regard *quid* as acc. of relation, "as to what there is need of
doing it."

14 **Saltem accurate**] (*fallas*).
"You should at least do it carefully,
to give the appearance of being
afraid of me should I discover it."

16 **Quid retulit**] "What good
was it (to order and threaten you)?"

DA. Quid credas? Quasi non tibi renunciata sint haec sic
   fore.

SI. Mihin' quisquam? DA. Eho an tute intellexti hoc ad-
   simulari? SI. Inrideor.   (500) 20

DA. Renunciatumst: nam qui istaec tibi incidit suspicio?

SI. Qui? quia te noram, DA. Quasi tu dicas, factum id
   consilio meo.

SI. Certe enim scio. DA. Non satis me pernosti etiam,
   qualis sim, Simo.

SI. Egon' te? DA. Sed, si quid narrare occepi, continuo
   dari

tibi verba censes falso: itaque hercle nil iam muttire
   audeo.   25

SI. Hoc ego scio unum, neminem peperisse hic. DA. Intellexti.

Sed nihilo secius mox deferent puerum huc ante ostium.

Id ego iam nunc tibi renuntio, here, futurum, ut sis sciens:

ne tu hoc posterius dicas Davi factum consilio aut dolis.

Prorsus a me opinionem hanc tuam esse ego amotam
   volo.   (510) 30

22 **Quasi tu dicas**] "That's as much as to say, that" &c. Donatus' explanation "dicas, i.e. credas; non enim dicimus nisi quod credimus" is unnecessary.

23 **enim**] may be explained by an ellipse. "I do say so, for...:" or bearing in mind the asseverative force of *enim* [especially in answers, cf. *Hec.* V. 4. 10; *Heaut.* I. 2. 14) as simply strengthening the assertion, "I tell you I know it."

etiam] "even yet," cf. I. 1. 89.

26 **Intellexti**] "You understand:" i.e. you have already found it out, cf. the use of the Greek aor. in such expressions as ἐδεξάμην τὸ ῥηθέν, where English must employ a present tense (see Jebb to Soph. *El.* 668) cf. Hor. *S.* II. 1. 16.

27] Davus intends to frighten

Chremes out of his consent to the marriage of Philumena to Pamphilus, by letting him discover the connection of the latter with Glycerium (see Act V. Sc. 2); and that he may do so without Simo at the same time discovering it, he cunningly prepares Simo for disbelieving the story, by predicting that it will be got up as a fraud.

28 **sciens**] this part. is used frequently in Plaut. and Ter. in an adjectival force, especially with verbs *sum* and *facio* (*Heaut.* IV. 8. 32): coupled with *prudens*, *Eun.* I. 1. 27, and opp. to *imprudens*, *Phor.* IV. 3. 55: both these also in Cicero. *sis sciens* here merely =*scias*, and can hardly be taken as an indication of the use of auxiliary verbs in Lat. such as Greek τετολμηκὼς ἔχει &c.

Si. Unde id scis? Da. Audivi, et credo: multa concur-
    runt simul,
qui coniecturam hanc nunc facio.   Iam primum haec se e
    Pamphilo
gravidam dixit esse: inventum est falsum. Nunc, postquam
    videt
nuptias domi apparari, missast ancilla illico
. obstetricem accersitum ad eam, et puerum ut adferret
    simul.   35
Hoc nisi fit, puerum ut tu videas, nihil moventur nuptiae.
Si. Quid ais? Quum intellexeras
id consilium capere, cur non dixti extemplo Pamphilo?
Da. Quis igitur eum ab illa abstraxit, nisi ego? Nam
    omnes nos quidem
scimus, quam misere hanc amarit.   Nunc sibi uxorem
    expetit.   (520) 40
Postremo id mihi da negoti: tu tamen idem has nuptias
perge facere ita, ut facis: et id supero adiuturos deos.

---

34 illico] Donatus, "quod Graeci
dicunt αὐτόθεν ἐπέμφθη." *Illico* (in
loco) is used of time as = at that
point of time, where the thing appears, i.e. at once: or as we say "on
the spot," Hand, *Turs.* III. p. 208,
cf. Spanish "luego" = "at once."
cf. *Eun.* V. 7. 11. *Ad.* II. 1. 2,
where however Donatus "addit
modo locum non tempus significat."
36 moventur] according to Donatus = *differuntur*, "are put off,"
cf. IV. 2. 23, *promoveo* nuptias. But
better = "disturb," cf. such expressions as *movere tribu, senatu*, and
Cic. *Phil. Ea non muto, non moveo.*
37 Quum intellexeras] "At
the moment when you had found
out: *quum* with the indic. plup. denotes coincidence, not succession of
events in past time (cf. I. 1. 69 note,
and Madvig, *Gr.* 368). "After," or
"in consequence of discovering"

would have been *quum intellexisses.*
38 consilium] So Bentley for
the old reading *consilii*, cf. I. 1. 132
note.
extemplo = ex tempulo (dim. of
tempus) = ex tempore, on the spur of
the moment, or from *templum* = "a
place of watching," cf. *illico.*
40 misere] "vehemently," so frequently in Plaut. and Ter. cf. *Eun.*
III. 1. 22; *Ad.* IV. 1. 6; Hor. *Sat.*
I. 9. 8.
41 idem] "on the other hand,"
used when something new is said of
a person or thing already mentioned
and thus either denotes *similarity*
("at the same time," "while") or
opposition, cf. the use of *immo* (μὲν
οὖν), which denotes either contradic-
tion, or restatement in another form,
of what has been said.
42 facere] This use of the infin.
to denote a purpose or result is

SI. Immo abi intro: ibi me opperire, et quod parato opus
        est para.

Non inpulit me, haec nunc omnino ut crederem:
atque haud scio, an, quae dixit, sint vera omnia: 45
sed parvi pendo: illud mi multo maxumumst,
quod mihi pollicitust ipsus gnatus. Nunc Chremem
conveniam: orabo gnato uxorem: si impetro,
quid alias malim, quam hodie has fieri nuptias?
Nam gnatus quod pollicitust, haud dubiumst mihi, (530) 50
si nolit, quin eum merito possim cogere.
Atque adeo in ipso tempore eccum ipsum obviam.

properly admissible only with verbs
that involve reference to another
action to complete their meaning,
e. g. verbs expressing *will*, *power*,
resolve &c. Thus *volo*, *statuo* &c.
are incomplete by themselves, and
require an infinitive of what is wished or determined to be done. But in
poetry even verbs which require no
such completion of their meaning,
or verbs which only figuratively
denote wish, inclination &c. are
followed by this infin. Thus *perge*
here implies going on with determination to do, so *instare* frequently
in Vergil. Cf. *ardet abire fuga: in-
cumbunt generis lapsi sarcire ruinas*,
G. IV. 248. In Greek the use of
the infin. with or without ὥστε, to
denote result, purpose &c., is much
more common, especially in certain
Homeric phrases, βῆ ἰέναι, συνέηκε
μάχεσθαι &c. Cf. *Eun.* Prol. 18.
Phormio IV. 3. 361: and see Madvig,
Gr. sect. 389.

48 **si impetro**] As the mood of
si is generally determined by the
mood of the apodosis, the subj.
malim might seem to require si
impetrem. But *malim*, *velim* &c.,
though in form subjunctive (potential), practically convey a *direct*

statement of a wish, and partake
more of the assertory character. of
the indic. mood than that of the
subj.: it states the supposition or
conception of an action. So when
we say "I should like" we mean
I *do* like; and in Greek γενοίμην ἂν
often *means* γενήσομαι (and is actually found in a construction which
is only admissible on that view, e.g.
οὐκ οἶδ' ἂν εἰ πείσαιμι: εἰ πείσαιμι ἂν
= εἰ πείσω).

49 **alias**] can hardly = *aliter*, for
such use is entirely post-Aug., and
first occurs in the Lat. of the jurists:
Tac. has *non alias quam* = under no
other circumstance than; and Cicero
twice has *alias* = elsewhere (*facete
is quidem sicut alias*, as in other
passages, *Fin.* I. 3. 7). Bentley
reads *quando alias*, quoting Acron.
ad Hor. *Sat.* I. 4. 36. It must =
"at any other time" with reference
to *hodie*: "If Chremes consents,"
says Simo, "the wedding shall come
off at once, this very day: what day
so good as the present?" Parry's
objection, that Chremes would give
his answer at once as well as at any
other time, is beside the mark:
Simo speaks of his own intentions
with regard to Pamphilus.

ACTUS III. SCENA III.

SIMO. CHREMES.

SI. Iubeo Chremetem.   CH. O, te ipsum quaerebam.   SI.
    Et ego te.   CH. Optato advenis.
Aliquot me adiere, ex te auditum qui aiebant, hodie filiam
meam nubere tuo gnato : id viso tun' an illi insaniant.
SI. Ausculta paucis : et quid ego te velim et tu quod quaeris
    scies.
CH. Ausculto : loquere quid velis.   5
SI. Per te deos oro, et nostram amicitiam, Chreme,
quae incepta a parvis, cum aetate adcrevit simul,
perque unicam gnatam tuam, et gnatum meum,   (540)
cuius tibi potestas summa servandi datur,
ut me adiuves in hac re : atque ita uti nuptiae   10
fuerant futurae, fiant.   CH. Ah ne me obsecra:

Sc. III.] Simo asks Chremes to
give his daughter to Pamphilus at
once, meeting the objection of the
Glycerium story, by what he has
heard from Davus of Pamphilus'
estrangement from her. Chremes
reluctantly consents. Metre : 1—4,
iambic tetrameter : 5, iambic dimeter : 6—42, iambic trimeter : 43, 48,
iambic tetram. catal. (including v. 1
of sc. 4).

1 Iubeo] sc. salvere, *Ad.* III. 4.
14 *optato* adverb, cf. *auspicato,
consulto,* &c. and Verg. *Aen.* X. 405.

4 Ausculta paucis] "Hear me
a moment," lit. "in" or "with a
few words:" cf. *Eun.* V. 8. 37, *audite paucis:* Bentley reads *Ausculta :
paucis......scies* (cf. *paucis dabo,
Heaut.* Prol. 10. *Ad.* V. 3. 20).
Donatus mentions a v. l. *pauca* which
would of course belong to *ausculta :*
and it is likely that he so understood *paucis,* as he makes no further
remark.

6 Per te deos oro] A formula
apparently imitated from Greek
πρός σε τῶν θεῶν, common in Latin
poetry and found in prose, e.g. Livy,
XXIII. 9.

11 fuerant] We should use the
imperfect "were to have been."
This idiomatic use of the plup.
brings out more emphatically that
the marriage was all over, by taking
the mind back to a point in past
time. It was even then a thing of
the past, how much more now?
Cf. Verg. *Aen.* X. 612, *Si mihi quae
quondam fuerat, quamque esse decebat, Vis in amore foret,* the power
that once I had, but have long lost :
cf. VII. 532. To express it in colloquial language the plup. infers that
some time ago it was a case of
"had been," which is stronger than
saying that it is now a case of *has
been.*

quasi hoc te orando a me impetrare oporteat.
Alium esse censes nunc me, atque olim quum dabam?
Si in remst utrique ut fiant, accersi iube.
Sed si ex ea re plus malist, quam commodi,   15
utrique : id oro te in commune ut consulas,
quasi illa tua sit, Pamphilique ego sim pater.
SI. Immo ita volo, itaque postulo ut fiat, Chreme :   (550)
neque postulem abs te, ni ipsa res moneat. CH. Quid est?
SI. Irae sunt inter Glycerium et gnatum. CH. Audio.   20
SI. Ita magnae, ut sperem posse avelli. CH. Fabulae.
SI. Profecto sic est. CH. Sic hercle, ut dicam tibi :
amantium irae amoris integratiost.
SI. Hem, id te oro, ut ante eamus. Dum tempus datur,
dumque eius lubido occlusast contumeliis,   25
prius quam harum scelera et lacrumae confictae dolis
reducunt animum aegrotum ad misericordiam,
uxorem demus. Spero consuetudine et   (560)
coniugio liberali devinctum, Chreme,
dein facile ex illis sese emersurum malis.   30
CH. Tibi ita hoc videtur: at ego non posse arbitror
neque illum hanc perpetuo habere, neque me perpeti.
SI. Qui scis ergo istuc, nisi periclum feceris?

---

13 **atque**] See infr. IV. 2. 15.

olim] "at that time." The original signification of the word,
which from a definite point in past
time came to signify an indefinite
time="formerly:" thence, without
allusion to past time="sometimes,"
"at any time" (Verg. *Aen.* V. 125):
and lastly transferred to future time
="some day or other," "hereafter"
(*Aen.* IV. 625: Hor. *Od.* II. 10, 17).

dabam] "offered," was willing to
give. So Greek ἐδίδουν.

14 **utrique**] "to either of us." *in
rem*, "to the purpose," *Hec.* II. 2. 7.

16 **id oro te**] Bentley, metri
gratia, for *id te oro.*

28] Wagner reads "Spero consuetudine Conjugi eum liberalis devinctum" on the ground that Terence does not end a verse with a
monosyllable and elision, except
with *es* or *est*. But is this reason
enough for the alteration? Terence
is no purist in respect to other rules
of metrical euphony.

29 **liberali**] i.e. with a free woman, opp. to *peregrina*, III. 1. 11.

30 **emersurum**] The transitive
use of *emergo* is not found in Plautus
nor the Augustan writers. In *Ad.*
III. 2. 4, the pass. is used imperso-
nally.

33 **periclum**] so *Eun., fac peri-*

CH. At istuc periclum in filia fieri, grave est.

SI. Nempe incommoditas denique huc omnis redit: 35
si eveniat, quod di prohibeant, discessio:
at si corrigitur, quot commoditates, vide.
Principio amico filium restitueris;
tibi generum firmum, et filiae invenies virum.   (570)
CH. Quid istic? Si ita istuc animum induxti esse utile, 40
nolo tibi ullum commodum in me claudier.
SI. Merito te semper maxumi feci, Chreme.
CH. Sed quid ais? SI. Quid? CH. Qui scis eos nunc
     discordare inter se?
SI. Ipsus mihi Davos, qui intumust eorum consiliis, dixit:
et is mihi suadet, nuptias quantum queam ut maturem. 45
Num censes faceret, filium nisi sciret eadem haec velle?
Tute adeo iam eius verba audies. Heus, evocate huc
     Davum.
Atque eccum: video ipsum foras exire.   ⌐   (580)

---

culum in literis. "periculum est tentamentum," Donatus.

35 **incommoditas**] "inconvenience." Simo uses the least offensive words, so *discessio* for *divortium* (*per discessionem*, Cic. *Phil.* IX. of voting on opposite sides in the senate).

36 **eveniat**] the subj. expresses a supposition; the indic. of *corrigitur* the certainty which Simo feels that all will turn out well.

37 **restitueris**] expresses the immediate result of Chremes' consent.

40 **Quid istic**] "Well, well." "concedentis et veluti victi verbum," Donatus; in full, "quin istic dicis?" "Why go on arguing?" *Ad.* I. 2. 53.

41 **in me claudier**] cf. *Eun.* I. 2. 84, *nunc ubi meam benignitatem sensisti in te claudier in me* = "in the case of me," in so far as I am concerned, and *in te* in *Eun.* = "in your case," "as far as you are concerned:" so that there is not such

dissimilarity between the two passages as some (v. Parry, note) suppose. Translate here, "I don't wish you to have any advantage obstructed as far as I am concerned." For *in me, in te,* may both come under the meaning "in the case of," cf. Verg. *Aen.* II. 541, *Talis in hoste fuit Priamo: Ecl.* VII. 83. The commentators appear first to create a difficulty by drawing a distinction between the use of *in* in these two passages, and then trouble themselves with unnecessary attempts at reconciliation. Bentley alters *in me claudier* to *intercludier*, and in *Eun.* for *nunc ubi...in te claudier* reads *num tibi...intercludier*, without any authority.

46 **censes**] parenthetical "think you?"

47 **adeo**] used with personal pronouns (cf. Verg. *Ecl.* IV. 11: *G.* I. 24) to direct attention in a transition, and often best express-

ACTUS III.　SCENA IV.

DAVUS.　SIMO.　CHREMES.

DA. AD te ibam. SI. Quidnam est?

DA. Cur uxor non adcersitur? Iam advesperascit. SI. Au·
din' tu illum?

Ego dudum non nihil veritus sum, Dave, abs te, ne faceres
idem,

quod volgus servorum solet, dolis ut me deluderes:

propterea quod amat filius. DA. Egon' istuc facerem? SI.

　　　Credidi: '　　　　　　　　　　　　　　　　5

idque adeo metuens vos celavi, quod nunc dicam. DA.

　　　Quid? SI. Scies:

nam propemodum habeo fidem. DA. Tandem cognosti qui

　　　siem?

ed by emphasis in pronunciation,
"*You* too," &c. From its first sense
of "insomuch as," "to such an extent," it passes to that of a mere
emphatic particle, and so is used especially with numbers, something
like our "full twenty" and the like.
Occasionally it has nearly the force
of *immo*: e.g. *adolescens tuus atque
adeo noster*, cf. Cic. *Cat.* I. 2, *hostem
intra moenia atque adeo in senatu
videmus* = "I had almost said."

Sc. IV.] Davus, coming to press
the marriage with Philumena (as
agreed Act II. Sc. 3), is alarmed at
hearing that Chremes has consented
to it.

Metre: 1 (with sc. 3. 48), iambic
tetram. catal.; 2—25, 27, iamb.
tetram.; 26, iamb. dimeter.

2] Bentley omits *tu illum* metri
gratia: but the v. is a regular iambic
tetrameter, the last syllable being
hypermetric and elided before *Ego*.
Examples of this are found in
Terence (*And.* IV. 1. 9; *Eun.* IV. 1.
11; *Phorm.* II. 1. 63; *Ad.* II. 2. 9).

Cicero preserves a passage of Pacu-
vius (*Tusc.* III. 26) in which it
occurs: Ennius does not use it.
Lucretius only once (v. 849, cf. Lachmann, ad I. 118): Vergil, Horace,
Catullus occasionally. The theory
of hypermetric verses must be that
the lines are scanned continuously
as one system; and whoever introduced the practice in Lat. must
have done so from a misapprehension
of the Greek metres, only one class
of which (the anapaestic) admits such
a system. It is unknown in Homer,
and οὐκ οἶδ' at the end of a verse of
Callimachus is the only known instance in Greek hexameters. The
Greek tragedians do employ it
(though not "infinitis locis," as
Wagner, *Georg.* II. 69).

3 **abs te**] cf. supra, I. 1. 78.

7] *tibi* which some editions read
after *habeo* may possibly be a gloss,
and as such is omitted by Bentley
metri gratia: it certainly "nocet
metro."

Sɪ. Non fuerant nuptiae futurae. Dᴀ. Quid? non? Sɪ. Sed
      ea gratia

simulavi, vos ut pertemptarem, Dᴀ. Quid ais? Sɪ. Sic res
  .   est. Dᴀ. Vide!

numquam istuc quivi ego intellegere. Vah, consilium cal-
      lidum.   . (590) 10

Sɪ. Hoc audi. Ut hinc te introire iussi, opportune hic fit
      mi obviam, Dᴀ. Hem,

numnam periimus? Sɪ. Narro huic, quae tu dudum narrasti
      mihi.

Dᴀ. Quidnam audio? Sɪ. Gnatam ut det oro, vixque id
      exoro. Dᴀ. Occidi.

Sɪ. Hem, quid dixti? Dᴀ. Optume inquam factum. Sɪ.
      Nunc per hunc nullast mora.

Cʜ. Domum modo ibo: ut apparentur, dicam: atque huc
      renuntio.   15

Sɪ. Nunc te oro, Dave, quoniam solus mi effecisti has
      nuptias—

Dᴀ. Ego vero solus. Sɪ. corrigere mihi gnatum porro enitere.

Dᴀ. Faciam hercle sedulo. Sɪ. Potes nunc, dum animus
      irritatus est.

Dᴀ. Quiescas. Sɪ. Age igitur, ubi nunc est ipsus? Dᴀ.
      Mirum, ni domi est.

---

12 periimus] "Are not we undone?" Davus begins to think he
gave bad advice to Pamphilus, that
he should consent to his father's
proposal.

13 audio] Donatus mentions a
reading *audiam* (fut.), quoting in
support of it the expr. in Menander
τί ποτ' ἀκούσω; Bentley adopts it as
better suited to the sense: Davus
wonders what he is going to hear.

14 Optume] Simo partly overhears *occidi*, v. 13, Davus turns it
aside as if he had said "*optume*,"
"Undone"..."Well done" might

keep up the effect in translation.

15 modo] seems to indicate that
it is now time to go home, that
there is nothing else to be done
(from the orig. *restrictive* sense of
the word): it can only be expressed
in translation by emphasis "*now* I
will go home."

17 enitere] "try hard." *enitor*
=to force one's way out, and so of
striving upwards.

Ego vero solus] "Yes, I alone
indeed." Davus had pressed Pamphilus against his wish, Act II.
Sc. 3.

•

SI. Ibo ad eum : atque eadem haec tibi quae dixi, dicam
    itidem illi. DA. Nullus sum.   (600) 20
Quid causae est, quin hinc in pistrinum recta proficiscar
    via ?
Nihil est preci loci relictum ; iam perturbavi omnia :
herum fefelli : in nuptias conieci herilem filium ;
feci hodie ut fierent, insperante hoc, atque invito Pamphilo.
Hem, astutias : quod si quiessem, nihil evenisset mali.   25
Sed eccum ipsum video : occidi.
Utinam mihi esset aliquid hic, quo nunc me praecipitem
    darem.

ACTUS III. SCENA V.

PAMPHILUS. DAVUS.

PA. Ubi illic est scelus qui me perdidit ? DA. Perii. PA.
    Atque hoc confiteor mihi
iure obtigisse ; quandoquidem tam iners, tam nulli consili
sum. Servon' fortunas meas me commisisse futili ?   (610)
Ego pretium ob stultitiam fero : sed inultum id numquam a
    me auferet.

---

23 in nuptias conieci] as though into chains, cf. II. 3. 12 supra.

25 astutias] "So much for tricks!" accusativus exclamantis, cf. supra, I. 5. 10.

Sc. v.] Pamphilus, informed by Simo of Chremes' consent to this marriage, comes to wreak vengeance upon Davus, who appeases him by undertaking to find a way out of the mess.

Metre: 1—14, iambic tetram.; 15 —18, troch. tetram. catal.

1] The scansion of this v. is difficult : *illic est* is pronounced as one syllable, *illest*, and *scelus* as monosyllable. Bentley makes great havoc, reading *Ubi illic est? scelus,*

qui me hodie: perii: atque hoc confiteor Iure......

2 nulli] archaic gen. of *nullus*. Plautus has *nullae* for fem. gen. and dat.

3 futili] (*fundo, futis*) lit. "that easily pours out." *Vas futile*, a vessel used at sacred rites, because of its narrow bottom and wide top spilt the water if set down, and therefore had to be held by the attendants (Donatus), hence "leaky" of people who cannot keep a secret (cf. *Eun.* I. 2, 23—25), as we say "a sieve." Here = "worthless." Cf. Verg. *Aen.* XI. 239 (in XII. 740, *f. glacies*, "brittle").

4 inultum] "Unpunished." So

DA. Posthac incolumem sat scio fore me, nunc si devito
    hoc malum.   5

PA. Nam quid ego nunc dicam patri? Negabon' velle me,
    modo

qui sum pollicitus ducere? Qua fiducia id facere audeam?

Nec, quid me nunc faciam, scio. DA. Nec quid me, atque
    id ego sedulo.

Dicam aliquid iam inventurum, ut huic malo aliquam pro-
    ducam moram.

PA. Oh. DA. Visus sum. PA. Ehodum, bone vir, quid
    ais? Viden' me consiliis tuis   10

miserum inpeditum esse? DA. At iam expediam. PA. Ex-
    pedies? DA. Certe, Pamphile.

PA. Nempe ut modo. DA. Immo melius spero. PA. Oh
    tibi ego ut credam, furcifer?

Tu rem inpeditam et perditam restituas? Hem quo fretus
    sim,   (620)

qui me hodie ex tranquillissima re coniecisti in nuptias.

At non dixi esse hoc futurum? DA. Dixti. PA. Quid
    meritus? DA. Crucem.   15

Sed sine paululum ad me redeam: iam aliquid dispiciam.
    PA. Hei mihi,

Cic. *Div. in Verr.* 16, *ut ceterorum
iniuriae sint impunitae et inultae.*
Of the person, Hor. *Sat.* II. 3. 189;
Od. III. 1. 140.

5 **si devito**] the indic. expresses
confidence that he can avoid it.

7] Lachmann (*ad Lucr.* II. 719)
emends *neque qua fiducia id audeam.* But why alter *fiducia* to
audacia (as Wagner) against all authority, to suit *Eun.* v. 4. 36?

8 **me**] ablative "as regards myself," more usual with prep. *de me.*

9 **moram**] is not cognate acc.
with *producam;* we might have
prod. hoc malum aliquam moram,

as in II. 1. 29, *aliquot dies profer*
(nuptias), when *moram* would be
acc. of duration of time. The constr.
is more like II. 1. 18, but easier to
explain (v. note to loc.): I will spin
out some delay for this evil (i.e. to
obstruct it: a sort of *dativus incommodi*).

12 **Nempe,** &c.] "Yes indeed, as
you did just now." Da. "No, better I hope."

15 **esse hoc**] So Bentley (on
auth. of some MSS.), for *hoc esse,*
by which reading a dactyl stands
for a trochee, which is inadmissible
in the 3rd foot.

quum non habeo spatium, ut de te sumam supplicium, ut
    volo :
namque hoc tempus, praecavere mihi me, haud te ulcisci,
    sinit.

ACTUS IV. SCENA I.

CHARINUS. PAMPHILUS. DAVUS.

CH. Hoccine credibile, aut memorabile ;
tanta vecordia innata cuiquam ut siet,
ut malis gaudeant, atque ex incommodis
alterius sua ut comparent commoda? Ah
idne est verum?   Immo id est genus hominum pessumum,
    in   (630) 5
denegando modo quis pudor paulum adest :
post ubi tempus promissa iam perfici,
tum coacti necessario se aperiunt :
et timent : et tamen res premit denegare :
ibi tum eorum inpudentissima oratio est :   10
quis tu es? quis mihi es? cur meam tibi? heus,

Act. IV. Sc. I.] Charinus accuses Pamphilus of ingratitude: but being at last convinced by him of the real case, turns upon Davus, who allows himself wrong, but promises to set things right.

Metre: 1—13, cretic with admixture of dactyls; 14—16, 19—25, trochaic tetrameter; 17, 18, 26—30, 39, 40, 58, 59, iambic tetrameter; 31—38, 41—57, iambic trimeter.

5 verum] "fair," "right." So Hor. Epp. I. 7, sub fin., Sat. II. 3. 312. Verg. Aen. XII. 694.

6, &c.] Those upon whom (quis =quibus) shame acts just so far as to prevent their refusing a request, but no further to the fulfilment of their engagement: when the time

comes they feel no shame in altogether repudiating it. Cf. Plautus, Epid. II. I. I, Plerique omnes homines, quos quum nihil refert pudet, ubi pudendum est. Ibi deseret eos pudor, quum usus est ut pudeat: Livy, XXXIX. 4, Nae simul pudere, quod non oportet, coeperit; quod oportet, non pudebit.

9 premit] is accepted by Bentley from Faernus instead of the reading cogit.

11 quis mihi es] "Who, may I ask, are you?" cf. Hor. Quid mihi Celsus agit? Donatus's interp. "What are you to me?" i. e. what relation? agrees with the next verse, proxumus sum egomet mihi.

proxumus sum egomet mihi.   Attamen ubi fides

si roges, nihil pudet;   hic ubi opust

non verentur: illic ubi nil opust, ibi verentur.

Sed quid agam? adeamne ad eum, et cum eo iniuriam hanc

     expostulem?   (640)   15

ingeram mala multa?   Atque aliquis dicat, nihil promo-

     veris.

Multum: molestus certe ei fuero;   atque animo morem

     gessero.

PA. Charine, et me et te imprudens, nisi quid di respici-

     unt, perdidi.

CH. Itane imprudens?   Tandem inventast causa.   Solvisti

     fidem.

PA. Quid tandem?   CH. Etiam nunc me ducere istis dic-

     tis postulas?   20

PA. Quid istuc est?   CH. Postquam me amare dixi, com-

     placitast tibi.

Heu me miserum, qui tuum animum ex animo spectavi meo.

PA. Falsus es.   CH. Nonne tibi satis esse hoc visum soli-

     dumst gaudium,

nisi me lactasses amantem, et falsa spe produceres?

---

cur meam tibi] sc. *rem* habes? i.e. meddle in my concerns. Cf. the exp. *tuas res tibi habe*, "keep to your-self," as a formula of divorce.

18 respiciunt] of regard from a superior to an inferior, cf. Juv. III. 185, *ut te respiciat clauso Veiento labello*. Hor. *Od*. I. 2. 35; Verg. *Ecl*. I. 28.

19 Itane] ironical, and so im-plying disbelief, cf. *Ad* I. 5. 8. *Solvisti fidem*, ironical, "you have kept your word."

20 ducere] cf. *Phorm*. III. 2. 15.

23 Falsus] in its original parti-cipial sense, "You are mistaken, deceive yourself." Cf. *Eun*. II. 2. 43; Plaut. *Men*. V. 2, "*Id quam facile sit mihi, haud sum falsus*."

solidum] "plenum, idoneum, in-tegrum," Don. Cf. *Eun*. v. 3. 2, s. *beneficium*, "a real," "substan-tial" kindness. Orig. = all of one piece (? Gk. ὅλος, as *Festus*), "*men-sa solida quatuor pedum*," Pliny: "whole," hence "firm," "hard;" and then "substantial," "perfect," see Forcellini.

24 lactasses] "wheedle" (cf. v. 4. 9), generally explained as transf. from *lacto* (*lac*), to feed with milk: Forc. (s. v. *lacto*) derives from *lacio* (cf. *iacio*, *iacto*, &c.) = "deceive," and referred by Fes-tus to a subst. *lax* = "*fraus*." In Lucr. IV. 1207 (the only passage quoted by Forc. s. v. *lacio*), "*lacere in fraudem*," ib. 1146, *lacimur*, are

Habeas.　PA. Habeam? ah nescis quantis in malis verser
　　　　miser;　　　　　　　　　　　　　　　25 (650)
quantasque hic suis consiliis mihi confecit sollicitudines
meus carnufex—CH. Quid istuc tam mirumst, de te si ex-
　　　emplum capit?
PA. Haud istuc dicas, si cognoris vel me vel amorem meum.
CH. Scio: cum patre altercasti dudum: et is nunc propte-
　　　rea tibi
suscenset: nec te quivit hodie cogere, illam ut duceres.　30
PA. Immo etiam, quo tu minus scis aerumnas meas,
haec nuptiae non adparabantur mihi:
nec postulabat nunc quisquam uxorem dare.
CH. Scio: tu coactus tua voluntate es.　PA. Mane:
nondum scis.　CH. Scio equidem illam ducturum esse te.　35
PA. Cur me enicas? Hoc audi. Numquam destitit　(661)
instare, ut dicerem me esse ducturum patri:
suadere, orare, usque adeo, donec perpulit.

readings of Lambinus for *iacere* and
iacimus, and according to Munro
(IV. 1207, notes 1), without cause;
and in v. 1068 M. prefers *iactant*
(the passage quoted by Forc. s.v.
"*lacio*" in support of connection
with *lacio*). On the other hand cf.
delecto, deliciae.
　25 **Habeas**] "Quando concedi-
mus mala importune postulantibus."
Don. "I wish you joy of it."
　26 **confecit**] Parry compares this
change from subj. *verser* with l. 5.
37, *credidit ... habuerim*, but that
passage (if rightly explained in my
note *ad loc.*) cannot well be classed
with this, if we have here ind. and
subj. in two exactly parallel clauses.
On such an assumption I see no
really conclusive solution of the
difficulty. I should rather suppose
(as in I. 5. 37), that the clauses are
not really parallel and similar in
construction, but that the dependent interrogation ends at *miser;*

where we may suppose Pamphilus
to pause a moment, and then start-
ing a-fresh, "And as to the anxiety
which, &c.," he is interrupted at
the word *carnufex* by Charinus,
whose words take up that epithet
and virtually apply it to Pamphilus
—"'Rascal:' no wonder, if he takes
you for his model." Pamphilus then
(v. 27) deprecates this uncompli-
mentary inference, and never finishes
the sentence begun v. 25.
　31 **quo minus scis**] "In so far
as you know too little," &c., i.e.
"So little do you know"—cf. such
expressions as tu quâ tu es virtute,
hoc facis. Of course it must not be
confounded with *quominus*, c. subj.
to denote a negative purpose.
　37 **esse**] so far as the metre is
concerned, appears superfluous;
but *dicerem* might be pronounced
dissyl. as *fores*, &c. l, m, n, r between two vowels often admit syni-
zesis.

CH. Quis homo istuc? PA. Davos... CH. Davos? PA. inter-
    turbat. CH. Quamobrem? PA. Nescio:
nisi mihi deos satis scio fuisse iratos, qui auscultaverim. 40
CH. Factum hoc est, Dave? DA. Factum. CH. Hem,
    quid ais, scelus?
At tibi di dignum factis exitium duint.
Eho, dic mihi, si omnes hunc coniectum in nuptias
inimici vellent, quod, ni hoc consilium, darent?
DA. Deceptus sum, at non defetigatus. CH. Scio. (670) 45
DA. Hac non successit, alia adgrediemur via.
Nisi id putas, quia primo processit parum,
non posse iam ad salutem converti hoc malum.
PA. Immo etiam: nam satis credo, si advigilaveris,
ex unis geminas mihi conficies nuptias.   50
DA. Ego, Pamphile, hoc tibi pro servitio debeo,
conari manibus, pedibus, noctesque et dies:
capitis periclum adire, dum prosim tibi:
tuumst, si quid praeter spem evenit, mi ignoscere.
Parum succedit, quod ago: at facio sedulo. (680) 55
Vel melius tute reperi, me missum face.
PA. Cupio: restitue, in quem me accepisti locum.

40 nisi] more usually *nisi quod,* · "Only, I am sure." Cf. *Heaut.* v. 2. 6.

deos iratos] insinuates madness, for "quem deus vult perdere, prius dementat." Cf. *Phorm.* I. 2. 24.

42 At] frequent in execrations or prayers. Cf. Verg. *Aen.* II. 535; *Eun.* II. I. 41; *Hec.* I. 2. 59; Hor. *Epod.* 5. I; Cic. *Verr.* III. 46, *At per deos immortales quid est quod de hoc dici possit.*

45 Scio] ironical (as vv. 28, 33 supra), refers to *defetigatus*—"Oh, not at all!"

47 putas] of a wrong or imaginary thought.

51 pro servitio] "As your slave."

servitium does not = *servus:* for when used personally it is (like *remigium*) collective; but "In virtue of my place as your slave," (cf. *pro dignitate,* &c.) is the meaning.

56 missum face] "Dismiss me." Cf. *Phorm.* v. 7. 53; *Eun.* I. 2. 10. Also in prose, "*missam facere legionem.*" Caesar.

57 restitue, &c.] "Restore me to the position in which you found me;" Greek attraction for *restitue in locum quo me accepisti.* Another reading *restitue quem a me accepisti locum* (Bentley) is not so well supported, and makes less sense.

DA. Faciam. PA. At iam hoc opus est. DA. Hem, st!
 mane : concrepuit a Glycerio ostium.
PA. Nihil ad te. DA. Quaero. PA. Hem, nuncne demum?
 DA. At iam hoc tibi inventum dabo.

ACTUS IV. SCENA II.

MYSIS. PAMPHILUS. CHARINUS. DAVUS.

MY. Iam ubiubi erit, inventum tibi curabo, et mecum adductum
tuum Pamphilum : tu modo, anime mi, noli te macerare.
PA. Mysis. MY. Quis est? Ehem Pamphile, opportune te
 mihi offers. PA. Quid est?
MY. Orare iussit, si se ames, hera, iam ut ad se venias :
videre ait te cupere. PA. Vah, perii : hoc malum inte-
 grascit.   5
Siccine me atque illam opera tua nunc miseros sollicitari?
Nam idcirco adcersor, nuptias quod mi adparari sensit. (691)

58 **concrepuit**] i. e. struck from within as a warning that some one is coming out. Greek ψοφεῖν τὴν θύραν (strepere) as opposed to κόπτειν (pulsare), to knock from without. Schol. on Aristophanes, *Nub.* 132.

59 **inventum dabo**] a favourite periphrasis in comic writers (cf. *Eun.* III. 2. 25; *Phor.* IV. 7. 81), also found in Vergil (*Aen.* I. 63, IX. 323, XII. 437). It has the force of a *futurum exactum*. With simple acc. it often gives the notion of exhibiting prominently, bringing about a result, &c. Cf. Greek phrase ἀτιμάσας ἔχω, where the verb is accurately defined by the use of an auxiliary. This is almost the only example in Latin of an auxiliary other than *sum ;* though *habeo* with past part. (*expertum habeo*, &c.) perhaps contains an anticipation of the later Latin use as an auxiliary verb, whence the French " avoir."

Sc. II.] Mysis appears, and relating Glycerium's distress, persuades Pamphilus to repeat his vows of attachment to her. Davus hits upon a scheme for setting things right, putting Charinus contemptuously on one side, and arranges preliminaries with Mysis.

Metre : iambic tetrameter catalectic.

6 **Siccine sollicitari**] v. note I. 5. 10.

CH. Quibus quidem quam facile potuerat quiesci, si hic qui-
    esset.

DA. Age, si hic non insanit satis sua sponte, instiga.   MY.
    Atque edepol.

ea res est : proptereaque nunc misera in moerore est.   PA.
    Mysis,   10

per omnes tibi adiuro deos, numquam eam me deserturum ;

non, si capiundos mihi sciam esse inimicos omnes homines.

Hanc mi expetivi, contigit : conveniunt mores : valeant,

qui inter nos discidium volunt : hanc, nisi mors, mi adimet
    nemo.

CH. Resipisco.   PA. Non Apollinis magis verum, atque hoc,
    responsum est.   15

Si poterit fieri, ut ne pater per me stetisse credat,   (700)

---

8 Quibus] i. e. *nuptiis, quiesci,* impersonal. Forc. quotes no other passage for this use.   Translate, "And how easily might you have been safe from this marriage (lit. in regard to this marriage), if Davus here had kept quiet.

potuerat...quiesszt] Note this use of the auxiliary verbs in conditional sentences. The performance of the action, not the power or lawfulness, &c., is conditional. The auxiliary is therefore put in the indicative mood, while the apodosis qualifies the verb of action. Cf. Juv. X. "*Antoni gladios potuit contemnere si sic omnia dixisset.*" Sall. *Jug.* "*Si victoria, praeda, laus...dubia essent, tamen omnes bonos reipublicae subvenire decebat.*"

13 valeant] "Away with those who..."

15 Resipisco] Charinus takes heart again on hearing Pamphilus speak so strongly of his attachment to Glycerium. In some editions the word is less appropriately assigned to Mysis.

magis atque] This use of *atque* and *ac* after comparatives and such

words as *aeque, juxta,* &c., may be illustrated by that of *et* where *quum* would be expected, as after *vix ea fatus erat,* and similar expressions in Vergil, *Aen.* II. 692 (where see Conington's note), III. 8, &c.; and both referred to an early usage of language which before elaborate grammatical structure and subordination of sentences expressed comparison and relation by simple juxta-position. Thus e.g. in Greek the relative use of the demonstrative pronoun ὅς is a further development, not yet complete in the Greek of Homer : while in our own language the uncultivated idiom of provincials gives us, "That man, he did it," for the more correct "That is the man who did it"—preferring, in other words, the "co-ordinate" to "subordinate" sentences. Such remnants of unartificial style find naturally a place in the colloquial language of the comic writers. Cf. supra, III. 3. 13; *Eun.* I. 2. 2; Cat. 61. 176, "*Illi non minus ac tibi Pectore uritur intimo Flamma.*"

16 ut ne] cf. I. I. 34, note.

ouo minus hae fierent nuptiae, volo.   Sed si id non poterit,
id faciam, in proclivi quod est, per me stetisse ut credat.
Quis videor?   CH. Miser aeque, atque ego.   DA. Consilium
    quaero.   CH. Fortis !
PA. Scio, quid conere.   DA. Hoc ego tibi profecto effectum
    reddam.   20
PA. Iam hoc opus est.   DA. Quin iam habeo.   CH. Quid est?
    DA. Huic, non tibi habeo, ne erres.
CH. Sat habeo.   PA. Quid facies?   Cedo.   DA. Dies mi hic
    ut satis sit vereor
ad agendum : ne vacuum esse me nunc ad narrandum
    credas :
proinde hinc vos amolimini : nam mi impedimento estis.
PA. Ego hanc visam.   DA. Quid tu? quo hinc te agis?
    CH. Verum vis dicam?   DA. Immo etiam   25
narrationis incipit mi initium.   CH. Quid me fiet?   (710)
DA. Eho tu impudens, non satis habes, quod tibi dieculam
    addo,

18 **in proclivi**] i. e. "easy." Cf.
Sall. *Or. ad Caes.* ch. 8, fin. *cuius
si dolum caveris alia omnia in proclivi erunt.* Plaut. *Capt.* II. 2. 86.
*Tum hoc quidem tibi in proclivi
quam nubes est quando pluit:* the
original meaning with implied sense
of easiness. Gellius (X. 24) says
that *proclivi* and *proclive* were used
indifferently by the ancients. So
Lucr. II. 455, *procursus item proclive volubilis exstat.*

20 **Scio quid conere**] These words
have caused difficulty, but the meaning seems clear. Pamphilus says
ironically, "I know what you are
trying"—implying, "I don't think
you will succeed."   So Donatus,
"Si Pamphili est persona, cum
εἰρωνείᾳ dicitur; si Charini, simplex
laudatio est." Bentley's correction
si quid conere (i. e. "very good, if
only you try hard"), and Parry's

ingenious suggestion, *scin' quid conere* (a literal translation of Greek
οἶσθ' ὃ δρᾶσον, "mind what you are
about"), are not required.

21 **ne erres**] "Make no error"
is a slang expression of our own
day.

23 **amolimini**] "Take yourselves
out of my way." The word implies
something heavy and troublesome
to move (Tac. *Ann.* I. 50, *amoliri
obstantia silvarum;* cf. *Hist.* I. 13,
amoliri uxorem), and is intended to
be contemptuous. Davus now that
he has got his head, assumes the
tone of a superior towards those who
want his help.

27 **dieculam**] "respite ;" occurs,
besides this passage, once in Cicero
(*Att.* V. 20, s. fin.), and once in
Plautus (*Pseud.* I. V. 88), in the
same sense.

quantum huic promoveo nuptias? CH. Dave, at tamen...
    DA. Quid ergo?
CH. ut ducam. DA. Ridiculum. CH. Huc face ad me ut
    venias, si quid poteris.
DA. Quid veniam? Nil habeo. CH. At tamen si quid.
    DA. Age, veniam. CH. Si quid;   30
domi ero. DA. Tu, Mysis, dum exeo, parumper opperire
    hic.
MY. Quapropter? DA. Ita facto 'st opus. MY. Matura.
    DA. Iam inquam hic adero.

ACTUS IV. SCENA III.

MYSIS. DAVUS.

MY. Nihilne esse proprium cuiquam? Di, vostram fidem:
summum bonum esse herae putavi hunc Pamphilum,
amicum, amatorem, virum, in quovis loco
paratum: verum ex eo nunc misera quem capit   (720)
laborem? Facile hic plus mali est, quam illic boni.
Sed Davos exit. Mi homo, quid istuc obsecrost?   6
Quo portas puerum? DA. Mysis, nunc opus est tua
mihi ad hanc rem exprompta memoria atque astutia.

---

32 **facto'st opus**] see note to III. 2. 10.

Sc. III.] Mysis soliliquises on her mistress' troubles. Enter Davus, with a child which he directs her to place at Chremes' door: but on the sudden appearance of Chremes, runs off, leaving Mysis in great perplexity.

Metre: iambic trimeter.

1 **nihilne esse?...fidem**] See note to I. 5. 10. *proprium*, "lasting," Greek βέβαιος, as in Eur. *Frag.* βέβαια δ' ουδείς θνητός ευτυχεί γεγώς.

5 **laborem**] So Bentley on auth. of Faernus: i.e. "distress" as often in Vergil and others: others *dolorem*. *Facile* = "clearly." Donatus quotes *facile princeps* from Cicero. *hic* refers to the immediately foregoing *verum —laborem: illic* to v. 2, *summum bonum*, &c.

8 **memoria**] Donatus and others: *malitia*, Bentley after Faernus. *exprompta* = in medium prolata, now you must display all the attention you can (to remember what I say).

My. Quidnam incepturus? DA. Accipe a me hunc ocius,

atque ante nostram ianuam adpone. My. Obsecro,   10

humine? DA. Ex ara hinc sume verbenas tibi,

atque eas substerne. My. Quamobrem id tute non facis?

DA. Quia si forte opus sit ad herum iurandum mihi,

non adposuisse, ut liquido possim. My. Intellego :   (730)

nova nunc religio in te istaec incessit, cedo?   15

DA. Move ocius te, ut, quid agam porro, intellegas.

Pro Iupiter! My. Quid est? DA. Sponsae pater inter-

venit.

Repudio, quod consilium primum intenderam.

My. Nescio, quid narres. DA. Ego quoque hinc ab dextera

venire me adsimulabo : tu, ut subservias   20

orationi, utcumque opus sit, verbis vide.

My. Ego quid agas nihil intellego : sed, si quid est,

quod mea opera opus sit vobis, aut tu plus vides,

manebo, ne quod vostrum remorer commodum.   (740)

---

11 **ara**] Two altars stood on the stage: on the right, sacred to Apollo (in comedy) and Bacchus (in tragedy); on the left, to the presiding deity of the games—here Cybele. Or there may be allusion to the altar of Apollo, which stood before Greek houses : cf. Arist. *Vesp.* 875. γείτον Ἀγυιεῦ τοῦ 'μοῦ προθύρου. *verbenas*, all sacred leaves, laurel, olive or myrtle ; so Servius on *Aen.* XII. 120, quoting this passage and comparing the line of Menander which gives μυρρίνας. On the derivation of the word Donatus, "verbenae quasi herbenae, redimicula sunt ararum:" Acron on Hor. *Od.* IV. 11. 7, compares the change Henetos (Ἔνετοι, Hdt.) to Uenetos, ἔσπερος, *vesperus*.

13 **iurandum**] seems to = *ius iurandum*, as in Plaut. *Cist.* II. 1. 26. *opus* is the predicate, "if an oath to my master is a necessity for me," cf. on I. 4. 37. Bentley alters to *jurato:* the construction is then

like *opus facto*, III. 2. 10.

14 **liquido**] "with a clear conscience:" Cic. *Fam.* II. *alia sunt quae liquido negare soleo* ("frankly"): *Verr.* V. sq. *manifesta res est cum nemo esset quin hoc se audisse liquido diceret.*

15] As our text stands *cedo* = "tell me." Weise and others punctuate *incessit. Cedo;* i.e. "give me (the child)," cf. *Hec.* IV. 4. 86: and Donatus' comment, "Cedo, porrigentis est manum," points to this.

18 **Repudio**] I reject (probably *retro pudio*), "push back with the foot," cf. tripudium.

intenderam] According to some a metaphor for spreading nets, "the plan I had first set"; or perhaps from aiming with a bow (as Verg. *Aen.* IX. 590, *nervo intendisse sagittam*).

consilium] probably his first intention to go and tell Simo of the discovery of the child.

ACTUS IV. SCENA IV.

Chremes. Mysis. Davus.

CH. Revertor, postquam, quae opus fuere ad nuptias
Gnatae, paravi, ut iubeam accersi. Sed quid hoc?
Puer herclest: Mulier, tun' adposuisti hunc? My. Ubi est?
CH. Non mihi respondes? My. Nusquam est. Vae miserae
  mihi,
reliquit me homo, atque abiit. DA. Di vostram fidem,   5
quid turbae apud forum est! quid illic hominum litigant!
Tum annona carast.—Quid dicam aliud, nescio.
My. Cur tu obsecro hic me solam? DA. Quae haec est
  fabula?
Eho Mysis, puer hic unde est? quisve huc attulit?
My. Satin sanu's, qui me id rogites? DA. Quem igitur
  rogem,   (750) 10

Sc. IV.] Chremes begins to question Mysis about the child, when Davus bursts in with scraps of gossip from the forum, pretending not to see Chremes, and then questions Mysis about the child to draw from her what Chremes may overhear. Mysis does not take up her cue as he wishes; and the skill with which he elicits the desired answers from the unintelligent and reluctant serving woman is the main point. Metre: iambic trimeter.

6 quid...litigant] "what a crowd of men are going to law there!" *litigant* agrees κατὰ σύνεσιν with the notion of multitude in the phrase *quid hominum*, cf. *Ad.* IV. 4. 26; but generally grammatical ideas prevail over logical, e.g. *at o deorum quicquid in coelo regit*, Hor. *Epod.* 5. 1. Donatus mentions another reading, *litigat.*

7 annona carast] "provisions are dear." annona (*annus*, cf. Greek

ἐπηέτανος) = provisions sufficient for a year's consumption: then "price of provisions," *a. vilis, cara, laxa, varia, gravis*, &c. It is also used absolutely in sense both of *abundance* and *deficiency* (Plaut. *Trin.* II. 4. 83, *Cena hac annona est sine sacris hereditas*), cf. its use in Hor. *Epp.* I. 12. 24: Juv. IX. 100.

Quid dicam nescio] an aside to the spectators.

10 Satin sanu's, &c.] "Are you in your senses to ask *me* that?" A relative clause when it denotes the reason of the leading proposition, or the attendant circumstances under which an action takes place, is put in the subj. mood, cf. *Eun.* IV. 7. 32, *iamdudum ego erro qui tam multa verba faciam:* and strengthened by *utpote praesertim.* Also when the relative clause states the circumstances notwithstanding which an action takes place: *qui* then = "although."

qui hic neminem alium videam? CH. Miror, unde sit.

DA. Dictura es quod rogo? MY. Au. DA. Concede ad
　　dexteram.

MY. Deliras: non tute ipse? DA. Verbum si mihi
unum, praeterquam quod te rogo, faxis cave.

MY. Male dicis? DA. Unde est dic clare. MY. A nobis.

　　　　DA. Attatae!　　　　　　　　　　　　　　　　　15

Mirum vero, inpudenter mulier si facit

meretrix. CH. Ab Andria est haec, quantum intellego. ·

DA. Adeon videmur vobis esse idonei,

in quibus sic inludatis? CH. Veni in tempore. ·

DA. Propera adeo puerum tollere hinc ab ianua: (760) 20
mane: cave quoquam ex istoc excessis loco.

MY. Di te eradicent: ita me miseram territas.

DA. Tibi ego dico, annon? MY. Quid vis? DA. At etiam
　　rogas?

---

12 **Concede ad dexteram**] an
"aside."

13 **non tute ipse**] sc. *dedisti
puerum.* Mysis left in perplexity at
the end of the last scene does not
yet take her cue from Davus, till
reminded by an "aside," *verbum si
faxis...cave.* Bentley omits *si*, and
connects *cave* with *faxis:* Weise
reads *sis* (=si vis, cf. *Eun.* IV. 7.
29): both unnecessarily assuming
that *cave si faxis* must be taken
together as = *cave faxis* or *cave ne
faxis*, the usual phrases. *Si faxis* is
the protasis of a conditional sentence, *cave* the apodosis. "If you
say one word more than I ask you,
look out."

15 **Male dicis?**] Do you threat-
en me? Bentley alters to *Quin
dicis undest dare?* on which see note
to II. 2. 9.

17 **meretrix**] is placed by some
editors in v. 16, and *ancilla* read
after *est:* but this is an evident
gloss, and is rejected as such by

Bentley and most modern editors.
Weise and others retain *ancilla*,
omitting *meretrix*, which is not
mentioned by Donatus, though implied in his note, "primo causa
impudentia natura est (expressed by
the word "mulier"), deinde con-
ditio" (evidently by the word "meretrix"). *mulier meretrix* occurs in
Plautus (*Mercator*, IV. 1. 19), Quid,
mulier? mulier meretrix: cf. *Homo
servus, Phorm.* II. 1. 62.

20 **adeo**] has not here its first
meaning to such an extent as above
v. 18, but is merely an emphatic
particle "ad urgentis vim congruit
et moram tolli vult," cf. Greek συλ-
λάβετε...γ' αὐτὸν, Soph. *Phil.* 1003:
as such often used with personal
pronouns. *Tuque adeo,* &c. Verg.
Ecl. IV. cf. supra, II. 5. 4.

21 **excessis**] an old form of
subj. pres. like *faxis,* 1. 14. *quoquam*
"any whither." *manē, cavĕ*, note the
variation of prosody in two words
thus side by side.

Cedo, cuium puerum hic adposuisti? dic mihi.

MY. Tu nescis? DA. Mitte id, quod scio: dic, quod rogo.

MY. Vestri. DA. Cuius nostri? MY. Pamphili. DA. Hem,
    quid? Pamphili?   26

. MY. Eho, annon est? CH. Recto ego semper fugi has
    nuptias.

DA. O facinus animadvertendum. MY. Quid clamitas?

DA. Quemne ego heri vidi ad vos adferri vesperi?

MY. O hominem audacem. DA. Verum. Vidi Cantharam

suffarcinatam. MY. Dis pol habeo gratias,   (771) 31
quum in pariundo aliquot adfuerunt liberae.

DA. Nae illa illum haud novit, cuius causa haec incipit.

Chremes, si positum puerum ante aedis viderit,

suam gnatam non dabit? tanto hercle magis dabit.   35

CH. Non hercle faciet. DA. Nunc adeo, ut tu sis sciens,

nisi puerum tollis, iam ego hunc in mediam viam

24 **cuium**] This adjective from the genitive *cuius* is found in Vergil (*Ecl.* III. 1) and in Cicero (*Verr.* III. 54, *cuia res sit, cuium periculum*).

26 **nostri Pamphili**] Davus repeats Mysis' words in a louder tone that Chremes may overhear.

29 **Quemne**, &c.] "What, the boy whom I saw carried to your house yesterday evening?" Cf. *Phorm.* v. 7. 9; Catullus, 64. 180. Davus by the insinuation that the story of birth is false irritates Mysis into saying what he wishes.

30 **Cantharam**] Some of the old commentators imagined a play on "cantharus," with allusion to the Athenian practice of exposing children ἐν χύτραις, whence ἐγχυτρίζειν, as *Vesp.* 289, and a reading *cantharus* even occurs, but against MS. evidence and Donatus, who says, Canthara, nomen est anus.

31 **suffarcinatam**] "with a bundle under her dress," cf. Plaut. *Curc.* II. 3. 9, "*Qui incedunt suffar-*

cinati cum libris cum sportulis?" and so Apuleius, of a person "stuffed" with food, *ego quamquam iam bellule suffarcinatus, exhibitas escas appctebam.*

gratias] Bentley's correction *gratiam* is adopted by modern editors because *agere gratias* but *habere gratiam* is used, cf. however Cic. *Phil.* III. ch. 10, *Gratias et agere et habere debemus.* Mysis says, "Thank Heaven there was more than one free woman present at the birth," i. e. witnesses whose evidence, according to Roman custom, would outweigh that of a slave (aliquot as opposed to one slave). Five *matronae* were required to establish the legitimate birth of a child.

34 **Chremes...non dabit**]. An ironical repetition of Glycerium's thoughts: Da. "She thinks this will stop Chremes giving his daughter to Pamphilus, He'll give her the more readily." Chr. (aside) "No indeed he won't."

provolvam : teque ibidem‚pervolvam in luto.

MY. Tu pol homo non es sobrius. DA. Fallacia

alia aliam trudit. Iam susurrari audio, (780) 40

civem Atticam esse hanc. CH. Hem. DA. Coactus legibus

eam uxorem ducet. MY. Au, obsecro, an non civis est?

CH. Iocularium in malum insciens paene incidi.

DA. Quis hic loquitur? O Chreme, per tempus advenis.

Ausculta. CH. Audivi iam omnia. DA. Anne tu omnia?

CH. Audivi, inquam, a principio. DA. Audistin' obsecro?

　　　Hem 46

scelera ! Hanc iam oportet in cruciatum hinc abripi.

Hic ille est : non te credas Davom ludere.

MY. Me miseram : nihil pol falsi dixi, mi senex.

CH. Novi omnem rem. Est Simo intus? DA. Est. MY.

　　　Ne me attigas, (790) 50

sceleste ! Si pol Glycerio non omnia haec...

DA. Eho inepta, nescis quid sit actum? MY. Qui sciam?

DA. Hic socer est. Alio pacto haud poterat fieri,

ut sciret haec, quae volumus. MY. Hem, praediceres.

DA. Paullum interesse censes, ex animo omnia, 55

ut fert natura, facias, an de industria?

39 **Fallacia...trudit**] aside to the audience. "Proverbium, cui memorem mendacem esse oportere subiacet." Donatus.

43 **malum**] might = the story he has just overheard; "Here's a queer piece of fraud I have stumbled on unawares:" or the marriage of his daughter to Pamphilus, which he has just escaped by hearing all this; cf. *Phormio* I. 2. 84, *iocularem audaciam*.

44] Davus pretends suddenly to be aware of Chremes' presence.

48 **Hic ille est**] "Here's the very man" (Chremes), i.e. of whom he spoke v. 34, Greek ὅδε ἐκεῖνος.

non credas] cf. Verg. *G.* I. 456: II. 315: and note to I. I. 34. It is however possible that these apparent

uses of the direct negative in prohibitions may be otherwise explained by the potential use of the subjunctive mood; so that *non credas* = "You cannot suppose," which has practically the imperative force.

54 **praediceres**] "You should have told me beforehand;" cf. note I. I. III. It is apodosis of a conditional sentence, *si recte faceres, praediceres*. The imperf. is found thus in both clauses of a conditional sent. instead of plup.; cf. Cic. *Phil.* VIII. 4, *Num tu igitur Opimium, si tum esses* (if you had lived at the time) *crudelem putares*. In poetry even pres. subj. is used: cf. Verg. *Aen.* V. 325.

55 **ex animo**] "from the heart." *Eun.* I. 2. 95.

ACTUS IV.   SCENA V.

CRITO.   MYSIS.   DAVUS.

CR. In hac habitasse platea dictumst Chrysidem,
quae sese inhoneste optavit parere hic divitias
potius, quam in patria honeste pauper vivere :
eius morte ea ad me lege redierunt bona.   (800)
Sed quos percontor video.   Salvete.   MY. Obsecro,   5
quem video ?   Estne hic Crito, sobrinus Chrysidis?
Is est.   CR. O Mysis, salve.   MY. Salvos sis, Crito.
CR. Itan' Chrysis?   hem.   MY. Nos quidem pol miseras
    perdidit.
CR. Quid vos? quo pacto hic? satin' recte?   MY. Nosne ?
    Sic
ut quimus, aiunt, quando, ut volumus, non licet.   10

Sc. v.] Crito, cousin to Chrysis, and of right her heir before Glycerium (falsely passing for her sister) appears ; a character somewhat abruptly introduced and without contributing much to the argument : but his appearance serves to recall the fact that Glycerium is *not* the sister of Chrysis, and thus make way for the καταστροφή. Metre : iambic trimeter.

2 **optavit**] "chose;" cf. Verg. *Aen.* I. 425, *Pars optare locum tecto*: Livy XLII. 32, *sine sorte se Macedoniam optaturum.*

3. **vivere**] Bentley and most modern editors read *viveret;* thereby avoiding the difficulty of *optavit se pauper vivere*, and producing an exact parallel to Plaut. *Aul.* Prol. 11, *Inopemque optavit potius eum relinquere quam eum thesaurum commonstraret.* But is it necessary to regard the *sese* of v. 2? *Optavit se parere* is the ordinary construction, and the natural parallel to it *op-*

tavit se pauperem vivere; but surely *optavit pauper vivere* is perfectly intelligible, and consistent with the use of *opto*, approaching to that of *volo*. The objection of a sudden change of construction applies equally to the reading *viveret*.

8 **Itan' Chrysis**] sc. *periit*, omitted to avoid δυσφημία: so the common euphemisms *fuisse, vixisse, abiisse ad plures.* Cf. Greek πλείονες μακαρῖται. Mysis substitutes *perdidit* for the suppressed *periit*.

9 **satin' recte**] sc. *agitis*, a formula of enquiry after friends. Cf. *Eun.* v. 6. 8.

10] An allusion is here traced to a line of Caecilius " Vivas ut possis, quando non quis ut velis," one of the very few reminiscences of anything Roman in Terence. The *Andria* was exhibited on recommendation of Caecilius. A Greek verse *apud Zenobium* is quoted ζῶμεν γὰρ οὐχ ὡς θέλομεν, ἀλλ' ὡς δυνάμεθα.

CR. Quid Glycerium? iam hic suos parentes reperit?

MY. Utinam. CR. An nondum etiam? Haud auspicato huc
     me adpuli:

nam pol, si id scissem, numquam huc tetulissem pedem:

semper enim dicta est eius haec atque habita est soror:

quae illius fuerunt, possidet: nunc me hospitem   (811)   15

lites sequi, quam hic mihi sit facile atque utile,

aliorum exempla commonent: simul arbitror,

iam aliquem esse amicum et defensorem ei: nam fere

grandiuscula iam profectast illinc.   Clamitent,

me sycophantam: hereditates persequi,   20

mendicum: tum ipsam despoliare non libet.

MY. O optume hospes, pol Crito antiquum obtines.

CR. Duc me ad eam: quando huc veni, ut videam.   MY.
     Maxume.

DA. Sequar hos: nolo me in tempore hoc videat senex.

---

13 **tetulissem**] The reduplicated
form is common in Terence and
Plautus. Cf. Lucr. VI. 672.

16 **lites sequi**] = "*hereditatem
persequi*," (as infra v. 20) Donatus;
but rather "To embark in," plunge
into a law-suit. Cf. *bellum sequi,
otium sequi*, "Make a pursuit of."
Cf. *Ad.* II. 2. 40; *Phorm.* II. 3. 61.
But perhaps it is merely a literal
translation of δίκην διώκειν.

facile utile] ironical. A stranger,
he insinuates, is not likely to get
justice here. Cf. *Phorm.* II. 1. 46.
Strangers were obliged to have their
suits tried at Athens, which was a
frequent cause of complaint.

18 **defensorem**] sc. Pamphilum.
She would be the defendant, if
Crito brought an action to claim
the property as next heir.

19 **illinc**] from Andros.

20 **sycophantam**] A term of entirely Greek associations. The συ-
κόφανται, or informers, at Athens

(originally informers against illegal
exporters of figs), are the constant
objects of Aristophanes' invective.

persequi] i.e. hunt after until I
secure it. "Run down the inherit-
ance."

21 **libet**] The reading of Donatus,
Bentley, &c., is preferable to *licet*,
as more expressive of Crito's gene-
rous unwillingness to press his claim
against Glycerium.

22 **antiquum obtines**] "You hold
fast (*obtinere*, cf. *Ad.* V. 3. 28) the
olden manners" (sub. *morem*). Cf.
Hec. V. 4. 20; Shakespeare, *As You
Like It*, II. 3. 56,

  "O good old man, how well in
     thee appears
  The constant custom of the
     antique world,
  When service sweat for duty,
     not for meed!"

Cf. also Plaut. *Capt.* I. 1. 37, *anti-
quis adolescens moribus.*

24 **in tempore**] cf. I. 1. 77.

ACTUS V. SCENA I.

CHREMES. SIMO.

CH. Satis iam, satis, Simo, spectata erga te amicitiast mea:
satis pericli coepi adire: orandi iam finem face.   (822)
Dum studeo obsequi tibi, paene inlusi vitam filiae.
SI. Immo enim nunc quum maxume abs te postulo atque
      oro, Chreme,
ut beneficium verbis initum dudum, nunc re comprobes.   5
CH. Vide quam iniquus sis prae studio: dum id efficias,
      quod cupis,
neque modum benignitatis, neque quid me ores, cogitas:
nam si cogites, remittas iam me onerare iniuriis.
SI. Quibus?   CH. Ah rogitas? perpulisti me, ut homini
      adulescentulo,

Sc. 1.] Chremes, enlightened by what he has just overheard, reproaches Simo with the unworthiness of the match designed for his daughter, and entreats to be let off his part of the agreement. Simo, remembering Davus' suggestion (III. Sc. 2), that a scene of this kind would be got up, maintains that the whole story is untrue.

Metre: trochaic tetrameter catalectic.

3 inlusi v. fil.] *Illudo* in active sense but rarely bears this secondary meaning = to fool away, and so "destroy." Cf. Tac. *Ann.* 1. 71, *corpus illudere;* Hor. *S.* II. 7. 108, *Illusi pedes.* But more frequent as neut. verb in this sense, cf. Verg. *G.* 1. 181; II. 375; Tac. *Hist.* II. 94.

4. Immo enim] (cf. *Eun.* II. 3. 64). Simo hardly understands Chremes' general accusation, and "draws in" another suggestion, that Chremes should fulfil his promise

(*enim τάρελκον est figura.* Don.).

6] Chremes specifies his complaint against Simo.

prae studio] ὑπὸ σπουδῆς. Cf. *Eun.* 1. 2. 18; *Heaut.* II. 3. 67. This use of *prae* is similar to that of *pro* in expressing *pro virili parte* (*pro imperio* = imperiously, Livy, II. 56). *Prae* and *pro* are both dative forms connected with *per*, but the causal sense is more conspicuous in *prae.*

8 remittas onerare] A construction rarely found (never in Cic. or Caesar), cf. Hor. *Od.* II. 11. 3; Sall. *Jug.* 52. 5, *neque remittet quid ubique hostis ageret explorare.* The infin. is not an "object clause," but is used substantivally, and answers to Greek infin. with article. Latin from its want of the article employs the infinitive as a substantive much less frequently than Greek even in nom. and accus. cases.

in alio occupato amore, abhorrenti ab re uxoria,   (830) 10
filiam darem in seditionem atque in incertas nuptias,
eius labore atque eius dolore gnato ut medicarer tuo.
Impetrasti; incepi, dum res tetulit.   Nunc non fert: feras.
Illam hinc civem esse aiunt: puer est natus: hos missos face.
SI. Per ego te deos oro, ut ne illis animum inducas credere,
quibus id maxume utilest, illum esse quam deterrimum.   16
Nuptiarum gratia haec sunt ficta atque incepta omnia.
Ubi ea causa, quamobrem haec faciunt, erit adempta his,
        desinent.
CH. Erras: cum Davo egomet vidi iurgantem ancillam.   SI.
        Scio.   CH. At
vero voltu; quum ibi me adesse neuter tum praesenserat. 20
SI. Credo; et id facturas Davus dudum praedixit mihi.   (841)
Et nescio quid tibi sum oblitus hodie ac volui dicere.

ACTUS V.   SCENA II.

DAVUS. CHREMES. SIMO. DROMO.

DA. Animo nunc iam otioso esse impero... CH. Hem Da-
        vum tibi.

10 re uxoria]=*uxore*, "Such a thing as a wife." Cf. *res frumentaria* = *frumentum*, Caesar. So *res bellica, judiciaria,* &c.   Or perhaps="matrimony."

11 in seditionem, &c.] "For nothing but quarrelling and a shaky marriage tie," *seditio* (*sedire* contrary to *coire*) may=separation, divorce, as *discessio, supra* III. 3. 36. Or "quarrels," cf. Cic. *Att.* II. I. 5, "Ego illam (Clodiam) odi. Ea est enim *seditiosa*, ea cum viro bellum gerit;" and Plaut. *Am.* I. 2. 13, "Amphitruo uxori turbas conciet... tum meus pater eam *seditionem* in tranquillum conferet."

incertas] "unsettled," "shaky." Cf. Verg. *Ecl.* v. 5, *incertas Zephyris mutantibus umbras,* i.e. flicker-

ing. Martial, II. 66, *comarum Annulus incerta non bene fixus acu; incertus vultus,* Sall. *Jug.* 106. 2.

12 labor] "distress," "misery." So frequently in Verg. e.g. *G.* I. 150; III. 452.

13 tetulit] cf. *supr.* I. 2. 17 (*Eun.* IV. I. 7); Cic. *Mur.* 5, *Quod natura fert;* Sall. *Cat.* 21, *Alia omnia, quae bellum atque libido victorum fert.*

15 ut ne] cf. I. I. 34, note. *Credere*=ὥστε πείθεσθαι. On this construction of infin. in Latin see Madvig, *Gr.* 389.

21 facturas] sc. *eas.*
praedixit] *supra* III. 2. 28.

Sc. II.] Before Glycerium's house. Davus comes out full of something he has heard indoors, which (he says

Si. Unde egreditur? Da. meo praesidio atque hospitis.
Si. Quid illud mali est?

Da. Ego commodiorem hominem, adventum, tempus, non
vidi. Si. Scelus,

quemnam hic laudat? Da. Omnis res est iam in vado. Si.
Cesso adloqui?

Da. Herus est: quid agam? Si. O salve, bone vir. Da.
Ehem o Simo, o noster Chreme,   5

omnia adparata iam sunt intus. Si. Curasti probe.

Da. Ubi voles, accerse. Si. Bene sane : id enimvero hinc
nunc abest.

Etiam tu hoc respondes, quid istic tibi negotist? Da. Mihin'?
Si. Ita.   (850)

Da. Mihine? Si. Tibi ergo. Da. Modo introii. Si. Quasi
ego, quam dudum, rogem.

Da. Cum tuo gnato una. Si. Anne est intus Pamphilus?
Crucior miser.   10

Eho, non tu dixti, esse inter eos inimicitias, carnufex?

to himself) has smoothed everything. Simo and Chremes overhear him: and on being questioned, he tells them that Glycerium is of Athenian birth. Though for once telling the truth, he is not unnaturally supposed to be concocting some fresh story, and is locked up by his angry master.

Metre: 1—15, 17—18, troch. tetr. catal.; 16, 19—24, iamb. tetr.; 25—30, iamb. trim.

2 **hospitis**] sc. Critonis, v. Act. IV. Sc. 5.

3 **commodiorem**] "more convenient," i.e. Crito, for coming so opportunely with the real account of Glycerium's parentage.

4 **in vado**] in shallow water, i.e. in safety. Plaut. *Rud.* I. 2. 81, *ut in vado'st, iam facile enabit.* Cf. *in portu navigo,* III. 1. 21, *in tranquillo, Eun.* V. 8. 8.

Cesso adloqui] Note the usual force of *cessare*=to abstain from beginning, not to "cease" from doing what is begun.

5 **noster**] "Most worshipful Chremes." Davus means to be respectful. So as an expression of approbation *En noster! Eun.* I. 2. 74. Donatus thinks "*noster*" signifies that Glycerium has been found to be Chremes' daughter.

7 **id enimvero hinc nunc abest**] "Sure enough that's the one thing we want now (to complete the marriage)", i.e. that Philumena should be summoned. *enimvero,* cf. I. 3. 1, note.

8 **Etiam respondes?**] "And now (*etiam* = *et iam,* cf. *Eun.* II. 2. 55) do you answer me this :" a polite command like *quin* with indic. (Madvig, *Gr.* § 351. 3). Cf. *Ad.* IV. 2. 11; *Heaut.* II. 2. 6.

DA. Sunt. SI. Cur igitur hic est? CH. Quid illum censes?
　　cum illa litigat.

DA. Immo vero indignum, Chreme, iam facinus faxo ex me
　　audias.

Nescio quis senex modo venit: ellum, confidens, catus:

quem faciem videas, videtur esse quantivis preti :　　　　15

tristis severitas inest in voltu, atque in verbis fides.

SI. Quidnam adportas? DA. Nil equidem, nisi quod illum
　　audivi dicere.

SI. Quid ait tandem? DA. Glycerium se scire civem esse
　　Atticam. SI. Hem,　　　　　　　　　　　　(860)

Dromo, Dromo. DR. Quid est? SI. Dromo. DA. Audi.
　　SI. Verbum si addideris. Dromo.

DA. Audi obsecro. DR. Quid vis? SI. Sublimem hunc
　　intro rape, quantum potes.　　　　　　　　20

DR. Quem? SI. Davom. DA. Quamobrem? SI. Quia lubet.
　　Rape inquam. DA. Quid feci? SI. Rape.

DA. Si quicquam invenies me mentitum, occidito. SI. Nihil
　　audio.

Ego iam te commotum reddam. DA. Tamenetsi hoc verum
　　est? SI. Tamen.

---

12 **Quid illum censes**] sc. *facere;*
cf. *Ad.* IV. 5. 22.

14 **ellum = ecce illum**] A colloquial abbreviation common in Plaut.;
ecce is thus combined with all parts
of *is iste ille: eccum, And.* III. 2. 52;
eccos, Heaut. II. 3. 15. Cf. Hand,
Turs. II. 343—351.

confidens] in bad sense "impu-
dent:" sc. *Phormio,* I. 2. 73.
Cicero explains it *Tusc.* III. 7,
" *Confidens* mala consuetudine lo-
quendi in vitio ponitur, ductum
verbum a confidendo, quod laudis
est."

16 **tristis**] "grave," not necessarily sad or gloomy, *index tristis et integer,* Cic. *Verr.* I. 10. Tacitus distinguishes *tristis* and *severus* when

he says of Piso (*Hist.* I. 14), "aesti-
matione recta *severus,* deterius in-
terpretantibus *tristis* habebatur."

fides] "that which makes one
believe," τὸ πιθανὸν ἀξιοπιστία:
called by Arist. *Rhet.* III. 34, πίστις,
by Cic. *Top.* 12, "*fides;*" also
= "evidence," "authority;" (*titu-
lorum* Cic. *Arch.* 5: *literarum*) cf.
Verg. *Aen.* IX. 79.

20 **Sublimem...rape**] "Up with
this fellow and take him indoors
as fast as you can." *Sublimem rapere
ferre,* &c. = to snatch one off, so that
he is lifted, as it were, from the
ground. Cf. *Ad.* III. 2. 18; Plaut.
Mil. V. 1, *Ducite istum; si non se-
quitur, rapite sublimem foras.*

23 **commotum**] "I'll now dis-

Cura adservandum vinctum. Atque audin'? quadrupedem
    constringito.

Age nunc iam: ego pol hodie, si vivo, tibi   25
ostendam, quid herum sit pericli fallere,

et illi patrem. CH. Ah ne saevi tantopere. SI. O Chreme,
pietatem gnati. Nonne te miseret mei?   (870)
Tantum laborem capere ob talem filium?
Age Pamphile: exi Pamphile: ecquid te pudet?   30

ACTUS V. SCENA III.

PAMPHILUS. SIMO. CHREMES.

PA. Quis me volt? Perii, pater est. SI. Quid ais, omnium?
    CH. Ah,
rem potius ipsam dic, ac mitte male loqui.
SI. Quasi quicquam in hunc iam gravius dici possiet.
Ain' tandem, civis Glyceriumst? PA. Ita praedicant.
SI. Ita praedicant? O ingentem confidentiam!   5

turb your mind a bit." Referring to
Davus' *animo otioso* in v. 1, which
Simo had overheard.

24 quadrupedem] i.e. hand and
foot. Cf. Suet. *Calig.*, *Bestiarum
more quadrupedes in cavea coer-
cuit;* and the famous riddle of the
Sphinx, describing man in infancy
as τετράπους, crawling on his hands
and feet.

29 capere] Infinitivus indignantis.
Cf. I. 5. 10.

Sc. III.] Simo upbraids Pamphilus
for his conduct; Pamphilus entreats
that his own excuses and Crito's
evidence may be heard. Simo at
Chremes' request consents.

Metre: 1—24, iamb. trim. 25—32,
iamb. tetr. cat.

1 **omnium**] "Aposiopesis" of
nequissime, or some such word.
Simo in his anger cannot think of a
word strong enough.

4 **tandem**]=*tamen*, according to
Donatus, but cf. *Eun.* I. 2. 100, for
tandem in interrogation.

praedicant] Stronger than *dicunt*,
conveying the notion of open and
public declaration. Pamphilus, "So
they declare." Simo, "Declare, do
they?"

5. **confidentiam**] "presumption."
Cf. *confidens* v. 2. 14.

Num cogitat quid dicat? num facti piget?

Num eius color pudoris signum usquam indicat?

Adeo impotenti esse animo, ut praeter civium   (880)

morem atque legem, et sui voluntatem patris,

. tamen hanc habere studeat cum summo probro?   10

PA. Me miserum.   SI. Hem, modone id demum .sensti,

   Pamphile?

Olim, istuc, olim, quum ita animum induxti tuum,

quod cuperes, aliquo pacto efficiundum tibi:

eodem die istuc verbum vere in te accidit.

Sed quid ego? cur me excrucio, aut cur me macero?   15

Cur meam senectutem huius sollicito amentia an

Ut pro huius peccatis ego supplicium

sufferam? Immo habeat, valeat, vivat cum illa. PA. Mi pater.

SI. Quid mi pater? quasi tu huius indigeas patris.   (891)

---

8 **Adeo...esse**] Infin. indignantis. Cf. I. 5. 10, *adeone esse*, and note. Lachmann *ad Lucr.* II. 16, has collected instances from Terence.

impotenti] "headstrong," "without self-control:" *impotens, iracundus*, &c. Cic. *Phil.* V. 9. 24.

civium morem, &c.] The Athenian law, cf. I. 3. 16.

9 **voluntatem patris**] perhaps alludes to the *patria potestas* of Roman law.

13 **quod cuperes**] The relative proposition is in subj. mood, as forming part of the thought that was in Pamphilus' mind, implied in the primary clause by *animum induxti tuum sub. ut efficeres*. *Quod cupiebas* would simply be Simo's own statement. See Madvig, *Gr.* 368. Sometimes the subj. is employed when the thought is the speaker's own, entertained at some other time. "Occurrebant colles campique et Tiberis et hoc coelum, sub quo natus educatusque *essem*," Livy, V. 54.

14 **istuc verbum**] i.e. *Me mise-*

rum! v. 11. *accidit* pres. or perfect? probably the latter. "What you just said was true enough of you on that same day (i.e. quum ita animum induxti)". *Accidere in* = to fit, apply to, is rare: *cadere* is common enough, especially in philosophical and rhetorical language, used often by Cicero: cf. Verg. *Ecl.* IX. 17, *Heu! cadit in quemquam tantum scelus?* Pliny, XXXV. 10. 36, *Non cadit in alium tam absolutum opus.*

18 **sufferam**] Rare but quite classical in this sense (= "to endure calamity"), being used by Cicero (*suff. poenam sceleris, Cat.* II. 13. 28), Lucretius (*s. volnera*, V. 1304), though the simple *ferre* is far more common. From Plaut. and Ter. it seems to have prevailed more in the language of every-day life than the classical language of literature; this would account for the French "*souffre*," our "*suffer*," derived from what at first sight appears an exceptional usage.

19 **huius**] i.e. "me," like Greek ὅδε. Cf. II. 1. 10; *Heaut.* II. 3. 115;

Domus, uxór, liberi inventi invito patre.   20
Adducti qui illam civem hinc dicant: viceris.
Pa. Pater, licetne pauca? Si. Quid dices mihi?
Ch. Tamen, Simo, audi. Si. Ego audiam? quid audiam,
Chreme? Ch. At tandem dicat sine. Si. Age dicat: sino.
Pa. Ego me amare hanc fateor. Si id peccare est, fateor
        id quoque.   25
Tibi, pater, me dedo. Quidvis oneris impone: impera.
Vis me uxorem ducere? hanc amittere? Ut potero, feram.
Hoc modo te obsecro: ut ne credas a me adlegatum hunc
        senem.   (900)
Sine me expurgem, atque illum huc coram adducam. Si.
        Adducas? Pa. Sine, pater.
Ch. Aequum postulat: da veniam. Pa. Sine te hoc exo-
        rem. Si. Sino.   30
Quidvis cupio, dum ne ab hoc me falli comperiar, Chremes.
Ch. Pro peccato magno paulum supplici satis est patri.

Verg. *Aen.* IX. 205, "Est *hic*, est animus lucis contemptor," and Forbiger's note.

21 **Adducti**] perhaps in sense of "inciting," "moving," in a bad sense, though this is more frequent with *seducere, inducere.* The literal sense seems simpler, "You've fetched people to say." Cf. *Eun.* IV. 4. 27, *quos secum adduxit Parmeno.*

24 **Age dicat**] This use of the imperat. *age* with a third person shews how completely it had passed in colloquial language into a mere exclamation, cf. *Phorm.* IV. 3. 57, *age, age iam ducat.* This is quoted by lexx. under a separate head, as "a sign of assent;" but this is hardly necessary, for the general use as an exclamation = "Come now,"

"Well then," would cover this.

28 **adlegatum**] "Suborned," "instigated." Cf. Plaut. *Poen.* III. 5. 28, *Eum allegaverunt qui...diceret.* Cf. *allegatus* subst.; *meo allegatu* venit, Plaut. *Trin.* V. 2. 18. But would not the ordinary meaning of *allegare* = "despatch," "commission," include these passages?

29 **Adducas?**] echoes *adducam* just before. It may be a deliberative subjunctive = "are you to bring him?" or *sinam* may be supplied— "*I* let you bring him?"

31 **dum ne**] *Dum* expresses the object or design in general, *ne* that it is a negative object; the subjunctive mood really depending on both conjunctions, as in constr. *ut ne*, cf. I. I. 34, note.

ACTUS V.   SCENA IV.

CRITO. CHREMES. SIMO. PAMPHILUS.

CR. Mitte orare.   Una harum quaevis causa me ut faciam
monet,

vel, tu, vel quod verum est, vel quod ipsi cupio Glycerio.

CH. Andrium ego Critonem video? Is certe est. CR. Salvos sis, Chreme.

CH. Quid tu Athenas insolens? CR. Evenit. Sed hicinest
Simo?

CH. Hic. CR. Simo, men' quaeris? SI. Eho, tu Glycerium
hinc civem esse ais?   5

CR. Tu negas? SI. Itane huc paratus advenis? CR. Qua
re? SI. Rogas?   (910)

Tune inpune haec facias? tune hic homines adulescentulos
imperitos rerum, eductos libere, in fraudem inlicis?

sollicitando, et pollicitando eorum animos lactas? CR.
Sanun' es?

SI. ac meretricios amores nuptiis conglutinas?   10

PA. Perii: metuo, ut substet hospes. CH. Si, Simo, hunc
noris satis,

Sc. IV.]   Crito, after some angry
language from Simo, tells the story
of Glycerium's appearance in Andros; Chremes discovers that she
is his own daughter, and at once
consents to her marriage with Pamphilus. Simo is reconciled.

Metre: 1—25, trach. tetr. cat.;
26—53, iamb. tetr.

2 **verum**] Either = "right," i. e.
"because it is right to tell what I
know," cf. IV. 1. 5; or "true," i.e.
"because what I have to say is true."

ipsi cupio] Cf. Cic. *Q. F.* I. 7. 3.
Quid? ego Fundanio non cupio? non

amicus sum?

4 **Quid...insolens?**] sc. venisti.
"what has brought you to Athens
against your wont?" cf. *insolens ma-
larum artium*, Sall. *Cat.* 3. 4.

6 **paratus**] "Have you come with
your part so well got up?" cf. *Phorm.*
II. 3. 80.   Liv. X. 3. 10.

9 **lactas**] cf. IV. 1. 23, note.

11 **noris**] "did you know him well
enough, you would..." The action,
supposed as the condition of another
action, is in subj. mood, without, as
well as with, a conjunction, cf. *Andria*, VI. 31. The omission of conjunc-

non ita arbitrere : bonus est hic vir. SI. Hic vir sit bonus?
Itane adtemperate evenit hodie in ipsis nuptiis,
ut veniret antehac numquam? Est vero huic credendum,
    Chremes?

PA. Ni metuam patrem, habeo pro illa re illum quod mo-
    neam probe.   15

SI. Sycophanta. CR. Hem. CH. Sic, Crito, est hic : mitte.
    CR. Videat qui siet.   (920)

Si mihi pergit quae volt dicere, ea quae non volt audiet.

Ego istaec moveo aut curo? Non tu tuum malum aequo
    animo feres?

Nam ego quae dico, vera an falsa audieris, iam sciri potest.

Atticus quidam olim navi fracta ad Andrum eiectus est, 20

et istaec una parva virgo. Tum ille egens forte adplicat

primum ad Chrysidis patrem se. SI. Fabulam inceptat.
    CH. Sine.

CR. Itane vero obturbat? CH. Perge. CR. Tum is mihi
    cognatus fuit,

tion is common in other cases, cf. *Ad.*
I. 2. 38; *Heaut.* III. 1. 78; Forb. *ad*
G. II. 519, *Venit hiems; teritur Si-*
cyonia bacca. Such omission is natural in quick emphatic speech, and
is a relic of the earlier phase of language which employs coordinate
rather than subordinate sentences.

12 **sit**] potential; "This man an
honest fellow!"

13 **evenit**] Simo sneeringly repeats the expression used by Crito V. 4.

15 **pro illa re**] "a-propos of that
matter," cf. Verg. *Aen.* IV. 337, *Pro*
re pauca loquar : Hand, *Turs.* IV.
p. 584.

16 **Sic...mitte**] "He's like this,
Crito: never mind him," cf. *Eun.*
III. 1. 18; *Phorm.* III. 2. 42.

Videat qui siet.] "Let him look to
his own nature." It is his look out
what kind of man he is. I don't care.

17 **pergit**] Bentley *perget.*

18 **Ego istaec moveo aut curo**]

"Have I any kind or part in your
troubles? *moveo,* "to set in motion,"
"begin;" *Motum ex Metello consule...*
bellum, Hor. *Od.* II. 1. 1. *curo* as in
exp. *faciendum curare,* &c. "to see
or look after."

19 **audieris**] refers to what Davus
said sc. 2. v. 18, *civem Atticum*
Glycerium esse, not to what Crito
is about to say. Tr. "From what
I now tell you you can judge if what
you have heard be true or false."

21 **adplicat se**] "attaches himself to my father," i.e. as client to
patron, by the *ius applicationis* (vid.
Dict. Ant. s. v. Banishment); cf. Cic.
de Or. I. 39, *Qui Romam in exsilium*
venisset, cui Romae exsulare ius es-
set, si ad aliquem quasi patronum se
applicavisset. For the relationship
thus secured, vid. *Dict. Ant.* s. v.
Cliens.

23 **Itane vero obturbat?**] Weise
puts the interrogative after *vero;* a

qui eum recepit. Ibi ego audivi ex illo sese esse Atticum.
Is ibi mortuus est. CH. Eius nomen? CR. Nomen tam
    cito tibi? CR. Phania. CH. Hem,   25
perii. CR. Verum hercle opinor fuisse Phaniam: hoc
    certo scio,   (930)
Rhamnusium se aiebat esse. CH. O Iuppiter. CR. Eadem
    haec, Chreme,
multi alii in Andro audivere. CH. Utinam id sit, quod
    spero. Eho, dic mihi,
quid eam tum; suamne esse aibat? CR. Non. CH. Cuiam
    igitur? CR. Fratris filiam.
CH. Certe meast. CR. Quid ais? SI. Quid tu ais? PA.
    Arrige aures, Pamphile.   30
SI. Quid credis? CH. Phania illic frater meus fuit. SI.
    Noram et scio.
CH. Is hinc, bellum fugiens meque in Asiam persequens
    proficiscitur;
tum illam relinquere hic est veritus. Postilla nunc primum
    audio

---

reading suggested by frequent use
of *itane vero?* as exclamation. *obturbat*, "interrupts," cf. Tac. *Ann.* VI.
24, *obturbabant patres specie detes-
tandi.* So Don. and Forc.
  18] sc. Chrys. pater.
  24 ex illo] sc. Phania.
  31 Quid credis] Bembine MS.:
others *qui credis.*
  Noram (sc. Phaniam) **et scio**] (fratrem esse Chremetis). Note the distinction between *nosco* and *scio*, both
expressed in English by "know."
"He was an acquaintance of mine,
and I know all about him now."
  33 Postilla] (not *post illâ* as Bentley) a formation analogous to *postea,
interea*. From analogy of *intereâ*,
and Enn. apud Cic. *Div.* I. 20, *postilla germana soror errare videbar*,
the a is long. This ă is variously
explained (1) as =a-ce and therefore
acc. plur. neut. (Donaldson, *Varron.*

ch. X. § 4): (2) That *ea, illa* &c., in
these words are ablatives. The asso-
ciation of *inter* and *post* with acc. case
is no proof that in early Latin they
may not have been used with other
cases, in the adverbial sense which is
the earliest of all prepositions (analogous to this would be ἐκ πόντοφιν=
from *on* the sea, ἀπὸ πασσαλόφιν from
on the peg in Hom.). And the word
interutraque Lucr. II. 517 might be
alleged: but there *inter* is explained
as belonging per tmesim to *iacent*
following, see Lachmann's note. (3)
That in all these cases a final m is
lost, i.e. *post ea quam=post eam
quam; ea-m, illa-m* being adverbial
accusatives like *quam*, which survives in classical Latin. The final m
is often omitted in remains of old
Latin, see esp. the epitaphs of the
Scipios. It may, however, be main-
tained that the view which makes

quid illo sit factum.   PA. Vix sum apud me : ita animus
    commotust metu,
spe, gaudio, mirando hoc tanto tam repentino bono.   35
SI. Nac istam multimodis tuam inveniri gaudeo.   PA. Credo,
    pater.   (940)
CII. At mi unus scrupulus etiam restat, qui me male habet.
    PA. Dignus es
cum tua religione, odium! Nodum in scirpo quaeris.   CR.
    Quid istuc est?
CH. Nomen non convenit.   CR. Fuit hercle huic aliud
    parvae.   CH. Quod, Crito?
Numquid meministi?   CR. Id quaero.   PA. Egon' huius
    memoriam patiar meae   40
voluptati obstare, quum egomet possim in hac re medicari
    mihi?
Non patiar.   Heus, Chreme, quod quaeris, Pasibula.   CII.
    Ipsast.   CR. East.
PA. Ex ipsa millies audivi.   SI. Omnis nos gaudere hoc,
    Chreme,
te credo credere.   CII. Ita me Di ament, credo.   PA. Quid
    restat, pater?
SI. Iam dudum res reduxit me ipsa in gratiam.   PA. O
    lepidum patrem.   45

these formations simply neut. plurals,
lengthened as many short syllables
are, is the simplest.

36 multimodis] with *inveniri*,
"I am glad she is so fully (in various
ways) proved to be your daughter,"
or with *gaudeo*, "I am very glad."

37 At] used appropriately for in-
troducing an objection.

male habet] "worries me;" cf. II.
6. 5, Lucr. III. 826. *bene habere, male
habere* are occasionally used as Greek
καλῶς, κακῶς ἔχειν, cf. *Phormio*, II.
3. 82; *Eun.* I. 2. 73.

38 odium] So Bemb. and Vat.
MSS.. Donatus, and the best edd.

It is suggested that *dignus odium* =
dignus ad odium; but it is better
with Stallbaum and others to make
an aposiopesis after *dignus es*, and
tr. *odium* as vocative "you wretch!"
cf. the use of *scelus*.

Nodum in scirpo quaeris] "You
are looking for a knot in a bulrush,"
i.e. for a difficulty where there is
none. *Quaerunt in scirpo, soliti
quod dicere, nodum*, Ennius apud
Fest. p. 257.

40 Id quaero] "I am trying to
remember it."

45 lepidum] "Charming."

De uxore, ita ut possedi, nil mutat Chremes. CII. Causa
    optumast : (950)
nisi quid pater ait aliud. PA. Nempe id. SI. Scilicet.
    CH. Dos, Pamphile, est
decem talenta. PA. Accipio. CII. Propero ad filiam. Eho
    mecum, Crito :
nam illam me credo haud nosse. SI. Cur non illam huc
    transferri iubes ?
PA. Recte admones. Davo ego istuc dedam iam negoti.
    SI. Non potest. 50
PA. Qui? SI. Quia habet aliud magis ex sese et maius.
    PA. Quidnam? SI. Vinctus est.
PA. Pater, non recte vinctust. SI. Haud ita iussi. PA. Iube
    solvi, obsecro.
SI. Age fiat. PA. At matura. SI. Eo intro. PA. O faus-
  .   tum et felicem diem.

ACTUS V. SCENA V.

CHARINUS. PAMPHILUS.

CH. Proviso quid agat Pamphilus. Atque eccum. PA. Ali-
    quis forsan me putet
non putare hoc verum : at mihi nunc sic esse hoc verum
    liquet.

---

46 nil mutat] "wishes to make no change;" cf. *And.* I. I. 13, *ita ut possedi*, perhaps (as Stallb.) referring to the Praetor's formula *ut possidetis, ita possideatis.*

51 magis ex sese] "More directly concerning himself," cf. *bene et e republica aliquid facere, ex mea re,* &c.

52] Pa. "He has been wrongly chained up, father." Si. "I ordered it to be done rightly enough." Simo in joke takes the word *recte* to apply not to the cause, but to the *manner* of Davus' imprisonment, i.e. *quadrupedem constringi.*

Sc. v.] Charinus finds Pamphilus rejoicing in his good fortune. Davus reappears.

Metre: iamb. tetram.

1 Proviso] "I am coming out to see." "Proviso duas res significat; et provideo et video," Donatus ad *Adelph.* v. 6. 1: cf. *Eun.* III. 1. 4. Only in Plaut. and Ter.

Ego Deum vitam propterea sempiternam esse arbitror, (960)
quod voluptates eorum propriae sunt: nam mi immorta-
    litas
partast, si nulla aegritudo huic gaudio intercesserit.   5
Sed quem ego mihi potissimum optem nunc, cui haec nar-
    rem, dari?
CH. Quid illud gaudi est? PA. Davom video. Nemost,
    quem mallem, omnium:
nam hunc scio mea solide solum gavisurum gaudia. '

ACTUS V. SCENA VI.

DAVUS. PAMPHILUS. CHARINUS.

DA. Pamphilus ubinam? PA. Hic est, Dave. DA. Quis
    homost? PA. Ego sum Pamphilus.
Nescis quid mi obtigerit. DA. Certe: sed quid mi obti·
    gerit scio.

4 propriae] "lasting," *perenne ac proprium*, Cic. *Serv.* 4; cf. Verg. *Ecl.* VII. 31; *Aen.* VI. 872; Hor. *Sat.* II. 6. 5.

The Epicurean sentiment of vv. 3, 4. is taken direct from the Eunuchus of Menander.

nam mi immortalitas parta est] Colman's translation aptly borrows from Shakespeare, *Othello*, II. 1:
"If it were now to die,
'Twere now to be most happy; for I fear
My soul hath her content so absolute
That not another comfort, like to this
Succeeds in unknown fate."
"Both speeches (Pamphilus' and Othello's) are of the highest joy and rapture, and founded on the instability of human happiness; but in my mind the English poet has the

advantage." Colman might have made this admission stronger; for while the comparison of the two passages is fully justified by their external and verbal similarity, the sentiment as handled by Shakespeare rises far above the mere echo of Menander's Epicureanism, which (as we see from v. 3) runs through the passage before us. Cf. *Eun.* III. 5. 3, 4.

8 solide] "wholly" (*solide scio*, Plaut. *Trin.* IV. 2. 8); cf. the use frequently in Cic. of the adj. = sound, substantial, real, *solidum gaudium*, and the like.

Sc. VI.] Pamphilus tells Davus of his good fortune, and Charinus intreats D.'s intervention with Chremes. Davus pronounces the Epilogue.

Metre: trochaic tetram. catalectic,

PA. Et quidem ego. DA. More hominum evenit, ut quod·
    sim nactus mali

prius rescisceres tu, quam ego illud quod tibi evenit boni.

PA. Mea Glycerium suos parentes repperit. DA. Factum
    bene. CH. Hem.   (970) 5

PA. Pater amicus summus nobis. DA. Quis? PA. Chremes.
    DA. Narras probe.

PA. Nec mora ulla est, quin eam uxorem ducam. CH. Num
    ille somniat

ea quae vigilans voluit? PA. Tum de puero, Dave? DA.
    Ah desine:

solus est quem diligunt Di. CH. Salvos sum, si haec vera
    sunt.

Conloquar. PA. Quis homost? Charine, in tempore ipso
    mi advenis.   10

CH. Bene factum. PA. Audisti? CH. Omnia. Age, me in
    tuis secundis respice.

Tuus est nunc Chremes: facturum quae voles scio esse omnia.

PA. Memini: atque adeo longumst nos illum expectare
    dum exeat.

Sequere hac me. Intus apud Glycerium nunc est. Tu,
    Dave, abi domum:

---

3. "Ill news flies apace."

9 solus est quem diligunt Di]
"Say no more about him; he's dead,
happiest of us all, for whom the gods
love, die young." Another reading
is es: the expression is then one of
strong congratulation to Pamphilus.
As Parry remarks, it is difficult to see
what point there is in thus "killing
off" the child. But est is best supported: and, but for Ah desine, we
might argue, why should not Davus
be supposed to call the child favour-
ed by heaven, because all this ends in
his being regarded as the legitimate
son and heir? [See Wagner's note.]

11 respice] "Take thought for
me." Respicere and respectare, frequently of protecting deities; cf. supra IV. 1. 8; Phorm. V. 3. 34; Verg.
Ecl. 1. 28, Di tibi, si qua pios respect-
ant numina....Praemia digna ferant.
Also (as here) of persons taking
thought for, bethinking themselves
of others, cf. Ad. III. 2. 55; Tac. Hist.
IV. 4, mox deos respexere, restitui
Capitolium placuit. For our passage cf. Soph. O. C. 1554, εὐδαίμονες
γένοισθε, κἀπ' εὐπραξίᾳ μέμνησθέ
μου.

12 Tuus est] is explained by what
follows.

Propera, accerse, hinc qui auferant eam. Quid stas? quid

        cessas? DA. Eo.   (980) 15

Ne exspectetis dum exeant huc: intus despondebitur:

intus transigetur, si quid est quod restet. ω plaudite.

---

17 **Plaudite**] Bentley assigned this to the "cantor" (who recited all parts set to music, the actor going through the necessary gestures) after all the actors had left the stage, cf. Hor. *A. P.* 155, *donec cantor* '*Vos plaudite*' *dicat,* and the ω which all MSS. give is according to him a corruption of CA, i.e. Cantor. Others suppose it to stand for ᾠδός= cantor; others again that ω the last letter of the alphabet designates the person that appears last in the play (the different characters in the Bembine MS. being indicated by letters).

Some later MSS. give a second ending (17 lines) in which Charinus's love affair is concluded. Wagner (following Ritschl) accepts them; but there is no evidence for their genuineness beyond a notice of Donatus. Wagner (supposing two representations of the Andria, for the second of which the present Prologue was written) thinks that these extra verses may have formed the end of the first performance, and that Terence may have cut them out before the second. But they most likely originated from some student or copyist interested in the final disposal of Charinus.

INTRODUCTION TO THE EUNUCHUS.

THE Eunuchus was acted B.C. 162 at the Megalesia, and was so popular as to be repeated. The poet received 8000 sesterces from the Aediles, more (as we are told in the Didascalia) than had ever been received for one play. It was deservedly the most popular of Terence's comedies: for though its leading incident is objectionable to modern ideas, the details of the action are worked out, and the characters delineated with greater delicacy and humour than in any other of his extant plays. The characters of the Parasite (Act II. Sc. 2) and of Thraso, the Braggadocio (corresponding to the Miles Gloriosus of Plautus), are drawn with a humour worthy of the true " Plautini sales," and (in the former case especially) with a pleasing variety from the somewhat hackneyed ideal of Plautus.

Donatus' criticism on the play is "in hac Terentius delectat facetiis, prodest exemplis, et vitia hominum paulo mordacius quam in ceteris carpit. Exempla autem morum hic tria praecipue ponuntur, urbani scilicet, parasitici, et militaris."

The plot is as follows: *Pamphila*, the daughter of an Athenian citizen, kidnapped in infancy, became the property of a courtezan at Rhodes, with whose daughter *Thais* she was brought up as a younger sister. Thais moved to Athens and there lived with a soldier named *Thraso*; who after a time went away to Caria, and on his return bought Pamphila at Rhodes from the uncle of Thais, and brought her to Athens as a present for Thais. Meanwhile Thais had a new lover,

6—2

Phaedria son of Laches: and here the play opens. Thraso discovering this makes his present conditional on Phaedria's dismissal. Thais in perplexity between her love for Phaedria and her desire to get Pamphila, whose story she has learnt in part, shuts her door against Phaedria; who, angry at first, agrees to give her time to get Pamphila from Thraso, and meanwhile sends to her house an Ethiopian slave and a eunuch as a present. At the same time Pamphila is being sent by Thraso to Thais in charge of his follower and parasite *Gnatho*. On her way *Chaerea*, Phaedria's brother, falls desperately in love with her: and with *Parmeno*, his father's slave, concocts the scheme on which the plot of the play turns; and during Thais' absence is admitted to her house in the Eunuch's clothes. Thais having meanwhile seen *Chremes*, the brother of Pamphila and almost succeeded in identifying her, is much annoyed at what has happened, which threatens to defeat her schemes for restoring Pamphila to her friends: and Phaedria is distressed at the mischief caused, as he supposes, by his present. Chaerea, however, promises to make amends by marrying Pamphila: and meanwhile *Pythias*, Thais' maid, drives Parmeno to explain the whole matter to *Laches*, father of Phaedria and Chaerea. A general explanation follows, and all parties are made happy with the exception of Thraso.

The "Eunuchus" has been translated or adapted by Baif, a Frenchman (temp. Charles IX), and by Fontaine, whose comedy "L'Eunuque" was founded on that of Terence, with alterations adapted to modern times.

EUNUCHUS.

PHAEDRIA, adulescens.
PARMENO, servus.
THAIS, meretrix,
GNATHO, parasitus.
CHAEREA, adulescens.
THRASO, miles.
PYTHIAS, ancilla,
CHREMES, adulescens.
ANTIPHO, adulescens.
DORIAS, ancilla.
DORUS, eunuchus.
SANGA, coquus.
SOPHRONA, nutrix.
LACHES, senex.

Acta ludis Megalensib. L. Postumio Albino L. Cornelio Merula Aedilib. curulib. Egere L. Ambivius Turpio L. Atilius Praenestinus. Modos fecit Flaccus Claudi Tibiis duabus dextris. Graeca Menandru. Acta II. M. Valerio C. Fannio Coss.

Acta II.] "Represented for the second time." Another reading is *facta secunda*, which is explained as = holding the second place in the order of Terence's comedies, and is adopted by Fleckeisen.

PROLOGUS.

Sɪ quisquam est, qui placere se studeat bonis
quam plurimis, et minime multos laedere,
in his poëta hic nomen profitetur suum.
Tum si quis est, qui dictum in se inclementius
existimavit esse, sic existimet,   5
responsum,. non dictum esse, quia laesit prior:
qui bene vertendo, et easdem scribendo male, ex
Graecis bonis Latinas fecit non bonas.
Idem Menandri Phasma nunc nuper dedit:
atque in Thesauro scripsit, causam dicere   10
prius unde petitur, aurum quare sit suum,
quam ille qui petit, unde is sit thesaurus sibi:
aut unde in patrium monumentum pervenerit.

1 **se**] pleonastic: cf. *And.* IV.
5. 2.

2 **multos**] perhaps = *malos* as
opposed to the few *boni*. Stallb.
compares Cic. *Rep.* VI. *in dissen-
sione civili, quum boni plusquam multi
valent*, and Accius, *Bonis probatum,
potius quam multis fore*. Or *minime
multos* = "as few as possible:" the
opposition then lies only between
placere and *laedere*.

7 **vertendo**] "translating," i.e.
from Greek to Latin, Hor. *Epp.* II.
I. 134, *Tentavit quoque rem* (Ro-
manus) *si digne vertere posset*.

scribendo] (Bentley, following Codex Bemb.) is explained *Bene vertere e Graec. est male Latine scribere*.
We may then paraphrase "Who, by
looking more to faithful translation
than elegance of style, has turned
good Greek into bad Latin dramas."

Stallb. *describendo*, which he explains
of distribution of characters (?).

9] Alluding to a recent production by L. Lavinius (the *vetus poeta*
of *And.* prol.) of a Menandrian play,
the *Phasma*. According to Donatus,
Terence condemns this play in toto,
the "*Thesaurus*" in one specified
passage, where the defendant is
made to speak first.

11 **unde**] = *ex quo*, "the defendant;" a legal phrase. So Cato ap.
Gell. XIV. 2. 26, *illi* unde *petitur, ei
potius credendum esse*. Cic. *Fam.* VII
11. 1, etc.

13 **in p. monumentum**] It was
a common custom to conceal treasure in tombs. Cf. Plaut. *Pseud.* I.
4. 19—Pseudolus says of a rich old
man, *Ex hoc sepulcro vetere viginti
minas Effodiam ego hodie, quas dem
herili filio*.

Dehinc, ne frustretur ipse se, aut sic cogitet:

defunctus iam sum, nihil est quod dicat mihi: 15

is ne erret, moneo, et desinat lacessere.

Habeo alia multa, quae nunc condonabitur;

quae proferentur post, si perget laedere;

ita ut facere instituit. Quam nunc acturi sumus

Menandri Eunuchum, postquam Aediles emerunt;   20

perfecit, sibi ut inspiciundi esset copia,

magistratus quum ibi adesset, occeptast agi.

Exclamat, furem, non poëtam, fabulam

dedisse, et nil dedisse verborum tamen:

---

15 **defunctus sum**] "My task is done," i.e. "I have already produced my drama" and got through the danger, cf. *Ad.* III. 4. 62; *Phorm.* v. 8. 32; Hor. *Epp.* II. 1. 22, *defuncta suis temporibus*, "that have lived their day."

17 **quae condonabitur**] "for which he shall be excused." The same construction occurs *Phorm.* v. 8. 54, *Argentum quod habes condonamus te;* Plaut. *Bacch.* v. 2. 24, *Si quam (rem) debes te condono.* Lexx. cite these passages as a separate use of the word *c. aliquem aliquid* = to present one with something: but they surely fall under the meaning "to pardon" (as Cic. *Mil.* 2, *ut crimen hoc nobis condonctis*), the construction only being different.

18 **perget laedere**] see *And.* III. 2. 42, note, and Madvig, *Lat. Gr.* § 389.

20 **postquam Aediles emerunt**] Dramas intended for exhibition at the *ludi scenici* were privately rehearsed before the Curule Aediles, on whom as presidents of the festivals (*Ludi Magni, Ludi Scenici* &c.) devolved the task of providing dramas for exhibition. Lavinius seems to have obtained admission to this private rehearsal, and to have then and there accused Terence of plagiarism from the *Colax* (κόλαξ) of Plautus.

Terence received from the Aediles 8000 sesterces for this play.

emĕrunt] Munro on *Lucr.* I. 406 quotes examples from Lucretius of this ĕ in 3 pers. plur. of the perfect. It occurs not unfrequently in Vergil, e.g. *Ecl.* IV. 61; *G.* II. 129; *Aen.* II. 774. Dr Wagner says "instances of ĕ in termination of perfects in the old comic poets, are not so numerous as one would be led to conclude from Munro's note;" they are not very numerous: but would one conclude otherwise from Munro, whose examples are all from Lucretius?

23 **fabulam dedisse et nil dedisse verborum**] "Has produced a play, but yet has not deceived us" (i.e. in passing it off as his own). Donatus suggests "*nihil addidisse de suo stilo*," i.e. "has given us a play, but not a word of his own in it." Another interpretation is "could not say a word in his own defence," i.e. so clearly was he found out in plagiarism. Neither of these latter, however, agrees with the familiar use of *verba dare* = "to deceive," cf. *And.* I. 3. 6. It is impossible to keep up the play upon the double sense of *dedisse.*

Colacem esse Naevi, et Plauti veterem fabulam :   25
parasiti personam inde ablatam et militis.
Si id est peccatum, peccatum imprudentiast
poetae : non quo furtum facere studuerit.
Id ita esse, vos iam iudicare poteritis.
Colax Menandri est : in ea est parasitus Colax,   30
et miles gloriosus : eas se non negat
personas transtulisse in Eunuchum suam
ex Graeca : sed eas fabulas factas prius
Latinas scisse sese, id vero pernegat.
Quodsi personis isdem uti aliis non licet :   35
qui magis licet currentem servum scribere,
bonas matronas facere, meretrices malas,
parasitum edacem, gloriosum militem,
puerum supponi, falli per servom senem,
amare, odisse, suspicari? Denique   40
nullum est iam dictum, quod non dictum sit prius.
Quare aequom est vos cognoscere atque ignoscere,
quae veteres factitarunt, si faciunt novi.

25 **Naevi et Plauti fabulam**] i.e. written originally by Naevius, but brought out and revised afterwards by Plautus.

27 **imprudentia**] "ignorance:" so in Cicero : cf. Verg. *G.* I. 373, *nunquam imprudentibus imber obfuit.*

28 **studuerit**] The subjunctive mood indicates the thought in the mind of the accuser. "It is not as he thinks, from any deliberate design to steal," cf. *And.* VI. 3. 13, and see Madv. 368.

33 **fabulas**] Wagner, following Ritschl, wishes to read *fabulis Latinis*, because *eas*, he says, must = *personas* (as in v. 31): for Terence mentions only *one* Greek play, from which he borrowed two characters, not knowing that they had already appeared in a Roman play derived from the same source.

34 **pernegat**] "he stoutly denies," cf. Greek δυσχυρίζομαι.

36] These vv. enumerate the standing characters of the Roman stage. Cf. Hor. *Epp.* II. I. 171; and Ovid, *Am.* I. 15. 17, *Dum fallax servus, durus pater, improba lena Vivent, dum meretrix blanda, Menandros erit.*

40 **Denique**] v. note *Heaut.* I. I. 17. "In fine there is not a word spoken now, that has not been spoken of old." *iam—prius* seem emphatic = *nunc—olim.* So Hor. *Od.* II. 4. 2, *Prius insolentem Serva Briseis... Movit Achillem.*

42] "'Tis but fair then for you to admit and allow the deed, if moderns do for once what their ancestors have done over and over." "*Et varie dixit,*" says Donatus, "factitarunt *et* faciunt, *et magna cum defensione*

Date operam, et cum silentio animum attendite,
ut pernoscatis, quid sibi Eunuchus velit.   45

ACTUS I. SCENA I.

PHAEDRIA. PARMENO.

PH. Quid igitur faciam? Non eam? ne nunc quidem
quum adcersor ultro? an potius ita me comparem,
non perpeti meretricum contumelias?
Exclusit: revocat. Redeam? Non, si me obsecret.
PA. Siquidem hercle possis, nihil prius neque fortius: (50)
verum si incipies, neque pertendes naviter,   ·   6
atque ubi pati non poteris, quum nemo expetet,
infecta pace, ultro ad eam venies; indicans

Terentii, semel facientis id quod saepe veteres."

44 **Date operam**] "Pay attention," perhaps originally a legal term, of judges hearing a case (Cic. *Verr.* II. 29, *In Petilium jubet operam dare, quod rei privatae judex esset*), so here of the audience. Of serving a friend, attending to his matters, *infr.* II. 2. 50: *malam operam dare* "to do an ill turn," Plaut. *Capt.* III. 3. 43.

45 **ut pern.**] "That you may get a clear idea."

Sc. I.] Phaedria is introduced deliberating with himself, and with Parmeno, how to take Thais' conduct to him, which he cannot endure, while he cannot bear to be away from her. Parmeno moralizes on the chances of love. Metre: iambic trimeter.

Cicero (*De Nat. Deor.* III. 29) and Quintilian (*Inst. Or.* IX. 2, 4) speak of this scene in terms of praise. Horace (*Sat.* II. 3, 260—271) gives an outline of the scene; and Persius (*Sat.* V. 172) imitates

the opening lines; *Quidnam igitur faciam? ne nunc quum accersor, et ultro Supplicat, accedam?* We may also compare the speech of Dido, Verg. *Aen.* IV. 534, "*En quid agam?*" &c.

1 **faciam, eam**] "deliberative" subjunctive.

2 **ultro**] "unexpectedly," i.e. after dismissal, cf. *And.* I. 1. 73, note.

3 **perpeti**] = *ut perpetiar*. The infinitive is admissible here after *me comparem*, in which lies the notion of preparing, resolving, &c. that requires another verb to complete it, cf. *And.* III. 2, 42.; Madv. § 389.

4 **Non si me obsecret**] *si* has the force of *etiamsi*; cf. *Heaut.* III. I. 33, Verg. *Aen.* V. 17.

5 **prius**] "better;" *bellante prior*, Hor. *Carm. Sec.* 21; *prior aetate et sapientia*, Sall. *Jug.* 10. This use of the comp. *prior* is unusual, not in Cicero or Caesar.

7 **pati**] without case following = καρτερεῖν, "to hold out:" cf. *Hec.* I. 2. 108; *Heaut.* IV. 5. 13; Luc. *Phar.* 5. 314. Hence the use of *patiens*.

te amare, et ferre non posse: actumst: ilicet:
peristi. Eludet, ubi te victum senserit.   10
Proin tu, dum est tempus, etiam atque etiam cogita,
here, quae res in se neque consilium neque modum
habet ullum, eam consilio regere non potes.
In amore haec omnia insunt vitia: iniuriae,
suspiciones, inimicitiae, indutiae,   (60) 15
bellum, pax rursum: incerta haec si tu postules
ratione certe facere, nihilo plus agas,
quam si des operam, ut cum ratione insanias.
Et quod nunc tute tecum iratus cogitas,
"egone illam, quae illum? quae me? quae non? Sine
                modo !   20
Mori me malim ! Sentiet qui vir siem !"
Haec verba una me hercle falsa lacrimula,
quam oculos terendo misere vix vi expresserit,
restinguet: et te ultro accusabit: et dabis
ei ultro supplicium.   PH. O indignum facinus : nunc ego

9 ilicet] The formula of dismissal from public ceremonies: in
Plautus and Terence when affairs
are desperate : with dative as an indignant farewell, *Phorm.* I. 4. 31;
Plaut. *Capt.* III. 1. 9.

10 Eludet] " She'll mock you."
Orig. of gladiators "to parry a blow,"
hence "to cheat;" further "to jeer,"
" banter," as here.

13] "You can't apply reason to
a case that has neither rhyme (mo-
dus) nor reason in it."

14] Horace imitates this catalo-
gue of the ills of love, *Sat.* II. 3. 267
—271: cf. Plaut. *Merc.* prol. 18—
36.

iniuriae, &c.] The plural denotes
repeated acts: so *irae, And.* III. 3.
20: *tristes Amaryllidis iras,* Verg.
Ecl. II. 14.

16] "If you stipulate for method
in matters of such mere chance, it's
much the same as trying to go mad
methodically."

20] *Egone illam (accedam), quae
illum (praeposuit)? quae me (spre-
vit)? quae non (me admisit)? sine
modo* "let me alone for that ;" often
expressing a threat as *Phorm.* II. 3.
73. Wagner compares German "lass
gut sein."

23 terendo misere] "by rubbing
her eyes hard:" cf. on *And.* III. 2. 49.

vix vi expresserit] "she scarcely
squeezed out." The action is well
indicated by the rhythm of these
words. For the idea, cf. Ov. *Met.*
VI. 628, *Invitique oculi lacrimis ma-
duere coactis;* Juv. XIII. 133, *Vexare
oculos humore coacto.*

24 ultro] may here bear its fundamental meaning of *insuper* (cf.
And. I. 1. 73, note), and so according
to Bentley it was understood by
Faernus. Or it may = without waiting for you to reproach her "she
will actually begin to accuse you."

et illam scelestam esse et me miserum sentio: (71) 26
et taedet: et amore ardeo: et prudens sciens,
vivus vidensque pereo: nec quid agam scio.
PA. Quid agas? Nisi ut te redimas captum quam queas
minimo: si nequeas paululo, at quanti queas: 30
et ne te adflictes.   PH. Itane suades?   PA. Si sapis.
Neque, praeterquam quas ipse amor molestias
habet, addas: et illas, quas habet, recte feras.
Sed ecca ipsa egreditur, nostri fundi calamitas:
nam quod nos capere oportet, haec intercipit.   (80) 35

ACTUS I.   SCENA II.

THAIS. PHAEDRIA. PARMENO.

TH. Miseram me! vereor ne illud gravius Phaedria
tulerit, neve aliorsum, atque ego feci, acceperit,

---

28 **vivus vidensque**] an alliterative proverb; Cic. *Sest. vivus ut aiunt, est et videns* (cf. Verg. *Ecl.* VI. 21, *videnti=vigilanti*), also Lucr. III. 1046, where its effect is strengthened by "*mortua cui vita est*" as here by *pereo*. "Alliteration," a favourite device of earlier Latin writers, is especially common with the letter *v* (pronounced *w*) "expressing pity, as its sound well fits it to do…or force or violence, because the words indicating such effects begin many of them with this letter." See Munro's *Lucretius* [Part II. *Introduction to notes*].

33 **habet**] "brings." So ἔχειν in Greek.

34 **nostri fundi calamitas**] "The blight of my harvest." His master is *fundus*, as being a source of income: cf. Plaut. *Truc.* V. 2. 15, *Solus summam hic habet apud nos. Nunc is est* fundus *nobis. Calamitas*, whether derived or not as some say from *calamus, culmus* (Donat. í loc. "Calamitatem rustici grandi-

nem dicunt, quod comminuat calamum, hoc est culmum, ac segetem"), is originally an agricultural term, *calamitas fructuum*, Cic. *Verr.* II. 3. 98; cf. Servius on Verg. *G.* I. 151, *ut mala culmos esset robigo:* hence according to him "*calamitas.*" It has been connected with *cado*, and was written *caaamitas* by Pompey.

35 **capere**] of receiving rents, produce, &c. Cic. *Paradox.* VI. 3, *Capit ille ex suis praediis sexcenta sestertia: ego centena ex meis;* cf. *Phormio*, V. 3. 7. Hence in jurists = "to inherit;" Juv. I. 55, *Si capiendi ius nullum uxori.*

Sc. II.]   Enter Thais lamenting Phaedria's misunderstanding of her conduct, for which she accounts to him by her anxiety to get possession of the girl promised by Thraso (see introduction to the play), and asks him to help her by going away for two days. Phaedria consents, though at first suspicious of some trick.

Metre: iambic trimeter.

2 **aliorsum**] "in another spirit"

quod heri intromissus non est. PH. Totus, Parmeno,
tremo horreoque, postquam aspexi hanc. PA. Bono animo es:
accede ad ignem hunc, iam calesces plus satis.　　　　　5
TH. Quis hic loquitur? Ehem, tun hic eras, mi Phaedria?
Quid hic stabas? Cur non recta introibas? PA. Ceterum
de exclusione verbum nullum. TH. Quid taces?
PH. Sane, quia vero hae mihi patent semper fores,
aut quia sum apud te primus. TH. Missa istaec face.　　　10
PH. Quid missa? O Thais, Thais, utinam esset mihi　　(91)
pars aequa amoris tecum, ac pariter fieret,
ut aut hoc tibi doloret itidem, ut mihi dolet ;
aut ego istuc abs te factum nihili penderem.
TH. Ne crucia te obsecro, anime mi, mi Phaedria.　　　15
Non pol, quo quemquam plus amem aut plus diligam,
eo feci : sed ita erat res, faciundum fuit.
PA. Credo, ut fit, misera, prae amore exclusti hunc foras.
TH. Siccine agis, Parmeno? Age : sed, huc qua gratia
te adcersi iussi, ausculta. PH. Fiat. TH. Dic mihi (100) 20
hoc primum, potin est hic tacere? PA. Egone? Optume.
Verum heus tu, hac lege tibi meam adstringo fidem :

lit. "other *wards*"...*in contrariam
partem*, cf. *in bonam partem*, &c.,
and Plaut. *Aul.* II. 4. 8, *aliorsum
dixeram*, i.e. looking *towards* another meaning.

atque] cf. *And.* IV. 2. 15, note.

5 **ignem**] i.e. Thais, his "flame,"
so Verg. *Ecl.* III. 66, *At mihi sese
offert ultro, meus ignis, Amyntas.*

9 **Sane, quia vero**] ironical. We
should emphasize *semper* and *primus.*
"Oh of course because your door is
always open to me..."

12 **pars aequa amoris tecum**]
i.e. as much of your love as you
have of mine.

pariter fieret] perhaps *amor* is
understood : or better impersonal,
as it will then apply to both the
alternatives that follow. Would it
were alike with us, that our feelings

were alike, i.e. either that we
loved, or cared nothing about, each
other.

16 **Non quo...amem**] The subjunctive marks a supposed reason
which is not true (see Madvig,
357 b). Cf. *Heaut.* III. 2. 43. *Quo*
= "that," "because," only after
negatives, as here.

18 **prae amore**] Cf. *And.* V. 1.
6 note.

19 **Siccine agis?**] An indignant
"aside :" "that's what you think, is
it?" cf. *infr.* IV. 7. 34: *Ad.* I. 2.
48.

Age] an exclamation expressing
the sudden transition, Phaedria
being now addressed : "corripientis
adverbium, non hortantis," Don.

22 **hac lege**] "On this condition," cf. *And.* I. 2. 29.

quae vera audivi, taceo et contineo optume:
sin falsum aut vanum aut fictum est, continuo palamst:
plenus rimarum sum, hac atque illac perfluo.   25
Proin tu, tacere si vis, vera dicito.
TH. Samia mihi mater fuit: ea habitabat Rhodi.
PA. Potest taceri hoc.   TH. Ibi tum matri parvolam
puellam dono quidam mercator dedit,
ex Attica hinc abreptam.   PH. Civemne?   TH. Arbitror: 30
certum non scimus: matris nomen et patris   (111)
dicebat ipsa: patriam et signa cetera
neque scibat, neque per aetatem etiam potuerat.
Mercator hoc addebat: e praedonibus,
unde emerat, se audisse, abreptam e Sunio.   35
Mater ubi accepit, coepit studiose omnia
docere, educere, ita uti si esset filia.
Sororem plerique esse credebant meam.
Ego cum illo, quocum tum uno rem habebam, hospite
abii huc: qui mihi reliquit haec, quae habeo, omnia. (120) 40

23 **contineo**] "I hold," as a vessel does water: the metaphor is kept up in the following lines.

24 **falsum**] A falsehood about what has happened: *vanum*, what never could happen: *fictum*, what might happen, but has not. Donatus distinguishes them, "Falsum loqui, mendacis est: Vanum stulti: Fictum callidi."

palamst] cf. *Ad.* I. 1. 46, n.: Lucr. II. 568.

25 **rimarum**] "leaks," cf. Hor. *Sat.* II. 6. 46, *quae rimosa bene deponuntur in aure*, i.e. an ear that does not take in and remember what it hears. *perfluo* must = I let it through, a meaning not found elsewhere, the verb being generally active as Lucr. II. 392. Bentley reads *perfluo*, quoting Plaut. *Trin.* II. 2. 45, *Benefacta benefactis alia tegito, ne*

perpluant, and *Mostell.* I. 2. 30, *Ventat nubes, lavat parietes: perpluunt tigna*. The interchange of words by copyists would no doubt be easy; but in the absence of any MS. evidence for *perpluo*, we must retain the text.

28 **Potest taceri hoc**] Donatus makes this allude to the fact, implied in Thais' words, that her mother was a "meretrix" living in another country than her own (cf. *ex peregrina = ex meretrice? And.* III. 1. 117). "No doubt that's true," says Parmeno sarcastically. It may however simply mean that the fact of where she lived is not worth telling.

hoc] may = *huc*, as Verg. *Aen.* VIII. 423 (Wagner): but it makes equally good sense as acc. neut. of *hic*.

PA. Utrumque hoc falsumst: effluet.   TH. Qui istuc?   PA.
    Quia
neque tu uno eras contenta, neque solus dedit:
nam hic quoque bonam magnamque partem ad te attulit.
TH. Itast; sed sine me pervenire quo volo.
Interea miles, qui me amare occeperat,   45
in Cariam est profectus: te interea loci
cognovi.   Tute scis, postilla quam intumum
habeam te: et mea consilia ut tibi credam omnia.
PH. Ne hoc quidem tacebit Parmeno.   PA. Oh, dubiumne
    id est?
TH. Hoc agite, amabo.   Mater mea illic mortuast (130) 50
nuper: eius frater aliquantum ad rem est avidior.
Is ubi hanc forma videt honesta virginem,
et fidibus scire: pretium sperans, illico
producit: vendit.   Forte fortuna adfuit
hic meus amicus: emit eam dono mihi,   55
inprudens harum rerum ignarusque omnium.
Is venit: postquam sensit me tecum quoque
rem habere, fingit causas ne det sedulo:

46 **interea loci**] = *interea*. The
partitive gen. *loci locorum* are sub-
joined to adverbs as well as
of place: *adhuc locorum*, "hitherto,"
Plaut. *Capt.* II. 3. 25; *post id locorum*,
Id. *Cas.* I. 32; Lucr. v. 791, *unde
loci mortalia saecla creavit*. In prose,
ad id locorum, Liv. XXII. 39: *postea
loci*, Sall. *Jug.* 102.

47 **postilla**] see *And.* V. 4. 33,
note.

50 **Hoc agite, amabo**] "Attend, please." Cf. *And.* I. 2. 15,
hoccine agis? and note. *Amabo te*
(never *vos*), a familiar conversational
idiom in Plautus: Terence always
omits the pronoun as here: Cicero
employs it in his Epistles; *cura,
amabo te, Ciceronem nostrum*, *Att.*
II. 2. With *ut* or *ne* following, *infr.*

III. 3. 31: Cic. *Q. Fr.* I. 4.

53 **fidibus scire**] It is doubtful
whether *scire* is here used abs. =
peritam esse; such expressions as
Latine scire, Graece scire, quoted
from Cicero, are evidently elliptical
(sub. *loqui*); and this might well be
an ellipse of *canere*. On the other
hand, *docere fidibus*, Cic. *Fam.* IX.
22, and *discere fidibus*, de *Sen.* 8,
might help the former interpretation.

54 **Forte fortuna**] "by a wonderful piece of luck:" cf. *Phorm.* V.
6. 1: Cic. *Div.* II. 7. 8, *quid est, quod
casu fieri aut forte fortuna putemus?*
There was a temple and a festival to
Fors Fortuna, see Ovid, *Fasti*, VI.
773.

58 **sedulo**] For this and a few

ait, si fidem habeat se iri praepositum tibi
apud me, ac non id metuat, ne, ubi acceperim,   (140) 60
sese relinquam, velle se illam mihi dare.
Verum id vereri.   Sed, ego quantum suspicor,
ad virginem animum adiecit.   PH. Etiamne amplius?
TH. Nihil: nam quaesivi.   Nunc ego eam, mi Phaedria,
multae sunt causae, quamobrem cupiam abducere: 65
primum quod soror est dicta: praeterea ut suis
restituam ac reddam.   Sola sum: habeo hic neminem,
neque amicum neque cognatum.   Quamobrem, Phaedria,
cupio aliquos parere amicos beneficio meo.
Id amabo adiuta me, quo id fiat facilius.   (150) 70
Sine illum priores partes hosce aliquot dies
apud me habere.   Nihil respondes?   PH. Pessuma,
egon quicquam cum istis factis tibi respondeam?
PA. Eu noster, laudo: tandem perdoluit: vir es.

other passages a distinct meaning
'designedly' is sometimes given, but
hardly, as it seems, with reason: for
the notion of design may always
underlie that of close application
(*sedeo*—sitting fast, persisting in).
The old derivation *se* (i.e. *sine*) *dolo*,
adopted by Donatus (here and *Ad.*
III. 3. 59) and Servius (*Aen.* II. 374),
was based on a mistaken view that
dolus=fraus: whereas *dolus* = any
trick or device, and the full legal
form was *sine dolo malo.* The
quantity *sēdulus* is paralleled by
sēdes, sĕdes: the form by *credulus*
from *credo.*

59 **se iri praepositum**] The exact
construction of this periphrasis for
Fut. Inf. Pass. is often misunderstood. *Iri* is an impersonal verb (cf.
itur, &c.) to which is added the supine in -*um* governing the case of the
verb. Thus *scribit milites missum
iri* is correct.   *Opinor, eum sibi fortunatum virum iri* is wrong, there
being nothing for *sibi* to depend
upon.   Where a verb has no supine,

this tense is expressed by *fore ut.*
68 **neque amicum**] She had
plenty of *amatores,* no real *amicus.*
69 **beneficio**] probably pronounced *ben'ficio.*
71 **priores partes habere**] cf.
Ad. v. 4. 26, note.
hosce aliquot] "These next
few days." *Hic* with words expressing time signifies the time
nearest to the present, either before
or after, cf. *infr.* II. 3. 40.   So
οὗτος in Greek refers to that which
is nearest before, ταῦτα τρία ἔτη,
"ante hos tres annos?" and as opposed to ὅδε: οὐκ ἔστι σοι ταῦτ', ἀλλά
σοι τάδ' ἐστί, Soph. *O. C.* 787.
73 **cum istis factis**] The colloquial use of *cum,* especially in expressions of indignation, cf. *And.* v.
4. 38: *Heaut.* IV. 6. 7: *Hec.* I. 2.
59, *Di te perdant cum istoc odio,* i.e.
cum tam odiosus sis. So Cic. *Phil.*
XIII. 18, *conservandus civis cum
tam pio iustoque foedere:* cf. the
English vulgarism "Get along with
your impudence!"

Ph. Haud ego nescibam, quorsum tu ires: "parvola　　75
hinc est abrepta: eduxit mater pro sua:
soror dictast: cupio abducere, ut reddam suis:"
nempe omnia haec nunc verba huc redeunt denique:
ego excludor: ille recipitur.　Qua gratia?
Nisi illum plus amas, quam me; et istam nunc times,　80
quae abductast, ne illum talem praeripiat tibi.　　　　(161)
Th. Ego id timeo?　Ph. Quid te ergo aliud sollicitat?
　　cedo.
Num solus ille dona dat?　Nunc ubi meam
benignitatem sensisti in te claudier?
Nonne, ubi mihi dixti cupere te ex Aethiopia　　　　85
ancillulam, relictis rebus omnibus
quaesivi?　Porro eunuchum dixti velle te,
quia solae utuntur his reginae: repperi,
heri minas viginti pro ambobus dedi.
Tamen contemptus abs te, haec habui in memoria: (170) 90
Ob haec facta abs te spernor.　Th. Quid istuc Phaedria?
Quamquam illam cupio abducere, atque hac re arbitror
id posse fieri maxume: verumtamen,
potius quam te inimicum habeam, faciam ut iusseris.
Ph. Utinam istuc verbum ex animo ac vere diceres:　95

77 **sŏrŏr dictast**] The final *r* was slurred in ordinary pronunciation. So II. 3. 27, *cŏlŏr verus;* cf. *And.* I. 5. 26.

78 **huc redeunt**] Cf. *And.* III. 3. 35.

81 **abductast**] Bembine MS.

84] "Have you ever found my liberality checked (or my pocket closed) where you were concerned?" Cf. note to *And.* III. 3. 41.

88 **reginae**] "Rich women," as *rex* = a great man, a patron. *Phorm.* II. 2. 24; Plaut. *Capt.* I. 1. 24; Hor. *Epp.* I. 17. 2, *Equus ut me portet, alat rex, Officium facio.* So βασιλεύς, Pind. *O.* VI. 79: and

ἄναξ frequently in Homer of the *master* in relation to slaves.

90 **Tamen,** &c.] = *quamvis contemptus, tamen habui* (the ordinary use of *tamen,* with a conditional or concessive clause following, is abbreviated); cf. Lucr. III. 553, *sed tamen in parvo licuntur tempore tabe,* and Munro's note.

91 **Quid istuc?**] (cf. *quid istuc? And.* III. 3. 40), a formula of reluctant assent, "well, well," *remoramur* or some such word being understood. "Say no more about that."

95 **ex animo**] "from the heart;" cf. *And.* IV. 4. 55: Lucr. III. 91, *Ex animo ut dicant;* IV. 1195:

"Potius quam te inimicum habeam!" Si istuc crederem
sincere dici, quidvis possem perpeti.

PA. Labascit: victust uno verbo, quam cito!

TH. Ego non ex animo misera dico? Quam ioco
rem voluisti a me tandem, quin perfeceris?   (180) 100
ego impetrare nequeo hoc abs te, biduum
saltem ut concedas solum. PH. Siquidem biduum:
verum ne fiant isti viginti dies.

TH. Profecto non plus biduum, aut... PH. Aut?   Nihil
          moror.

TH. Non fiet: hoc modo sine te exorem.   PH. Scilicet 105
faciundumst, quod vis.   TH. Merito amo te.   PH. Bene
          facis.

Rus ibo: ibi hoc me macerabo biduum.

Ita facere certumst: mos gerundust Thaidi.

Tu, Parmeno, huc fac illi adducantur. PA. Maxume.

PH. In hoc biduum Thais vale.   TH. Mi Phaedria,   110
et tu. Numquid vis aliud? PH. Egone quid velim? (191)
Cum milite isto praesens absens ut sies:
dies noctesque me ames: me desideres:

Cat. 109. 4, *Di magni, facile ut
vere promittere possit, atque id sincere
dicat, et ex animo.*

99 **Quam ioco** &c.] "What service, pray, have you ever desired
from me even in joke, without
getting all you wanted?" Donatus
brings out well the contrast intended
between this and Phaedria's reproach vv. 85, 87, "Non *munus*,
inquit, sed quod plus est, *rem*. Et
non *serio*, sed *ioco*, a facilitate prae-
stantis. Et *voluisti*, non enim *dixisti*.
Mirandum obsequium, ex voto animi
pendens."

100 **tandem**] So frequently in interrogative clause = "Pray now."
Cic. *Cat.* I. 1. 1, *Quousque tandem
abutere patientia nostra? And.* V.
3. 4, *Ain' tandem?*

104 **Nihil moror**] "I won't have

it," i. e. any more than the *biduum*.
Cf. Hor. I. *Ep.* XV. 16, *vina nihil
moror illius orae.*

106 **Bene facis**] "Thank you."
Bentley assigns these word to Thais
on the authority of Cod. Fabricius.

109 **illi**] sc. *Eunuchus et ancilla.*
Cf. *supra*, v. 86.

112 Addison (*Spectator*, No. 170)
in describing the exacting temper of
a jealous man, quotes this passage—
"Phaedria's request to his Mistress
upon leaving her for three Days, is
eminently beautiful and natural."
In a fine passage of Shakespeare's
Cymbeline [Act I. Sc. 2, vv. 25—33,
Globe Ed.] Imogen expresses in
somewhat similar language what
she intended to have said on parting
with Postumus.

me somnies: me exspectes: de me cogites:
me speres: me te oblectes: mecum tota sis: 115
meus fac sis postremo animus, quando ego sum tuus.
TH. Me miseram, forsitan hic mihi parvam habeat fidem,
atque ex aliarum ingeniis nunc me iudicet.
Ego pol, quae mihi sum conscia, hoc certo scio,
neque me finxisse falsi quicquam, neque meo   (200) 120
cordi esse quemquam cariorem hoc Phaedria.
Et quicquid huius feci, causa virginis
feci: nam me eius spero fratrem propemodum
iam reperisse, adulescentem adeo nobilem:
et is hodie venturum ad me constituit domum.   125
Concedam hinc intro, atque exspectabo, dum venit.

ACTUS II.   SCENA I.

PHAEDRIA.   PARMENO.

PH. Fac, ita ut iussi, deducantur isti. PA. Faciam. PH. At
    diligenter.

116 **meus animus**] cf. *animae dimidium meae*, Hor. *Od.* I. 3. 8.

119 **conscia**] *mihi sum conscia*, "know my own heart." Usually with a gen. case or object clause (as *Ad.* III. 2. 50). Cf. *conscia fama* Verg. *Aen.* x. 679, = "fame that knows my story;" *conscia virtus*, XII. 668 = "self-conscious:" and (of consciousness of *wrong*) Luc. IV. 1135, *conscius animus*, "conscience stricken" (cf. Hor. *Epp.* I. I. 61, *Nil conscire sibi, nulla pallescere culpa*).

122 **huius**] = *huiusmodi* (perhaps understood *rei*). Cf. *infr.* V. 5. 10.

126 **dum venit**] = "until he comes:" cf. Munro *on Lucr.* I. 222. Here there may be the same doubt

as in *And.* II. I. 29, between the meanings "until" and "whilst:" but the former is decidedly most agreeable to the sense; v. note *ad loc.*

Act. II. Sc. I.] Phaedria gives directions to Parmeno about taking his presents to Thais, and departs with full resolution to stay the whole three days in the country. Gnatho, the follower of Thraso, then appears with the girl promised to Thais by his master.

Metre: 1, 10, 11, trochaic tetrameter; 2, 4, 5, 8, 12, 18—25, trochaic tetrameter catal.; 6, 13—17, iambic tetrameter; 3, 7, 9, iambic dimeter.

1 **deducantur**] "Have them

PA. Fiet.   PH. At mature.   PA. Fiet.   PH. Satin' hoc man-
    datumst tibi?   PA. Ah

rogitare? quasi difficile sit.

Utinam tam aliquid invenire facile possis, Phaedria,   (210)

quam hoc peribit.   PH. Ego quoque una pereo, quod mi

    est carius :   5

ne istuc tam iniquo patiare animo.   PA. Minime : quin factum

    dabo.

Sed numquid aliud imperas?

PH. Munus nostrum ornato verbis, quod poteris : et istum

    aemulum,

quod poteris, ab ea pellito.

PA. Memini, tametsi nullus moneas.   PH. Ego rus ibo, at-

    que ibi manebo.   10

---

taken to her house. *Deducere* implies some special limit from whence
and whither. So in phrases *deducere coloniam : deducere nuptam* (from
her father's to her husband's house),
Hec. I. 2. 60 : *deducere navem* (from
the stocks into the sea), 'to launch,'
καθέλκειν.

3 **rogitare?**] Sometimes explained by ellipse of *vis* or *pergis :* but
better as accus. and infin. [sub. *te*],
analogous to the use of accus. in
exclamations. So frequently with
interrogative particle *ne* added, cf.
And. I. 5. 10.

5 **peribit**] i. e. is thrown away.
Phaedria then plays upon the word
pereo = "I am dying for love." *Quod*,
i. e. *ego.*

6 **factum dabo**] cf. *And.* IV. 1.
59, note.

9 **quod**] = *quod* or *quantum :*
more usually with subjunctive (potential), *quod sciam, quod meminerim : quod commodo tuo fiat*, Cicero :
*quod sine reipublicæ iactura fieri
posset*, Livy : cf. *And.* II. 6. 23,
note : but also with indic., *Cures
quae tibi mandavi, quod sine tua*

molestia facere poteris. Both constructions occur, Lucr. II. 850,
"*quod licet ac possis reperire*"
[Both Munro and Lachmann, however, in this passage and v. 1033,
read *quoad :* see Lachmann's note
to v. 1033]. Cf. *Heaut.* III. 1. 7,
quod potero : Ad. III. 5. 1, *quod
potes.* The potential construction is
no doubt more usual ; and it may be
observed that the indicative chiefly
occurs with verbs having in themselves a potential meaning (*posse,
licere, &c.*).

10 **nullus**] = *non, nullo modo :* cf.
Cic. *Att.* XV. 22, *Sextus ab armis
nullus discedit.* This idiom of attraction, by which the adverbial
notion is expressed adjectivally in
agreement with subject of sentences,
is familiar, especially with numeral
adverbs ; *Tuque o cui prima fremen-
tem Fudit equum tellus* (*Geor.* I. 12.) :
so with pronominal adverbs, *quo
numine laeso* = *quam, numine laeso*,
Aen. I. 10 ; *Anthea si quem iacta-
tum videat*, ib. 181 = *si qua Anthea
videat.*

PA. Censeo. PH. Sed heus tu. PA. Quid vis? PH. Censen' posse me offirmare et
perpeti, ne redeam interea? PA. Tene? non hercle arbitror:
nam aut iam revertere; aut mox noctu te adiget horsum
insomnia.

PH. Opus faciam, ut defetiger usque, ingratiis ut dormiam.

PA. Vigilabis lassus: hoc plus facies. PH. Ah, nil dicis,
Parmeno.   (221) 15

Eiiciunda hercle haec est mollities animi: nimis me indulgeo.
Tandem non ego illa caream, si sit opus, vel totum triduum?
PA. Hui,

univorsum triduum? vide quid agas. PH. Stat sententia.

PA. Di boni, quid hoc morbi est? Adeon homines immutarier
ex amore, ut non cognoscas eundem esse? Hoc nemo fuit
minus ineptus, magis severus quisquam, nec magis continens.
Sed quis hic est, qui huc pergit? Attat, hic quidem est
parasitus Gnatho

---

11 **Censeo**] "ironice, negantis se censere." Bentley. The word is proper to Senators delivering their opinion, and comes in burlesque grandiloquence from a slave.

13 **insomnia**] = ἀυπνία. Rare in singular. *neque insomniis neque labore fatigari*, Sall. *Cat.* 27. 2.

14 **ingratiis**] This and *gratiis*, the full forms of *gratis* and *ingratis* (Cic. *Verr.* 49), occur in Plautus (*Casin.* II. 5. 7. *Vobis invitis atque amborum ingratiis*), and Terence; cf. *Heaut.* III. 1. 37: *Phorm.* V. 6. 48. They mean "with the will," "against the will."

15 **hoc plus facies**] i. e. "you will keep awake so much the more for being tired."

16 **me indulgeo**] This rare and ante-classical construction occurs again, *Heaut.* V. 2. 35.

18 **Hui, univorsum triduum**] "What! three whole livelong days!" Dryden (*Essay of Dramatick Poesie*)

dwells upon the "elegance and propriety" of this expression: "The elegancy of which *univorsum*, though it cannot be rendered in our language, yet leaves an impression on our souls."

19 **Adeone......immutarier**] cf. *And.* I. 5. 10, note.

The soliloquy of Benedick in *Much Ado About Nothing*, Act II. Sc. 3, is in the same vein with this of Parmeno, but heightened by his falling in love immediately afterwards.

20 **nemo...quisquam**] cited on *And.* I. I. 61, in support of Donatus' view (see note *ad loc.*); but this is not to the purpose, as the words are in parallel clauses, and *quisquam* repeats *nemo*, the necessary negative being implied by the previous use of *nemo*. We have not therefore *nemo quisquam = nemo*, or *non quisquam*, but we have *nemo* followed up by and repeated in (*non*) *quisquam*.

militis: ducit secum una virginem dono huic: papae,
facie honesta. Mirum, ni ego me turpiter hodie hic dabo
cum meo decrepito hoc eunucho.   Haec superat ipsam
      Thaidem.   (231) 25

ACTUS II.   SCENA II.

Gnatho.   Parmeno.   ·

Gn. Di immortales, homini homo quid praestat stulto in-
     tellegens
quid interest!   Hoc adeo ex hac re venit in mentem mihi:
conveni hodie· adveniens quendam mei loci hinc atque or-
     dinis
hominem haud inpurum, itidem patria qui abligurierat bona.
Video sentum, squalidum, aegrum, pannis annisque obsitum.
Quid istum, inquam, ornati est?   "Quoniam miser, quod ha-
     bui, perdidi: hem   6
quo redactus sum! omnes noti me atque amici deserunt."

24 **turpiter me dabo**] "I shall cut a sorry figure." *Dare sese a-licui* = "to give oneself up, devote oneself to"...hence, "to present oneself, appear;" *dare se populo et coronae*, Cic. *Verr.* II. 3. 19.

Sc. II.] Gnatho appears, congratulating himself on his success in the rôle of a parasite to which he has given new principles (the chief of which is *omnia assentari*), and founded a school of "Gnathonici." Seeing Parmeno, he begins to exult over him on the strength of the present he brings from Thraso, promising him an easy time of it now as far as anything between Phaedria and Thais is concerned.

Metre: 1—23, trochaic tetrameter catalectic; 24—60, iambic tetrameter catalectic.

2 **adeo**] cf. *And.* IV. 4. 20, and *infra*, v. 16, *ego adeo*.

4 **haud inpurum**] "tolerably decent." Cf. *Heaut.* IV. 1. 16.

abligurierat] "had squandered." Literally = "lick off." Cf. *rem patris oblimare*, Hor. *Sat.* I. 2. 62.

5 **sentum**] "untidy." Cf. Verg. *Aen.* VI. 462, *loca senta situ*, "rough with neglect." Some connect the word with *sentis*, "a bramble:" but it is more probably a participial form from *sino* (whence *situs* = the mouldiness of disuse), analogous to *lentus* from *lino*.

6 **ornati**] gen. from *ornatus*, cf. *And.* II. 2. 28.

7 **noti**] = "acquaintances" (cf. Hor. *Sat.* I. 1. 85); not, as sometimes explained, active = "*qui me norunt*."

Hic ego illum contempsi prae me.   Quid homo, inquam, ig-
  navissime?

itan' parasti te, ut spes nulla reliqüa in te esset tibi? (240)

Simul consilium cum re amisti?   Viden' me ex eodem ortum
  loco?   10

Qui color, nitor, vestitus; quae habitudo est corporis?

Omnia habeo, neque quicquam habeo: nil quum est, nil
  defit tamen.

"At ego infelix neque ridiculus esse neque plagas pati
possum."   Quid? tu his rebus credis fieri?   Tota erras via.

Olim isti· fuit generi quondam quaestus apud saeclum prius :

hoc novum est aucupium : ego adeo hanc primus inveni
  viam.   16

---

8 **prae me**] "as compared with
myself." Cf. Hor. *Epp.* I. 11. 4,
*cunctane prae campo et Tiberino
flumine sordent?* It might however = "as my manner is." Cf.
supr. I. 2. 18, and *And.* I. 5. 6,
note.

9 **reliqüa**] "*Reliquus*" is always
quadrisyllabic in older writers : so
adsequĕ, consequĕ and the like, the
last two syllables of which were
never contracted into one any more
than in *perpetuus, ambiguus,* &c. See
Lucr. I. 560, and Munro's note.
The word was variously written *re-
licuus* and *reliquus,* v. Lachmann on
Lucr. v. 679. Cf. on this point of orthography Munro's *Lucretius,* Notes,
Part I. *Introduction* (sub fin.).

11 **nitor**] with its kindred *nitere,
nitidus,* implies "sleekness, plump-
ness of body:" so frequently in
Verg. In Hor. *Od.* I. 19. 5, III. 12.
5, *it* = "beauty:" but the reference
is always to something material and
sensuous.

13 **ridiculus esse...plagas pati**]
Two special rôles of parasites : "the
sayer of witty things" (γελωτό-
ποιος), the "*imi derisor lecti*" of
Horace (*Epp* I. 18. 11); and the
butt for practical jokes (*plagipatida,*

Plaut. *Capt.* I. 1. 20; cf. ib. III. 1.
12, and both scenes *passim,* descriptive of parasite manners and cus-
toms). The old-fashioned view of
the parasite's profession, according
to Gnatho, is now obsolete: he no
longer studies the rude art of making
himself a butt to others, but the
more refined one of humouring their
self-love, and acquiescing in their
whims.

14 **Tota erras via**] "You are
altogether out of the road: " cf. Ar.
Plut. 162, ἦ τῆς ὁδοῦ τὸ παράπαν
ἡμαρτήκαμεν; Lucr. II. 82, *Avius
a vera longe ratione vagaris.*

15. **quondam**] "at times" = *aliquando,* cf. Verg. *Aen.* II. 367
(Forbiger), Lucr. VI. 109. Like
olim (*Aen.* V. 105), this word, indicating at first a definite period in
time past, then time past in general
("formerly"), passes to the indefinite use that we have here, and is
even applied to future time, "some
day," cf. *Aen.* VI. 877, *nec Romula
quondam Ullo se tantum tellus iacta-
bit alumno.*

16 **aucupium**] i. e. "a means of
picking up a living." In better
days the parasite's occupation was a
regular business (*quaestus*).

Est genus hominum, qui esse primos se omnium rerum volunt
nec sunt; hos consector: hisce ego non paro me ut rideant,
sed eis ultro adrideo, et eorum ingenia admiror simul.   (250)
Quicquid dicunt, laudo: id rursum si negant, laudo id quo-
    que.   20
Negat quis? nego: ait, aio: postremo imperavi egomet mihi
omnia adsentari.   Is quaestus nunc est multo uberrimus.
PA. Scitum hercle hominem; hic homines prorsus ex stultis
    insanos facit.
GN. Dum haec loquimur, interea loci ad macellum ubi ad-
    ventamus,
concurrunt laeti mi obviam cupedinarii omnes: 25
cetarii, lanii, coqui, fartores, piscatores,
quibus et re salva et perdita profueram et prosum saepe.
Salutant: ad cenam vocant: adventum gratulantur.
Ille ubi miser famelicus videt me tanto honore, et   (260)
tam facile victum quaerere; ibi homo coepit me obsecrare,
ut sibi liceret discere id de me.   Sectari iussi: 31
si potis est, tanquam philosophorum habent disciplinae ex
    ipsis   .

19] "I don't lay myself out to make them laugh (by making jokes); but I force a laugh at all they say and admire their wit."

ultro] i.e. where it could not be expected, is unnecessary, that any one should laugh, cf. *And.* I. 1. 73.

adrideo] cf. Hor. *A. P.* 101, *Ut ridentibus arrident, ita flentibus adflent.*

20] Cf. Martial, XII. 40, *Mentiris; credo. Recitas mala carmina; laudo, Cantas; canto. Bibis, Pontiliane; bibo.*

22 **omnia**] Adverbial accus. *assentari,* scil. *eis.*

24 **interea loci**] Cf. v. 2. 46, note.

25 **cupedinarii**] "vendors of good things." Bentley reads *cupediarii,* fr. *cupediae,* "titbits," cf. Hor. *S.* II. 2. 55.

27] "Whom I had benefited while my fortune lasted, and often do so now that it is gone."

31 **Sectari iussi**] "I bade him follow in my train," i. e. as the pupils of philosophers followed them about (whence "secta" of the train of a candidate, cf. Cic. *Mur.* 34). *iussi* aorist. The Greek aor. denotes (I) momentary action; (II) a succession of momentary actions, what constantly or usually happens ("gnomic" aorist in maxims, proverbs, &c). The Perfect in Latin represents both (I) immediate and momentary, *G.* I. 330, *Terra tremit: fugere ferae;* (II) as here, customary action; *G.* I. 49, *Illius immensae ruperunt horrea messes,* cf. IV. 212.

32 **potis**] is found in connection with neuter and plural subject.

Vocabula, parasiti item ut Gnathonici vocentur.

PA. Viden' otium et cibus quid facit alienus. GN. Sed ego
cesso

ad Thaidem hanc deducere, et rogare ad cenam ut veniat? 35

Sed Parmenonem ante ostium [Thaidis tristem] video,

rivalis servum: salva res est: nimirum homines frigent.

Nebulonem hunc certumst ludere.   PA. Hice hoc munere
arbitrantur

suam Thaidem esse. GN. Plurima salute Parmenonem (270)

summum suum impertit Gnatho.   Quid agitur? PA. Statur.
GN. Video.   40

Numquidnam quod nolis vides?   PA. Te.   GN. Credo: at
numquid aliud?

PA. Quidum?   GN. Quia tristi's.   PA. Nil equidem   GN.
Ne sis: sed quid videtur

hoc tibi mancipium?   PA. Non malum hercle.   GN. Uro
hominem.   PA. Ut falsus animi est !

LUCR. I. 453, *quod nusquam potis est
sciungi: duae plus satis dare potis
sunt*, Plaut. *Poen.* I. 2. 17. So the
neut. form *pote* with masc. subj.
They are two indeclinable forms of
an adj. rarely used adverbially.

disciplinae] That Donatus so read
appears from his remark, "nisi forte
disciplinam pro discipulis posuerit."
Since the two clauses do not corres-
pond, Bentley on authority of two
MSS. read *discipuli*. 'Disciplina'
(preferred by Parry on the ground
potior lectio difficillima) does not
elsewhere occur as noun of multitude = *discipuli*, which must here be
its meaning.

37] Bentley reads *hice homines*,
metri gratia.

frigent] "are out of favour, are
coldly received:" so chiefly in Cicero,
*iacent beneficia Nuculae; friget An-
tonius, Phil.* VI. 5. 14; of speakers
or musicians ill received by their
audience, *Brut.* 50. So perhaps in

Hor. *Sat.* II. 1. 62, *Metuo, maiorum
ne quis amicus Frigore te feriat,* "*frigus*" may refer to the condition of
one coldly treated: though Persius
1. 107 ("*Vide sis maiorum ne tibi
forte Limina frigescant*"), an obvious
imitation of Horace, points to the
converse metaphor of growing cold
towards anyone. In that case "frigore" = the coldness shown.

38 **Plurima,** &c.] Gnatho wishes
the best of health to his best friend
Parmeno, cf. Plaut. *Epid.* I. 2. 23,
*herum quum Stratippoclem Salva
impertat Salute Epidicus*, and (in
deponent form) *Ad.* III. 2. 22. Cic.
always employs the ordinary construction: "*Terentia impertit tibi
multam salutem,*" *Att.* II. 12. 4.

43 **hoc mancipium**] the female
slave that Gn. has brought: *uro hominem*, I annoy the fellow.

Ut falsus animi est] How mistaken
he is! cf. *And.* IV. 1. 22. This genitive
and *mentis* (cf. Plaut. *Trin.*, *Satin*

Gn. Quam hoc munus gratum Thaidi arbitrare esse? Pa.
　　Hoc nunc dicis,
eiectos hinc nos : omnium rerum heus vicissitudo est.　　45
Gn. Sex ego te totos, Parmeno, hos menses quietum reddam;
ne sursum deorsum cursites; neve usque ad lucem vigiles.
Ecquid beo te? Pa. Men'? Papae. Gn. Sic soleo amicos.
　　Pa. Laudo.
Gn. Detineo te: fortasse tu profectus alio fueras.　　(280)
Pa. Nusquam.　Gn. Tum tu igitur paululum da mi operae :
　　fac ut admittar　　　　　　　　　　　　　　50
ad illam.　Pa. Age modo, nunc tibi patent fores hae, quia
　　istam ducis.
Gn. Num quem evocari hinc vis foras?　Pa. Sine biduum
　　hoc praetereat:
qui mihi nunc uno digitulo fores aperis fortunatus,
nae tu istas faxo calcibus saepe insultabis frustra.
Gn. Etiam nunc hic stas, Parmeno? Eho numnam hic re-
　　lictus custos,　　　　　　　　　　　　　55
ne quis forte internuntius clam a milite ad istam curset?
Pa. Facete dictum : mira vero, militi quae placeant.
Sed video herilem filium minorem huc advenire.

tu es sanus mentis aut animi tui) are
common after verbs and adjectives
expressing certain states of feeling—
animi dubius, Verg. G. III. 289: nec
me animi fallit, Lucr. I. 136 (where
see Munro's note): confusus atque
incertus animi, Livy, I. 7. The
genitive, as in other instances of the
"genitive of respect,"or"reference,"
fessi rerum, integer aevi, &c., denotes
the source or origin of the state or
feeling.

44 Hoc nunc dicis, &c.] What
you mean is, that we (Phaedria and
Parm.) have got our congé for this
house : but look you, everything is
liable to change.

50 Nusquam] "no whither." So

frequent in Plaut. and Ter. Cf. Cic.
Ep. Fam. X. 32, "Finibus meae pro-
vinciae nusquam excessi."

53 mihi] "as I see." This use of
the dative (Dat. Ethicus) is familiar
in both Latin and Greek, cf. Phorm.
v. 8. 21; Verg. Ecl. VIII. 6 (Forbiger).　Madvig, Gr. 248.

54 calcibus insultabis] Cf. Hor.
Od. I. 25. 1, Parcius iunctas quati-
unt fenestras Ictibus crebris iuvenes
protervi.

55] Gnatho, having gone in at v.
50, comes out again and pretends to
be astonished at finding Parmeno
still there.　Etiam = still (et iam =
even now): cf. Verg. G. III. 189;
Aen. VI. 485; Hec. III. 4. 16.

Miror, quid ex Piraeo abiit : nam ibi custos publice est nunc.
Non temere est : et properans venit : nescio quid circum-
    spectat.   (291) 60

ACTUS II. SCENA III.

CHAEREA. PARMENO.

CH. Occidi.

Neque virgo est usquam : neque ego, qui illam e conspectu
    amisi meo.

Ubi quaeram, ubi investigem, quem perconter, quam insis-
    tam viam,

incertus sum. Una haec spes est ; ubi ubi est, diu celari
    non potest.

O faciem pulchram : deleo omnes dehinc ex animo mulieres :

taedet quotidianarum harum formarum. PA. Ecce autem
    alterum,   6

de amore nescio quid loquitur. CH. O infortunatum senem!

Hic vero est, qui si occeperit, ludum iocumque dices

Sc. III.] Chaerea rushes in, raving of the beauty of a girl he has seen in the street, and followed until detained by a friend. Meeting Parmeno, he ascertains that she has just gone into Thais' house : and between them they concoct the scheme upon which the action of the play turns.

Metre : 1, trochaic clausulae ; 2—13, 15—27, 29, 30, 75—98, iambic tetrameter ; 14 iambic dimeter ; 28, 31—59, iambic trimeter ; 60—74, troch. tetram. catal.

3 quam insistam viam] So Verg. Georg. III. 164, viamque insiste domandi; Bentley reads quâ viâ: but ablat. is unusual construction. Forc. quotes no examples, as QVĀ=quam might easily be confounded by a copyist with QVA. Phorm. IV. I. 14

is usually quoted for abl. : but see note ad loc.

6 quotid.] i.e. usual, common : cf. Martial, XI. 1, Cultus sindone non quotidiana.

7 o infortu. senem] ascribed by Donatus and most old edd. to Parmeno, referring to the catastrophe of the play. Parry assigns them to Chaerea, as' an exclamation against his father's old friend who delayed him : and there is undoubtedly more point in the words so taken.

8, 9] On the arrangement of these vv. see Parry, note ad loc. Zeune's is here retained. Praeut, "compared with," like praequam, praequod, chiefly confined to the comic poets, see Forcellini.

fuisse illum alterum, praeut huius rabies quae dabit. (300)

Сн. Ut illum di deaeque senium perdant, qui hodie me remoratus est ;   10

meque adeo qui restiterim; tum autem qui illum flocci fecerim.

Sed eccum Parmenonem. Salve.   PA. Quid tu es tristis?
   quidve es alacris?

Unde is?   Сн. Egone? Nescio hercle, neque unde eam,
   neque quorsum eam :

ita prorsum oblitus sum mei.

PA. Qui quaeso?   Сн. Amo.   PA. Hem.   Сн. Nunc, Parmeno, te ostendes, qui vir sies.   15

Scis te mihi saepe pollicitum esse : Chaerea, aliquid inveni

modo quod ames : in ea re utilitatem faciam ut cognoscas
   meam :

quum in cellulam ad te patris penum omnem congerebam
   clanculum.

PA. Age inepte.   Сн. Hoc hercle factumst. Fac sis nunc
   promissa appareant :   (310)

sive adeo digna res est, ubi tu nervos intendas tuos.   20

Haud similis virgost virginum nostrarum : quas matres student

demissis humeris esse, vincto pectore, ut gracilae sient.

---

10 **Ut...perdant**] *ut* "optantis,"
cf. *Heaut.* IV. 66: Verg. *Aen.* X.
631 ; XI. 153.

remoratus est...restiterim] Cf.
And. I. 5. 38 ; Bentley emends,
remoratus sit. The indic. is simply
descriptive of *senium;* the subj. in-
troduces a thought in the speaker's
mind ; "who was such a fool as to
stay."

11] "Confound me for having
stopped—for having paid any attention to him."

15 **te ostendes**] To avoid the
hiatus necessary for scansion Bentley
suggests *ostende sis*, or *ostenderis.*
Weise reads *ted ostendes:* but this

Plautine form is unusual in Terence.

20 **sive**] not "since:" but "if
indeed," cf. *And.* II. 1. 19.

22 **vincto pectore**] i.e. "tight
laced," cf. IV. 1. 49 (of Hercules
with Omphale), "*Mollis et hirsutum
cepit mihi fascia pectus. Et manibus
duris apta puella fui.*"

gracilae] "slender-waisted." Donat. has *graciles:* but Faernus (apud
Bentley) says "legit Donatus *gracilae:*" et Val. Probus p. 1466, *Hic et
haec gracilis : sed Terentius nove, ut
gracilae sient.* Cf. Lucil. *ap. Non.*
8. 48, *Quod gracila est, pede quod
pernix, quod pectore puro.*

Siqua est habitior paulo, pugilem esse aiunt : deducunt cibum :
tametsi bona est natura, reddunt curatura iunceas ;
itaque ergo amantur. PA. Quid tua istaec? CH. Nova figura
        oris. PA. Papae.   25
CH. Color verus, corpus solidum et succi plenum. PA. Anni?
        CH. Anni? Sedecim.
PA. Flos ipse.   CH. Hanc tu mihi vel vi, vel clam, vel
        precario
fac tradas : mea nihil refert, dum potiar modo.
PA. Quid, virgo cuiast? CH. Nescio hercle. PA. Undest?
        CH. Tantundem. PA. Ubi habitat?   (320)
CH. Ne id quidem. PA. Ubi vidisti? CH. In via. PA.
        Qua ratione amisisti?   30
CH. Id equidem adveniens mecum stomachabar modo :
neque quemquam esse ego hominem arbitror, cui magis bonae
felicitates omnes adversae sient.
PA. Quid hoc est sceleris? CH. Perii. PA. Quid factumst?
        CH. Rogas?
Patris cognatum atque aequalem Archidemidem   35
novistin'? PA. Quidni? CH. Is, dum hanc sequor, fit mi
        obviam.
PA. Incommode hercle. CH. Immo enimvero infeliciter :
nam incommoda alia sunt dicenda, Parmeno.

24] "If she is in rather too good case, they say she is an athlete and cut off her rations; then, however good their natural condition, this treatment makes them as thin as rushes : and so they get lovers."

27 vi, clam, precario] the three unlawful methods of acquiring possession; cf. Hor. Epp. II. 2, 173, Nunc prece, nunc pretio, nunc vi, nunc morte supremâ Permutet dominos.

The scansion is difficult. Bentley omits flos ipse, making an iambic trimeter : Lindemann [ed. Capt.,

Trin., Mil. Glor. "De Prosodiâ Plauti," p. xxxvii.] suggests calim. Parry would repeat tu before clam comparing Hor. Od. I. 9. 5. Wagner reads Flos ipsus. CH. Hance.

34 sceleris] "bad luck," Plaut. Capt. III. 5. 104, Quod hoc est scelus! Quasi in orbitatem liberos produxerim." In Verg. Aen. II. 229, VII. 307, quoted by Parry, scelus seems rather = "punishment for crime:" but cf. sceleratum frigus = "noxious." Misfortune, as Parry observes, to the Greeks implied νέμεσις for fault.

Illum liquet mi deierare, his mensibus   (330)
sex, septem prorsus non vidisse proxumis,   40
nisi nunc, quum minime vellem, minimeque opus fuit.
Eho, nonne hoc monstri similest? quid ais? PA. Maxume.
CH. Continua adcurrit ad me, quam longe quidem,
incurvus, tremulus, labiis demissis, gemens:
heus, heus, tibi dico, Chaerea, inquit. Restiti.   45
Scin' quid ego te volebam? Dic. Cras est mihi
iudicium. Quid tum? Ut diligenter nunties
patri, advocatus mane mi esse ut meminerit.
Dum haec dicit, abiit hora. Rogo, num quid velit.   (340)
Recte, inquit. Abeo. Quum huc respicio ad virginem, 50
illa sese interea commodum huc advorterat
in hanc nostram plateam. PA. Mirum ni hanc dicit, modo
huic quae data est dono. CH. Huc quum advenio, nulla
     erat.
PA. Comites secuti scilicet sunt virginem?
CH. Verum; parasitus cum ancilla. PA. Ipsast: ilicet: 55
desine: iam conclamatumst. CH. Alias res agis.
PA. Istuc ago equidem. CH. Nostin, quae sit? Dic mihi;
     aut
vidistin? PA. Vidi, novi: scio, quo abducta sit.

---

39 **deierare**] διομνύναι, to swear solemnly: cf. Forb. on *Aen.* III. 260.

43 **quam longe**] *quam* with positive is rare: *vino quam possit excellenti*, Pliny; cf. *And.* I. I. 109, note.

48 **advocatus**] up to time of Tacitus = a friend who attended a trial to give advice or act as witness, cf. *Phorm.* II. 4, and the use of *adesse*, Hor. *Sat.* I. 9. 38: II. 6. 35. "*Advocatos adesse*," *Eun.* IV. 6. 26.

50 **Recte**] like "*benigne*" (Hor. *Epp.* I. 7. 16); Greek κάλλιστα (Ar. *Ran.* 508), πάνυ καλῶς (ib. 511); and French "*merci*" declines an offer courteously or ironically. "No thank you;" cf. *Heaut.* III. 2. 7.

51 **commodum**] adv. 1st. = εὐκαίρως: 2nd. "just now," cf. *Phorm.* IV. 3. 9.

53 **nulla erat**] "she was nowhere," cf. I. I. 10, note.

56 **conclamatumst**] "'tis all over." At the moment of death, the friends of the dying man raised a cry (conclamare), as though to arrest the soul's flight. Parry quotes Prop. IV. 7. 23, 24, *At mihi non oculos quisquam inclinavit euntes; Unum impetrassem, te revocante, diem.*

Alias res agis, &c.] "That's nothing to do with it." "It has, though, to your question." cf. *And.* I. 2. 15, note.

Ch. Eho Parmeno [mi], nostin? Pa. Novi. Ch. et scis
    ubi siet?   (350)

Pa. Huc deductast ad meretricem Thaidem : ei dono da-
    tast.   60

Ch. Quis is est tam potens, cum tanto munere hoc? Pa.
    Miles Thraso

Phaedriae rivalis. Ch. Duras fratris partes praedicas.

Pa. Immo si scias quod donum huic dono contra comparet,

tum magis id dicas. Ch. Quodnam quaeso hercle? Pa.
    Eunuchum. Ch. Illumne obsecro

inhonestum hominem, quem mercatus est heri, senem mu-
    lierem?   65

Pa. Istunc ipsum. Ch. Homo quatietur certe cum dono
    foras.

Sed istam Thaidem non scivi nobis vicinam. Pa. Haud diu est.

Ch. Perii, numquamne etiam me illam vidisse? Ehodum
    dic mihi :

estne, ut fertur, forma? Pa. Sane. Ch. At nihil ad nos-
    tram hanc. Pa. Alia res.   (360)

Ch. Obsecro hercle, Parmeno, fac ut potiar. Pa. Faciam
    sedulo, ac   70

dabo operam, adiutabo. Numquid me aliud? Ch. Quo
    nunc is? Pa. Domum,

ut mancipia haec, ita uti iussit frater, ducam ad Thaidem.

Ch. O fortunatum istum eunuchum, qui quidem in hanc de-
    tur domum !

---

61 **Duras fratris partes praedicas**] Ch. "My brother's part is hard
from what you say." Pa. "If you
knew what a present he has got to
match with this present, you would
say that all the more" (sc. *duras
partes esse*).

63 **comparet**] of matching gladiators, Suet. *Calig. gladiatores...non
solum* : "committi," et. "componi"

sed et "comparari" *dicebantur.*

64] Observe with what address
Terence proceeds to the main part
of his argument. The casual mention of the Eunuch suggests the
stratagem on which the whole play
turns.

69 **ad nostram**]=compared with;
"nothing *to* mine" is English idiom,
cf. IV. 4. 14, note.

PA. Quid ita? CH. Rogitas? summa forma semper per
  conservam domi

videbit, conloquetur: aderit una in unis aedibus.   75

Cibum nonnumquam capiet cum ea: interdum propter dor-
  miet.

PA. Quid si nunc tute fortunatus fias? CH. Qua re, Parmeno?

Responde. PA. Capias tu illius vestem. CH. Vestem? Quid
  tum postea?

PA. Pro illo te deducam. CH. Audio. PA. Te esse illum
  dicam. CH. Intellego.   (370)

PA. Tu illis fruare commodis, quibus tu illum dicebas
  modo: 80

cibum una capias, adsis, tangas, ludas, propter dormias:

quandoquidem illarum neque te quisquam novit, neque scit
  qui sies.

Praeterea forma et aetas ipsa est, facile ut pro eunucho
  probes.

CH. Dixti pulchre: numquam vidi melius consilium dari.

Age eamus intro nunc iam: orna me, abduc, duc, quantum potes.   85

PA. Quid agis? iocabar equidem. CH. Garris. PA. Perii,
  quid ego egi miser?

Quo trudis? perculeris iam tu me. Tibi equidem dico, mane.

CH. Eamus. PA. Pergin? CH. Certumst. PA. Vide ne
  nimium calidum hoc sit modo.

CH. Non est profecto: sine. PA. At enim istaec in me
  cudetur faba. CH. Ah!   (380)

---

77 **Qua re**] In what way but
this could we be happy?—and this
is not possible. *Qua re* appears to
have special emphasis, and is best
written as two words, cf. Munro,
Lucr. II. 960.

 82 **illarum quisquam**] *Quis* and
quisquam are sometimes feminine in
old Latin, cf. Plaut. *Aul.* II. 1. 48,
quis east quam vis ducere uxorem?

 83 **probes**] sc. *te*, "pass yourself
off for."

 88 **calidum**] "hot-headed," so
Greek θερμός.

PA. Flagitium facimus.   CH. An id flagitiumst, si in domum

· meretriciam   90

deducar, et illis crucibus, quae nos nostramque adulescen-
tiam

habent despicatam, et quae nos semper omnibus cruciant
modis,

nunc referam gratiam: atque eas itidem fallam, ut ab illis
fallimur?

An potius haec patri aequum est fieri, ut a me ludatur dolis?

Quod qui rescierint, culpent; illud merito factum omnes
putent.   95

PA. Quid istuc? Si certumst facere, facias: verum ne post
conferas

culpam in me. CH. Non faciam. PA. Iubesne? CH. Iubeo,
cogo, atque impero;

nunquam defugiam auctoritatem. PA. Sequere. CH. Di
vortant bene.

ACTUS III. SCENA I.

THRASO. GNATHO. PARMENO.

TH. Magnas vero agere gratias Thais mihi?   (390)

GN. Ingentes. TH. Ain' tu, laetast? GN. Non tam ipso
quidem

89 **istaec in me cudetur faba**]
"That bean will be cracked on my
head," i.e. "I shall suffer for it."
The proverb evidently alludes to the
recoiling of a suggestion on its author's head: whether (as Donatus)
from the threshing floor, which gets
all the blows that fall on what is
threshed, is uncertain.

91 **crucibus**] "pests;" cf. *Phorm.*
III. 3. 11: and the expression *in
malam crucem, Phorm.* II. 3. 21:
Plaut. *Capt.* III. 1. 9, *Ilicet para-
silicae arti in maximam malam
crucem.*

94 **patri**] Bembine MS. One
MS. has *pati.* Bentley reads *An
potius par atque aequum est, pater
ut a me...* The mention of Chaerea's
father is not very appropriate: but
it should be remembered that in
Comedy of this class the normal
relation of son and father is one of
deception and trial of wits. Chaerea
must of course be taking in some
one: if not these women, his father
is the obvious person.

Act III. Scene 1.] This scene
gives a picture of the braggadocio,
the *miles gloriosus* Thraso; "drawn

dono, quam abs te datum esse: id vero serio
triumphat.   PA. Huc proviso ut, ubi tempus siet,
deducam.   Sed eccum militem.   TH. Est istuc datum   5
profecto, ut grata mihi sint quae facio omnia.
GN. Advorti hercle animum.   TH. Vel rex semper maxumas
mihi agebat quicquid feceram; aliis non item.
GN. Labore alieno magno partam gloriam
verbis saepe in se transmovet, qui habet salem;   10
quod in te est.   TH. Habes.   GN. Rex te ergo in oculis....
        TH. Scilicet.   .   (400)
GN. gestare.   TH. Vero: credere omnem exercitum,
consilia.   GN. Mirum.   TH. Tum sicubi cum satietas
hominum, aut negoti si quando odium ceperat,
requiescere ubi volebat, quasi: nostin'?   GN. Scio.   15
Quasi ubi illam exspueret miseriam ex animo.   TH. Tenes.
Tum me convivam solum abducebat sibi.   GN. Hui,
regem elegantem narras.   TH. Immo sic homost:

out " by his toady Gnatho to boast
of his exploits. Cicero (de Am.
XXVI.) alludes to these two characters; *Nulla est igitur haec ami-
citia quum alter verum audire non
vult, alter ad mentiendum paratus
est. Nec parasitorum in comoediis
assentatio faceta videretur nisi essent
milites gloriosi; 'magnas vero agere
gratias Thais mihi.' Satis erat re-
spondere 'magnas;' 'ingentes' inquit. Semper auget assentator id
quod is, cuius ad voluntatem dicitur,
vult esse magnum.*
    Metre: iambic trimeter.
    5 **Est istuc datum**] "It has
been given me," i.e. by heaven, cf.
Hor. S. II. 2. 31; Pers. 5. 124,
*Liber ego. Unde datum hoc sumis,
tot subdite rebus?* Lucr. II. 302.
    6 **grata mihi sint**] "procures
me favour," *Heaut.* II. 3. 21: V. I.
61 (ingratum), cf. Cic. *Phil.* II. 46,
*quam sit...beneficio gratum, tyran-
num occidere* [i.e. *quantum apud*

cives gratiam paret. Forcellini.]
    11 **in oculis...gestare**]   "To
keep in one's eye," implies great af-
fection: so *ferre in oculis* opposed
to *odisse,* Cic. *Phil.* VI. 4, *Trebel-
lium oderat tum, cum ille tabulis
novis adversabatur; iam fert in oculis: ad Fam.* XVI. 27, *Te ut dixi,
fero oculis:* and *esse in oculis, Ep.
ad Att.* VI. *publicanis in oculis sumus.* With these instances the
suggestion of allusion to the Persian
title of a minister ὀφθαλμὸς βασιλέως
(Ar. *Ach.* 92: Herod. I. 114: Xen.
Ag. VIII. 2. 10) seems unnecessary.
    14 **odium**] here approaches the
sense of *taedium;* cf. inf. V. 5. 2: *Hec.*
II. 1. 22.
    15 **quasi...nostin'?**] "Grate ex-
pressit stulti infantiam militis, qui
ante vult intelligi quod sentit, quam
ipse dicat." Donatus.
    16 **exspueret**] "reject" (as some-
thing distasteful); cf. Lucr. II. 104.
    miseriam]   "miserable work."

perpaucorum hominum.　GN. Immo nullorum, arbitror,
si tecum vivit.　TH. Invidere omnes mihi,　　　20
mordere clanculum : ego non flocci pendere :　　(410)
illi invidere misere. Verum unus tamen
inpense, elephantis quem Indicis praefecerat:
is ubi molestus magis est, Quaeso, inquam, Strato,
eone es ferox, quia habes imperium in beluas?　　25
GN. Pulchre mehercle dictum et sapienter.　Papae,
iugularas hominem.　Quid ille?　TH. Mutus illico.
GN. Quidni esset?　PA. Di vostram fidem ! hominem per-
　　ditum
miserumque : et illum sacrilegum.　TH. Quid illud, Gnatho,
quo pacto Rhodium tetigerim in convivio,　　30

The ideas of "labour" and "dis-
tress" run into one another, as in
Greek ταλαιτωρεῖν, our "travail,"
Lat. "labor."

18 **elegantem**] "a man of taste;"
cf. infr. v. 8. 64.

sic homost] "That's his way,"
cf. *And*. v. 4. 16.

19 **perpaucorum hominum**] "a
man of very few friends;" cf. Hor.
Sat. 1. 9. 44, *Maecenas quomodo
tecum?...Paucorum hominum et
mentis bene sanae*. For this, the ordinary 'descriptive' use of gen.
cf. Madv. *Gr.* 287.

**perpaucorum hominum. Immo
nullorum arbitror**] Bentley to avoid
hiatus reads *hominum'st*. But hiatus, though rare in Terence, is admissible where there is a change of
speaker, or in the regular caesura of
the metre. See Introduction.

22 **miscere**] cf. *And*. III. 1. 40.

23 **inpense**] "extravagantly;"
cf. *Aen*. XII. 20, *tanto me impensius
aequum est Consulere*, i.e. "more ear-
nestly:" and iufra III. 5. 39, *impendio*.

27 **iugularas hominem**] "You
did for the man at once:" cf. Cic.
Verr. VII. ch. 64, *iugulari sua con-
fessione*, and the phrase *plumbeo

gladio iugulare = to overthrow with
a feather [see Forcellini s.v.], Cic.
Att. 1. 15. *Suo gladio iugulare* in
Ad. v. 8. 35 = to condemn out of
one's own mouth, q. v.

The pluperf. expresses the instantaneous nature of the act, "The
words were hardly out of your
mouth, when he was already crush-
ed." This idiom occurs in Verg.
Aen. VIII. 219, *Hic vero Alcidae
furiis exarserat atro Felle dolor*, i.e.
blazed forth at once—had already
burst out, directly he heard the
oxen's low, cf. XII. 430. We must
employ the aorist in translating
such use, and that of *Aen*. v. 397,
*Si mihi, quae quondam fuerat, fuit
illa iuventus*, where the thought
goes back to a point in past time,
at which something had already
ceased, instead of speaking of it as
past, in reference to the moment of
speaking : thus intensifying the idea
of its being past or gone.

28 **Quidni esset?**] "Of course
he was." Deliberative subjunctive :
lit. "Why was he not to be so?"

30 **tetigerim**] aorist : "I touched
up," possibly in allusion to phrase
acu rem tangere, Plaut. *Rud*. v. 2.

nunquam tibi dixi?   Gn. Nunquam: sed narra obsecro.
Plus millies audivi.   Th. Una in convivio   (421)
erat hic, quem dico, Rhodius adulescentulus.
Forte habui scortum: coepit ad id adludere,
et me inridere.   Quid ais, inquam, homo impudens?   35
lepus es, et pulpamentum quaeris?   Gn. Ha ha hae.
Th. Quid est?   Gn. Facete, lepide, laute, nil supra.
Tuumne, obsecro te, hoc dictum erat?   Vetus credidi.
Th. Audieras?   Gn. Saepe: et fertur in primis.   Th.
    Meumst.
Gn. Dolet dictum imprudenti adulescenti, et libero.   40
Pa. At te di perdant.   Gn. Quid ille quaeso?   Th. Per-
    ditus.   (430)
Risu omnes, qui aderant, emoriri: denique
metuebant omnes iam me.   Gn. Non iniuria.
Th. Sed heus tu, purgon' ego me de istac Thaidi,
quod eam me amare suspicatast?   Gn. Nil minus.   45
Immo auge magis suspicionem.   Th. Cur?   Gn. Rogas?
Scin', siquando illa mentionem Phaedriae
facit aut si laudat, te ut male urat?   Th. Sentio.
Gn. Id ut ne fiat, haec res solast remedio.
Ubi nominabit Phaedriam, tu Pamphilam   50
continuo.   Siquando illa dicet, Phaedriam   (440)
comissatum intromittamus: tu, Pamphilam
cantatum provocemus.   Si laudabit haec
illius formam, tu huius contra.   Denique

17: or to the meaning "to cheat,"
"come over."

36 lepus es...] "You are a
hare and want game yourself." So
a Greek proverb δασύπους ὢν κρέως
ἐπιθυμεῖς; Pulpamentum = any kind
of delicate food. The proverb is
said by Vopiscus (Vita Numeriani,
13) to be from Livius Andronicus,
who may have translated it from
the Greek. If so Gnatho's vetus

credidi in v. 38, has all the more
point, and would be appreciated by
the audience.

40 "Your joke must hurt that
thoughtless and forward young man."
Parry supplies mihi with dolet, "It
grieves me to think this was said to
the simple young gentleman" (libero = of good birth).   Some give
the line to Thraso, but without any
necessity.

par pro pari referto, quod eam mordeat.   55
TH. Si quidem me amaret, tum istuc prodesset, Gnatho.
GN. Quando illud, quod tu das, exspectat atque amat,
iam dudum te amat: iamdudum illi facile fit
quod doleat: metuit semper, quem ipsa nunc capit
fructum, ne quando iratus tu alio conferas.   60
TH. Bene dixti: ac mihi istuc non in mentem venerat.
GN. Ridiculum: non enim cogitaras: ceterum   (451)
idem hoc tute melius quanto invenisses, Thraso!

ACTUS III. SCENA II.

THAIS. THRASO. PARMENO. GNATHO. PYTHIAS.

TH. Audire vocem visa sum modo militis.
Atque eccum. Salve, mi Thraso.   THR. O Thais mea,

---

55 **par pro pari referto**] The MS. reading is altered by most editors, because *par pari referre* is the usual form of the saying. Servius quoting this passage to Verg. *Aen.* I. 265, omits *pro:* but MSS. of Cicero *ad Fam.* I. 9. 12 retain it. Bentley reads *tu* for *pro:* Wagner *porro*=in your turn. But *par pro pari* if unusual, is neither unintelligible nor ungrammatical: and where that is the case, it seems safer to avoid conjectural emendation, the besetting sin of editors.

56] The bragging self-conceit of Thraso is interrupted by a gleam of good sense.

58] "At this very moment she's in love with you; at this very moment you can easily manage to annoy her." Gnatho corrects Thraso's doubt (v. 56) as to Thais' love for him; she is now, he says, expecting Thraso's present, and therefore now really in love with him. *Iamdudum* need not always imply a long inter-

val of time (*iampridem*, "for a long time") but = what is close at hand, before or after; *iamdudum sumite poenas*, Verg. *Aen.* II. 103, cf. *Aul.* I. 4. 1. "*Dudum*" (from *diu*, connected with *dies*, and = a space of time, "a while") seldom in old Latin writers implies length of time, except in *haud dudum, quam dudum, iam dudum*. Plautus has *dudum—quum* = "just now—when," of time present or only just past: and sometimes *dudum* almost = *nuper*, cf. Cic. *Att.* II. 24, *quae dudum ad me, et quae etiam ante bis ad Tulliam de me scripsisti*, where it expressly contrasts with *ante*. Cf. Verg. *Aen.* V. 650: X. 599.

63 **melius quanto**] is of course adverb; but Bentley seems to have thought that *idem melius* agreed, for he says, "nam si idem est, quomodo melius." Verily, "aliquando bonus dormitat Homerus!"

Sc. II.] Thais comes out to talk to Thraso. Parmeno takes the

meum suavium, quid agitur? Ecquid nos amas
de fidicina istac? PA. Quam venuste! Quod dedit
principium adveniens! TH. Plurimum merito tuo.   5
GN. Eamus ergo ad cenam: quid stas? PA. Hem alterum:
ex homine hunc natum dicas? TH. Ubi vis, non moror.
PA. Adibo, atque adsimulabo quasi nunc exeam.   (460)
Ituran', Thais, quopiam es? TH. Ehem, Parmeno,
bene fecisti: hodie itura. PA. Quo? TH. Quid, hunc non
vides?   10
PA. Video, et me taedet. Ubi vis, dona adsunt tibi
a Phaedria. THR. Quid stamus? cur non imus hinc?
PA. Quaeso hercle ut liceat, pace quod fiat tua,
dare huic quae volumus, convenire et conloqui.
THR. Perpulchra credo dona, aut nostri similia.   15
PA. Res indicabit. Heus, iubete istos foras

opportunity of showing her the presents that Phaedria has sent by him,
and after some byeplay between him
and Gnatho Thais goes off to Thraso's house, leaving directions about
Chremes, whom she is expecting.
Metre: iambic trimeter.

4 Quam venuste ... adveniens]
"Beautifully put! What a beginning
he has made when he comes up!"
Parmeno ridicules the awkwardness
in at once reminding Thais of his present.

7 ex homine hunc natum dicas]
"Would you believe this fellow to
be a human being" (and not a beast)?
referring to Gnatho's characteristic
suggestion of eating. This explanation of the text seems better than
(dropping the?) "You would say
this fellow was the other's (Thraso's)
son." Dryden seems to have understood the words in the sense of
Colman's translation. "He's a chip
of the old block." He says, "This
contains the general character of
men and manners; one old man or
father, one courtezan, one lover, so
like another, as if the first of them

had begot the rest of every sort.
Ex homine hunc natum dicas."
Bentley's correction *abdomini* is very
ingenious but without authority;
"You would say this fellow was
born for his belly;" cf. Cic. in *Piso-
nem*, 17, *Ille gurges atque helluo
natus abdomini suo, non laudi et
gloriae*. Parry (who adopts *abdomini*) also quotes from Plutarch περὶ
κόλακος, XV. 93, Γαστὴρ ὅλον τὸ σῶμα,
πανταχῇ βλέπων ὀφθαλμὸς ἔργον τοῖς
ὀδοῦσι θηρίον. *abdomini* must be scanned as a trisyllable, cf. *nemini, Hec.*
III. I. I.

10 bene fecisti] "I am glad you
have come," a common colloquial
form, cf. I. 2. 106, *Hec.* III. 5. 56.
Donatus supposes Thais to be com-
plimenting Parmeno for no reason:
but it is better taken as an ordinary
term of courtesy, which agrees better
with the character of Thais, in
which the good motives (of doing
justice to Pamphila) predominate;
see Parry ad loc.

15 nostri] (Bembine MS.) sc.
doni. Other MSS. and most editions have *nostris*.

exire, quos iussi, ocius.　Procede tu huc.
Ex Aethiopia est usque haec.　THR. Hic sunt tres minae.
GN. Vix.　PA. Ubi tu es, Dore? accede huc.　Hem eunu-
　　chum tibi　　　　　　　　　　　　　　　　　　　(471)
quam liberali facie! quam aetate integra!　　　　　　　20
TH. Ita me di ament, honestus est.　PA. Quid ais, Gnatho?
numquid habes quod contemnas?　Quid tu autem, Thraso?
Tacent: satis laudant.　Fac periclum in literis,
fac in palaestra, in musicis: quae liberum
scire aequom est adulescentem, sollertem dabo.　　　　25
THR. Ego illum eunuchum, si opus sit, vel sobrius.
PA. Atque haec qui misit, non sibi soli postulat
te vivere, et sua causa excludi ceteros;　　　　　　　(480)
neque pugnas narrat, neque cicatrices suas
ostentat; neque tibi obstat, quod quidam facit:　　　30
verum ubi molestum non erit, ubi tu voles,
ubi tempus tibi erit, sat habet, si tum recipitur.
THR. Apparet servom hunc esse domini pauperis
miserique.　GN. Nam hercle nemo posset, sat scio,
qui haberet qui pararet alium, hunc perpeti.　　　　35

---

18 **usque**] "all the way from Aethiopia," cf. Verg. *Aen.* VII. 289, and
with other prepositions; *ad usque*
(also written *adusque*), *Aen.* XI. 262:
Hor. *Sat.* I. 5, 96, *via peior adusque
Bari moenia piscosi*: *Aen.* XI. 317,
fines super usque sicanos.

tres minae] an absurdly low price
for a female slave, cf. *Phormio*, III. 3.
24—5, where 30 minae is the price.
Thraso and Gnatho of course dis-
parage Phaedria's present.

21 **Ita me di ament**] "Heaven
love me! he's a good one." This use
of *ita* in asseverations and vows [cf.
Hor. *Sat.* II. 2. 124, *Et venerata
Ceres, ita culmo surgeret alto, Ex-
plicuit vino contractae seria frontis*:
Cic. *Cat.* IV. 6. 11, *ita mihi...liceat,
liceat ut ego non atrocitate animi*

movcor; Phorm. V. 3. 24] is parallel
to that of οὕτω, *Od.* VIII. 465, οὕτω
νυν Ζεὺς θείη οἰκαδέ τ᾽ ἐλθεμέναι...Ar.
Nub. 520.

23 **literis palaestra musicis**] the
three elements of a liberal education
among the Greeks: cf. Arist. *Pol.*
VIII. 2, and Parry's note here.

24 **musicis**] "music," the more
limited and less common use of
Greek μουσική, which is generally
used = "a liberal education" including γράμματα, cf. *Heaut.* Prol. 23.

25 **dabo**] "I'll warrant him accomplished in all that a young
gentleman of good birth ought to
know."

35 **qui pararet**] This second *qui*
is of course the old form of abl. "the
means of buying another."

P⒜ Tace tu: quem ego esse infra infimos omnis puto
homines: nam qui huic animum adsentari induxeris,
e flamma petere te cibum posse arbitror.   (490)

THR⒜ Iamne imus? TH. Hos prius introducam, et quae
        volo

simul imperabo: post continuo exeo.   40

THR⒜ Ego hinc abeo. Tu istanc opperire. P⒜ Haud
        convenit

una ire cum amica imperatorem in via.

THR⒜ Quid tibi ego multa dicam? Domini similis es.

GN. Ha ha hae. THR⒜ Quid rides? GN. Istud quod dixti
        modo:

et illud de Rhodio dictum quum in mentem venit.   45

Sed Thais exit. THR⒜ Abi, praecurre ut sint domi

parata. GN. Fiat. TH. Diligenter, Pythias,

fac cures, si Chremes forte huc advenerit,   (500)

ut ores, primum ut maneat: si id non commodumst,

ut redeat: si id non poterit, ad me adducito.   50

---

37 qui induxeris] The subjunctive
indicates the causal force of *qui*.

38 e flamma petere cibum] A
proverb implying extreme readiness,
as of people who would even steal
from a funeral pyre the food placed
there as an offering to the infernal
gods. *Bustirape!* is a term of abuse
in Plaut. *Pseud.* I. 3. 127: cf. *Rudens*, I. 2. 52; Catullus, 59; Schol.
ad Arist. *Nub.* 907. Donatus takes
the proverb in a more general sense
of poverty that runs any risk to get
food, "unde sine damno aut malo
nihil potest auferri."

39 imus?] Shall we go? cf. IV.
7. 17. Cic. *Or. imusne sessum?*
Verg. *Aen.* II. 322, *quam prendimus
arcem?* III. 88. 367. In all these
examples a question is asked as to
what is to be done instantly; and
the present tense shows that the
action, though grammatically future,
is practically all but present. In

this passage Thraso probably suits
the action to the word by beginning
to move.

42 una ire cum amica] This
order, followed by all editors, makes
the hiatus necessary for the scansion, *ūnă ĭrĕ cum ămĭ|că ĭm |*.
Parry avoids this by transposition,
una cum amica ire, pleading the
comparative rarity of genuine *hiatus*
as opposed to *Synaloepha* or coalescing of two syllables into one, which
was more congenial to Latin pronunciation. Cf. his Introduction,
pp. xlix, lvii.

43 similis] Bentley reads *simia;*
"ingeniosius quam verius," as Stallbaum justly remarks; for his only
support is the use of πιθηκίζω and
πιθηκισμός = "flattery" and a passage of Plaut. *Mostell.* IV. 1. 40,
vide ut fastidit Simia.

45 illud de Rhodio] III. 1. 30
above.

Py. Ita faciam. Th. Quid? quid aliud volui dicere?
Ehem curate istam diligenter virginem:
domi adsitis, facite. Thr. Eamus. Th. Vos me sequimini.

ACTUS III. SCENA III.

CHREMES. PYTHIAS.

Ch. Profecto quanto magis magisque cogito,
nimirum dabit haec Thais mihi magnum malum:
ita me video ab ea astute labefactarier,
iam tum quum primum iussit me ad se accersier.
Roget quis, quid tibi cum ea? ne noram quidem.   (510) 5
Ubi veni, causam, ut ibi manerem, reperit:
ait rem divinam fecisse, et rem seriam
velle agere mecum. Iam tum erat suspicio,
dolo malo haec fieri omnia. Ipsa accumbere
mecum; mihi sese dare: sermonem quaerere.   10
Ubi friget, huc evasit, quam pridem pater
mi et mater mortui essent. Dico, iam diu.
Rus Sunii ecquod haberem, et quam longe a mari.

Sc. III.] Enter Chremes, much perplexed at his summons to Thais, and speculating as to what she can want with him. Donatus observes of his character, "haec persona apud Menandrum adolescentis rustici est, et inconsequens oratio est:" but there is not much attempt at working out his character. The present scene merely fills a gap and suggests the dénouement. Metre: iambic trimeter.

2 nimirum] Donatus' note is worth giving: "Solve nimirum et fac non est mirum: nam ni ne significat, et ne non, ni pro ne, Virgilius Aen. III. 696:" (he might add Lucr. II. 734, on which see Munro's note. The passage in Vergil is questioned,

but it occurs in all MSS. and Servius ad loc. says that ni = ne). Ne pro non Plautus nevult pro nonvult: add to this the instances in which non is used instead of ne to convey a prohibition (Verg. G. I. 456; II. 315), and the chain of connection is complete.

7 ait rem divinam fecisse] An excuse of Thais for having kept Chremes waiting, "she had just been engaged in religious duties."

11 Ubi friget] sc. sermo, "when it flagged," cf. Fam. III. 8, Refrigerato iam levissimo sermone hominum provincialium? XI. 14, frigeo = I am at a standstill, out of work.

13 Sunii] appears to violate the usage of poets as to genitives of words

Credo ei placere hoc; sperat se a me avellere.

Postremo, ecqua inde parva periisset soror;   (520) 15

ecquis cum ea una; quid habuisset, quum perit;

ecquis eam posset noscere.   Haec cur quaeritet?

nisi si illa forte, quae olim periit parvola

soror, hanc se intendit esse, ut est audacia.

Verum ea si vivit, annos natast sedecim: 20

non maior: Thais, quam ego sum, maiusculast.

Misit porro orare, ut venirem, serio.

Aut dicat quod volt, aut molesta ne siet.

Non hercle veniam tertio.   Heus heus, ecquis hic?

Ego sum Chremes.   Py. O capitulum lepidissimum.   25

Ch. Dico ego mi insidias fieri?   Py. Thais maxumo   (531)

te orabat opere, ut cras redires.   Ch. Rus eo.

Py. Fac amabo.   Ch. Non possum, inquam.   Py. At tu

        apud nos hic mane,

dum redeat ipsa.   Ch. Nihil minus.   Py. Cur, mi Chremes?

Ch. Malam rem hinc ibis?   Py. Si istuc ita certumst tibi,

amabo, ut illuc transeas ubi illast.   Ch. Eo.   31

Py. Abi, Dorias, cito hunc deduce ad militem.

---

in -ius, -ium (And. I. I. 132 note).
Lachmann however (ad Lucr. v.
1006) defends this and Palladii
Verg. Aen. IX. 151 (a v. regarded
by some as spurious): Latin poets,
he says, did not observe the contracted usage in Greek words, con-
sidering the first i to be Greek.

16 quid habuisset] i.e. what
crepundia or trinkets by which children who had been exposed were to

be recognized, cf. IV. 6. 15, and
Parry's note ad loc.

19 intendit] "maintains," Greek
διισχυρίζεται. Both words give the
notion of maintaining a point earn-
estly and with effort: so intendere,
intentio are common legal terms.

26 Dico, &c.] "am I right in
saying there's a trap laid for me?"

28 amabo] cf. supra I. 2. 50
note.

ACTUS III. SCENA IV.

ANTIPHO.

AN. Heri aliquot adulescentuli coiimus in Piraeo,
in hunc diem ut de symbolis essemus. Chaeream ei rei
praefecimus: dati anuli: locus, tempus constitutumst.   (540)
Praeteriit tempus; quo in loco dictumst, parati nihil est.
Homo ipse nusquamst: neque scio quid dicam, aut quid
            coniectem.   5
Nunc mi hoc negoti ceteri dedere, ut illum quaeram.
Idque adeo visam, si domist. Quisnam hinc a Thaide exit?
Is est, an non est? Ipsus est. Quid hoc hominis? Quid
            hoc ornatist?
Quid illud malist? Nequeo satis mirari neque coniicere.
Nisi quicquid est, procul hinc lubet prius quid sit sciscitari.

ACTUS III. SCENA V.

CHAEREA. ANTIPHO.

CH. Numquis hic est? Nemo est. Numquis hinc me se-
            quitur? Nemo homost.

Act III. Sc. IV. V.] Antipho, one
of Chaerea's friends who have been
waiting to dine with him at the
Piraeus, comes to look for him, and
sees a strange figure coming out of
Thais' house.

1 **Piraeo**] Cic. *Att.* VII. 3.

2 **de symbolis essemus**] a literal
translation of Greek δειπνεῖν ἀπὸ
συμβόλων, "to club together for a
dinner;" cf. *And.* I. I. 61.

3 **praefecimus**] i.e. "appointed
him to manage it," not as Donatus,
συμποσίαρχον *fecimus*, appointed
him *magister bibendi*: for that would
be done at the feast by dice, according to the familiar allusion of Ho-

race, *Quem Venus arbitrum Dicet
bibendi.*

dati anuli] "We pledged ourselves." The interchange of rings
was a common formula in agree-
ments of any kind: Lindenbrogius
quotes Pliny, XXXIII. I, *ad sponsiones
etiamnunc anulo prosiliente:* and
the Athenian custom of the two
parties to a suit laying down their
rings. Dem. *adv. Pantaen.* p. 978,
προκαλοῦμαί σε ταυτί· δέχομαι· φέρε
τὸν δακτύλιον λαβέ· τίς δ' ἐγγυητής;
οὑτοσί.

Sc. v.] Chaerea comes out of
Thais' house rejoicing in the success

Iamne erumpere hoc licet mihi gaudium? Pro Iuppiter!

Nunc est profecto, interfici quum perpeti me possum, (550)

ne hoc gaudium contaminet vita aegritudine aliqua,

Sed neminemne curiosum intervenire nunc mihi,   5

qui me sequatur quoquo eam, rogitando obtundat, enicet,

quid gestiam, aut quid laetus sim, pro pergam, unde emer-
          gam, ubi siem

vestitum hunc nactus, quid mihi quaeram, sanus sim anne
          insaniam?

An. Adibo, atque ab eo gratiam hanc, quam video velle,
          inibo.

Chaerea, quid est quod sic gestis? Quid sibi hic vestitus
          quaerit?   10

Quid est, quod laetus sis? quid tibi vis? Satine sanu's?
          Quid me

adspectas? Quid taces? Ch. O festus dies hominis! amice,
          salve:

of his scheme. Antipho accosts him, and extracts a full account of the adventure.

Metre: 1, 2, troch. tetram. catal.: 10, 11, troch. tetram.: 3, 4, 9, 12, 13, 44—66, iamb. tetram. catal.: 5—8, 14—43, iamb. tetram.

1 **Nemo homo**] This adjectival use of *nemo* occurs again *Ad.* II. 3. 6; *Phorm.* IV. 2. 1; in Plautus; and two or three passages in Cicero.

2 **erumpere**] "to give vent to." The *active* use is less common but quite classical; cf. Lucr. I. 724, *eruptos ignes*: V. 598, *erumpere lumen*: Verg. *G.* IV. 368, *unde altus primum se erumpit Enipeus.*

3, 4. For the sentiment of these two vv. cf. *And.* V. 5. 4.

5 **neminemne intervenire?**] For the construction see *And.* I. 5. 10 note. Chaerea is so full of the success of his scheme, that he longs for some one, were it the greatest 'bore' he knows, to come up and

ask him, that he may have it out.

9 **gratiam inibo**] Parry translates, "Will do him this favour:" but the phrase more strictly means "to get into the good graces of a person," "to earn his favour." For example, when *A* is said *inire gratiam* with *B*, the *gratia* is conceived not as proceeding from *A* to *B*, but as sought by *A* in *B*. "I'll get up to him, and get out of him what I see he wants to let out," may perhaps express the play on *adibo, inibo.*

12 **O festus dies hominis!**] The reading of all the old copies and Donatus, who explains it *homo festi dies*. From Plaut. *Cas.* I. I. 49, *Sine, amabo, ted amari, meus festus dies*, we may perhaps gather that *festus dies* was a colloquial form of address to any one who was particularly welcome, "a sight for sore eyes:" and this seems the only way to extract sense from the ex-

nemost hominum, quem ego nunc magis cuperem videre,
　　quam te.　　　　　　　　　　　　　　　　　(560)

AN. Narra istuc quaeso quid sit.　CH. Immo ego te ob-
　　secro hercle ut audias.

Nostine hanc, quam amat frater?　AN. Novi; nempe, opinor,
　　Thaidem.　　　　　　　　　　　　　　　　　15

CH. Istam ipsam.　AN. Sic commemineram.　CH. Quaedam
　　hodie est ei dono data

virgo: quid ego eius tibi nunc faciem praedicem aut laudem,
　　Antipho:

quum ipsum me noris quam elegans formarum spectator siem?

In hac commotus sum.　AN. Ain' tu?　CH. Primam dices,
　　scio, si videris.

Quid multa verba? amare coepi.　Forte fortuna domi　20
erat quidam eunuchus, quem mercatus frater fuerat Thaidi:
neque is deductus etiam tum ad eam.　Summonuit me Par-
　　meno

ibi servus, quod ego arripui.　AN. Quid id est?　CH. Tacitus
　　citius audies:　　　　　　　　　　　　　　　(570)

pression as it stands. Bentley proposed *O festus dies! O meus amicus,
salve:* Weisse's Tauchnitz text reads
O festus dies, O mi amice, salve.
Parry's suggestion *O festi dies omi-
uis* (written *hominis,* as *olim, holim,
arundo, harundo* in MSS.) is happy: but unfortunately without authority.

　O festus dies] This "use of
Nominative for Vocative case" is
paralleled by such examples as *Vos,
o Pompilius sanguis,* Hor. *A. P.*
292. *Vacuas adhibe mihi maximus,
aures,* Lucr. I. 45. The so-called
'Vocative' case is- indeed little
more than a shorter form of the
Nominative, due to a change of
pronunciation in the latter when
used *rapidly* in addressing others.
In Latin it only exists as a distinct
form in 2nd declension words in
-*us:* in Greek the nominative is
used for it wherever its occurrence
would naturally be rare, e. g. ὦ
ποῦς.

　18　elegans] "of nice taste,"
"critical," cf. III. 1. 18.

　19　In hac commotus sum] "I
was much struck with her," so *sus-
pirare, insanire, ardere, uri,* in *puella.* The object of the feeling is regarded as the spot at or upon which
it is exercised: so often in c. abl. =
"in the case of;" *In eo potissimum
populus abutitur libertate, per quem
consecutus est.* Cf. *Aen.* II. 541,
*At non ille, satum quo te mentiris,
Achilles Talis in hoste fuit Priamo:*
Tib. III. 6. 19, *nec torvus Liber in
illis.*

ut vestem cum eo mutem, et pro illo iubeam me illoc de-
    ducier.

An. Pro eunuchon'? Ch. Sic est. An. Quid ex ea re tan-
    dem ut caperes commodi?   25

Ch. Rogas? viderem, audirem, essem una quacum cupiebam,
    Antipho.

Num parva causa, aut parva ratiost? Traditus sum mulieri.

Illa illico ubi me accepit, laeta vero ad se abducit domum:

commendat virginem. An. Cui? tibine? Ch. Mihi. An.
    Satis tuto tamen.

Ch. Edicit, ne vir quisquam ad eam adeat: et mihi, ne abs-
    cedam, imperat: 30

in interiore parte ut maneam solus cum sola. Adnuo

terram intuens modeste. An. Miser. Ch. Ego, inquit, ad
    cenam hinc eo:

abducit secum ancillas: paucae, quae circum illam essent,
    manent   (580)

noviciae puellae. Continuo haec adornant ut lavet.

Adhortor properent. Dum apparatur, virgo in conclavi sedet

suspectans tabulam quandam pictam; ibi inerat pictura haec,
    Iovem   36

quo pacto Danaae misisse aiunt quondam in gremium imbrem
    aureum.

Egomet quoque id spectare coepi: et quia consimilem luserat

iam olim ille ludum, inpendio magis animus gaudebat mihi;

deum sese in hominem convertisse, atque in alienas tegulas

---

34 haec] nom. fem. plur.; cf.
Phorm. V. 8. 23, haec itiones (Do-
natus): Heaut. IV. 7. 10, haec minae.
Plautus has haec commoditates (Aul.
III. 5. 59): and the Palatine MS. of
Vergil reads in Aen. VI. 852, haec
tibi erunt artes: in Cat. 64. 320 the
MSS. have Hae (Parcae) tum clari-
sona pellentes vellera voce; cf. Lucr.
III. 601, VI. 456. Hae does not
occur in Lucretius, and in his time

haec must have been the usual form,
and is sometimes preserved in the
best MSS. of Cicero, Vergil, Livy
and others.

40 in hominem] Into a shower
of gold, according to the well-known
story; whence Bentley reads in pretium; cf. Hor. Od. III. 16. 8, con-
verso in pretium deo. But Terence
does not want to show, as Horace,
that no road is impassable to gold.

venisse clanculum per impluvium, fucum factum mulieri. 41
At quem deum? qui templa caeli summa sonitu concutit.
Ego homuncio hoc non facerem? Ego illud vero ita fecerim
    ac lubens.   (590)
Dum haec mecum reputo, adcersitur lavatum interea virgo:
iit, lavit, rediit; deinde eam in lectum illae conlocarunt. 45
Sto exspectans, si quid mi imperent. Venit una, heus tu,
    inquit, Dore,
cape hoc flabellum, et ventulum huic sic facito, dum la-
    vamus:
ubi nos laverimus, si voles, lavato. Accipio tristis.
AN. Tum equidem istuc os tuum inpudens videre nimium
    vellem,
qui esset status, flabellum sic tenere te asinum tantum. 50
CH. Vix elocutast hoc, foras simul omnes proruunt se;
abeunt lavatum, perstrepunt, ita ut fit, domini ubi absunt.
Interea somnus virginem obprimit. Ego limis specto (600)
sic per flabellum clanculum: simul alia circumspecto
satine explorata sint. Video esse. Pessulum ostio obdo. 55
AN. Quid tum? CH. Quid, quid tum? Fatue. AN. Fateor.
    CH. An ego occasionem

The text is certainly puzzling, but confirmed by all MSS. Donatus suggests *in hominem*, "id est in hominis audaciam atque flagitia," "into human nature." But more probably it is a slip of the writer, as he thinks of many similar stories of gods becoming men for a like object.

41 per impluvium] "through the skylight," altered by Bentley to *per pluvium*, i. e. *imbrem aureum*: see Parry's note. The criticism, "if Jupiter had descended into the impluvium, he would have been almost as far from Danae's room as if he had been in the street," is curiously hypercritical, and apparently assumes that the *turris aenea* in which

Acrisius shut her, was built after the model of a house such as a Dictionary of Antiquities supplies.

42 qui concutit] A quotation from Ennius, who imitated Homer's μέγας ἐλέλιξεν Ὄλυμπον. The *sound* of the thunder (*sonitus*) is confounded with the thunderclap itself; cf. Lucr. II. 1100.

53 limis] sc. *oculis*, "askance," Greek λοξὸν βλέπειν, cf. Plautus *M. G.* IV. 6. 2 (Lindem.). *Limus* (orig. *limus cinctus*) "a waistband" occurs Verg. *Aen.* XII. 120, on which Servius *limum obliquum dicimus. Unde et Terentius oculis limis*, i. e. *obliquis*.

mi ostentam, tantam, tam brevem, tam optatam, tam inspe-
ratam
amitterem? Tum pol ego is essem vero, qui adsimulabar.
AN. Sane hercle ut dicis. Sed interim de symbolis quid
actumst?
CH. Paratumst. AN. Frugi es: ubi? domin'? CH. Immo
apud libertum Discum.   60
AN. Perlongest. CH. Sed tanto ocius properemus. AN.
Muta vestem.
CH. Ubi mutem? Perii: nam domo exulo nunc; metuo
fratrem,
ne intus sit: porro autem, pater ne rure redierit iam. (610)
AN. Eamus ad me, ibi proxumumst ubi mutes. CH. Recte
dicis.
Eamus: et de istac simul quo pacto porro possim   65
potiri consilium volo capere una tecum. AN. Fiat.

ACTUS IV. SCENA I.

DORIAS.

Ita me di ament, quantum ego illum vidi, non nihil timeo
misera,
ne quam ille hodie insanus turbam faciat, aut vim Thaidi.

Instead of this scene, Fontaine in his "Eunuch" substitutes one between Chaerea and Pamphila. Ch. professes honourable love, leaves her in the house of Thais, and at last obtains his father's consent to marry her. Fontaine no doubt considered the plot of the Eunuch unsuitable to modern ideas, and naturally enough. But to do Terence justice, he treats the subject with as much delicacy and modesty as it admits.

Act IV. Sc. 1.] Dorias, who had taken Chremes to Thraso's house, returns with her mistress' jewelry, Chremes' arrival having roused Thraso's jealousy and produced a quarrel between him and Thais.

Metre: 1—4, troch. tetram.: 2, 7, 9—14, troch. tetram. catal.: 3, 8, iamb. tetram.

1 Ita me di ament] see above, III. 2. 21 note.

Nam postquam iste advenit Chremes adulescens, frater vir-
    ginis,
militem rogat ut illum admitti iubeat: ille continuo irasci,
neque negare audere: Thais porro instare, ut hominem in-
    vitet.   5
Id faciebat retinendi illius causa: quia illa quae cupiebat
de sorore eius indicare, ad eam rem tempus non erat. (620)
Invitat tristis: mansit. Ibi illa cum illo sermonem occipit.
Miles vero, sibi putans adductum ante oculos aemulum,
voluit facere contra huic aegre: heus, inquit, puere, Pam-
    philam   10
adcerse, ut delectet hic nos. Illa exclamat, minime gentium:
in convivium illam? Miles tendere: inde ad iurgium.
Interea aurum sibi clam mulier demit, dat mihi ut auferam:
hoc est signi: ubi primum poterit, se illinc subducet scio.

11 **minime gentium**] "not for the
world." The construction falls under
the head of Partitive Genitive, like
ubi gentium? τοῦ γῆς: This verse is
'hypermetric,' the last syllable of
gentium being elided before *in* of v.
12. Terence uses this licence *And.*
IV. 1. 8: *Phormio*, II. 1. 63: *Ad.* II.
2. 9, III. 3. 21. It only occurs
once in Lucretius (v. 849, where
see Munro's note), but is more common in Vergil, e.g. *G.* II. 69, *In-
seritur vero et fetu nucis arbutus
horrida Et spumas miscent:* and frequently *que* is thus ὑπὲρ μέτρον,
Aen. I. 332, IV. 558, &c. Catullus
also uses it, *Nullum amans vere sed
identidem omnium Ilia rumpens* (Sap-
phic). The licence is unknown to
Homer and but rare (except in anapaestic metre) with the great dramatists. Those who introduced it
into the metres must have done so
under the mistaken view that the
lines formed one continuous metrical system, as in anapaestic metres;
for we find the invariable conditions
of its occurrence are (1) that the
hypermetric syllable is one that *may*
be elided; (2) that the first syllable
of the next line begins with a vowel
or aspirate: cf. Lachmann's note on
Lucr. II. 118.

13 **aurum**] her jewels; cf. *Heaut.*
II. 3. 47.

ACTUS IV. SCENA II.

PHAEDRIA.

Dum rus eo, coepi egomet mecum inter vias,
ita ut fit, ubi quid in animo est molestiae,
aliam rem ex alia cogitare, et ea omnia in   (630)
peiorem partem.   Quid opust verbis?   Dum haec puto,
praeterii inprudens villam,   Longe iam abieram,   5
quum sensi : redeo rursum, male vero me habens!
Ubi ad ipsum veni diverticulum, constiti :
occepi mecum cogitare, Hem, biduum hic
manendumst soli sine illa?   Quid tum postea?
Nihil est. Quid? nihil? Si non tangendi copia est,   10
eho ne videndi quidem erit? Si illud non licet,
saltem hoc licebit.   Certe extrema linea

Sc. II.] Phaedria returns, tired of his absence, and unable to live without at least seeing Thais.

Metre : iambic trimeter.

1 **Dum eo**] For the familiar usage of *dum* with present tense in clauses referring to *past* time, see Madvig, § 336, obs. 2.

inter vias] of time, and exactly = *dum eo*: cf. German "unterwegs." Inter *viam* (Cic. *Att.* IV. 3) is the more natural expression : Stallb. quotes Plaut. *Aul.* II. 8. 9, *Egomet mecum inter vias cogitare accepi*: and Lexx. *Poen.* V. 3. 43.

4 **puto**] which usually means to think, hold an opinion (often with the collateral notion of a wrong opinion), is sometimes used like *reputo* or *considero* = to think over : Plautus, *Cas.* III. 2. 25, *cum eam mecum rationem puto;* cf. Verg. *Aen.* VI. 332, *Multa putans.*

6 **male me habens**] cf. *And.* II. 3. 4 and note.

7 **diverticulum**] 'the turning to

my house' must not (as Parry, following Stallbaum, shows) be confounded with *deverticulum* = *diversorium*, καταγωγεῖον, an "inn" or house by the way-side. There must have been a tendency to confound the two words in common conversation and in MSS., and the difference may not have been strictly observed ; but it should not be forgotten that in *diverticulum* we have *dis-* or *di-* in the sense of separation from ; in *deverticulum* the force of *de* in reference to the "terminus ad quem" of the motion indicated, which is found in *deducere defero,* &c. Vergil, *Aen.* IX. 379, uses *divortia* = cross-roads, where roads diverge from each other.

12 **extrema linea amare**] "To love at a distance is something," i.e. only to see, if not to speak to, the beloved object. *Linea* is used = boundary, limit, end (*mors ultima linea rerum est*, Hor. *Epp.* I. 16. 79; *peccare est tanquam transire lineas,*

amare, haud nihil est: villam praetereo sciens.   (640)

Sed quid hoc, quod timida subito egreditur Pythias?

ACTUS IV. SCENA III.

PYTHIAS. DORIAS. PHAEDRIA.

Ubi ego illum scelerosum misera atque inpium inveniam?
      aut ubi quaeram?

Hocine tam audax facinus facere esse ausum? PH. Perii?
      hoc quid sit, vereor.

PY. Quin etiam insuper scelus, postquam ludificatust yir-
      ginem,

vestem omnem miserae discidit, tum ipsam capillo conscidit.

PH. Hem. PY. Qui nunc si detur mihi;   5

ut ego unguibus facile illi in oculos involem ven'efico?

Cicero), "and so *extrema linea* = "at the furthest limit," "a long way off." The reference to a *linea*, stretched across the racecourse, and which could not be passed till the signal was given, seems doubtful; for such a barrier would naturally be at the beginning of the course immediately in front of the racers (as the rope holding back the horses at the modern Carnival, or the *carceres* so often alluded to in connexion with chariot races), and *extrema linea* would point to the further end of the course. But however this may be, the expression is intelligible enough without any such special reference. Donatus and the other old commentators imagine five *lineae* or stages of love, of which the first (*visio*) is the *extrema linea* of the text.

Sc. III.] Pythias and Dorias rush on to the stage, hoping to catch the pseudo-eunuch who has done such mischief. Pythias tells the story to Phaedria, who goes to see what has become of Dorus.

Metre: 1, 2, troch. tetram.: 3, 7, 12, 13, troch. tetram. catal.: 4, 6, 8, 9, 11, 14, 15, 17, 25, iamb. tetram.: 16, iamb. trim.: 5, 10, iamb. dimeter.

2 Hocine...esse ausum] see note to *And.* I. 5. 10.

4 ipsam capillo conscidit] "Tore her hair." The ablative *capillo* defines more particularly the part *at* or *on* which, and so *in respect of* which, the action described by *conscidit* took place. Whether we call it ablative "of respect," or of "part affected," it is an adverbial use of the ablative case corresponding to the common adverbial use of the accusative (*scissa comam*), and often nearly identical with it in meaning. Here *ipsam capillum conscidit* might as naturally have been written; and these two adverbial usages of accus. and abl. "of respect" were doubtless but little discriminated. Parry prefers to explain the construction as "an enallage for *ipsi capillum discidit*."

PH. Nescio quid profecto absente nobis turbatumst domi.

Adibo.   Quid istuc? quid festinas? aut quem quaeris, Pythias?

PY. Ehem Phaedria, ego quem quaeram? In' hinc quo dignu's
    cum donis tuis   (650)

tam lepidis?   PH. Quid istuc est rei?   .   10

PY. Rogasne?   Eunuchum quem dedisti nobis, quas turbas
    dedit?

Virginem, quam herae dono dederat miles, vitiavit. PH.
    Quid ais?

PY. Perii.   PH. Temulenta es.   PY. Utinam sic sint, qui
    mihi male volunt.

---

7 **absente nobis**] "Aut subdistinguendum est, et subaudiendum *me; aut ἀρχαισμὸς* figura est, *absente nobis* pro *nobis absentibus*." Donatus. On the former view *nobis* is "dativus ethicus" with *turbatumst; absente* (*me*), abl. absol.: "We have had some disturbance at home in my absence." For support of the latter Donatus quotes from Pomponius and Varro *praesente* with plural subst.; but Varro's *id praesente legatis omnibus, exercitu,* is not conclusive from the proximity of *exercitu:* and a passage from Plautus, *Amphit.* II. 2. 204, *nobis praesente,* is not considered genuine by Weise. Parry quotes Cat. 105. 5, "*Restituis cupido atque insperante ipsa refers te Nobis;*" and this and our text might be sufficiently explained as a "constructio κατὰ σύνεσιν," since *nobis* really= *me.* There remain, however, Attius *praesente his* and Pomponius *praesente testibus,* and from XII. Tables *praesente ambobus,* to include which we might possibly conceive a colloquial usage of the ablatives *praesente absente* as mere adverbs="in the presence of," "away from," rejected by the greater precision of classical Latin to avoid grammatical confusion.

9 **in'?**]=*isne,* cf. *viden'? ain'?* So Bentley from Bembine and Vatican MSS.: Zeune *i hinc:* Stallbaum *abi hine.*

11 **Eunuchum quem dedisti**] cf. *And.* prol. 3, note.

12] As the text stands *virg'nem* is pronounced dissyllable, *quăm hĕrae* anapaest. This hiatus is doubtless rare: it does not occur in Vergil, but Lucretius employs it in one or two passages; and Gossrau in his Excursus de Hexametro Virgilii quotes Lucan, I. 231, *Vicinumque minax invadit Ariminum. Ignes...* Lachmann on Lucr. VI. 106 (*quae memorare quĕam inter se sing'lariter aptam*) wishes to transpose our passage thus, *Virginem herae quam—* a suggestion adopted by Parry. L. objects to the introduction of an apostrophe in the middle of words and between two consonants as "barbarus scribendi mos ab Anglis ante annos plus CC inventus," and "contractio Latinis auribus intolerabilis." But a licence so congenial to the tendency of all languages to "phonetic decay," recognized moreover and stereotyped in such Latin forms as *vinclum, circlus, hercle,* need scarcely alarm us into forced alteration, especially in the language of comedy, representing the careless pronunciation of everyday life. In this passage of Lucretius Munro retains the contracted *sing'lariter.*

Do. Au obsecro, mea Pythias, quod istuc nam monstrum fuit?

PH. Insanis: qui istuc facere eunuchus potuit? PY. Ego
      illum nescio   15

qui fuerit; hoc quod fecit, res ipsa indicat:

virgo ipsa lacrumat, neque quum rogites, quid sit audet dicere.

Ille autem bonus vir nusquam apparet. Etiam hoc misera
      suspicor,

aliquid domo abeuntem abstulisse. PH. Nequeo mirari satis,

quo ille abire ignavos possit longius: nisi si domum (661) 20

iorte ad nos rediit. PY. Vise amabo, num sit. PH. Iam
      faxo scies.

Do. Perii, obsecro tam infandum facinus, mea tu, ne audivi
      quidem.

PY. At pol ego amatores mulierum esse audieram eos max-
      umos,

sed nihil potesse: verum miserae non in mentem venerat:

nam illum aliquo conclusissem, neque illi commisissem vir-
      ginem.   25

ACTUS IV. SCENA IV.

PHAEDRIA. DORUS. PYTHIAS. DORIAS.

PH. Exi foras, sceleste: at etiam restitas,

fugitive? Prodi, male conciliate. DOR. Obsecro! PH. Oh,

17 **quum rogites**] "any time you ask her," ὅταν ἔρῃ: cf. Munro on Lucr. II. 41: and infra, V. I. 12.

24 **potesse**] the old form (=*potis esse*, as *possum*=*potis sum*), common in Plautus and Lucretius (e. g. I. 665, II. 215).

Sc. IV.] Phaedria comes back with Dorus, whom of course Pythias cannot identify. By cross-questioning Dorus, he finds out the whole story of Chaerea's misde-

meanour: but makes him deny it all, so as to leave Pythias and Dorias on a false scent. Metre: 1—35, iambic trimeter; 36—59, trochaic tetrameter catalectic.

1 **etiam**] "still;" see note to *And*. I. I. 89.

2 **male conciliate**] "you bad bargain." *Conciliare*="to buy" (i.e. to "win over," and so "procure"); cf. Plaut. *Pseud.* I. 2. 1, *ignavi, male habiti, et male conciliati. Male*

illuc vide, os ut sibi distorsit carnufex.

Quid huc tibi reditiost? quid vestis mutatio?   (670)

Quid narras? Paulum si cessassem, Pythias,   5

domi non offendissem, ita iam ornarat fugam.

Py. Habesne hominem, amabo? Ph. Quidni habeam? Py.

    Factum bene.

Do. Istuc pol vero bene. Py. Ubi est? Ph. Rogitas? Non

    vides?

Py. Videam? obsecro, quem? Ph. Hunc scilicet. Py. Quis

    hic est homo?

Ph. Qui ad vos deductus hodiest. Py. Hunc oculis suis   10

nostrarum numquam quisquam vidit, Phaedria.

Ph. Non vidit? Py. An tu hunc credidisti esse, obsecro,

ad nos deductum?   Ph. Namque alium habui neminem.

    Py. Au,

nec comparandus hic quidem ad illumst. Ille erat   (680)

honesta facie et liberali. Ph. Ita visus est   15

dudum, quia varia veste exornatus fuit:

nunc eo videtur foedus, quia illam non habet.

Py. Tace obsecro: quasi vero paulum intersiet.

Ad nos deductus hodie est adulescentulus,

quem tu videre vero velles, Phaedria.   20

Hic est vietus, vetus, veternosus, senex, ·

= badly, and so dearly bought; cf. Cic. *Att.* II. 4, *mihi placet ea, quae male empta sunt, reddi:* and for the opposite phrase, Cic. *Att.* XII. 23, *bene emitur quod necesse est,* i.e. is cheaply bought. Cf. also the French expressions "bon marché," "mal marché."

4] "What's the meaning of your return here?"

8 Istuc pol vero bene] "Aye, marry, very well" (Colman). Dorias ironically echoes Phaedria's *factum bene.*

11 quisquam] cf. II. 3. 83.

14 comparandus ad illum] cf.

II. 3. 70. This not very common use of *ad* in comparison (cf. supra, II. 3. 69: Cic. *Tusc.* I. 17, *Terram...ad universi caeli complexum quasi puncti instar*) arises from its use to imply juxtaposition, *ad limina,* &c., and is analogous to the use of παρά = in comparison with, i.e. "side by side with."

16 dudum] "but now," see note to III. 1. 58.

21 vietus] "a shrivelled up, drowsy old fellow, with a weasel's complexion." Donatus explains it as = "mollis, flaccidus, flexibilis; unde et *vimina,* et *vites,* et *vimenta:*"

colore mustelino. PH. Hem, quae haec est fabula?

Eo rediges me, ut, quid egerim, egomet nesciam.

Eho tu, emin' ego te? DOR. Emisti. PY. Iube mi
      denuo   :   (690)

respondeat. PH. Roga. PY. Venisti hodie ad nos? Negat.

At ille alter venit annos natus sedecim :   26

quem secum adduxit Parmeno. PH. Agedum hoc mi expedi

primum : istam quam habes, unde habes vestem? Taces?

Monstrum hominis, non dicturu's? DOR. Venit Chaerea.

PH. Fraterne? DOR. Ita. PH. Quando? DOR. Hodie. PH.
      Quam dudum? DOR. Modo.   30

PH. Quicum? DOR. Cum Parmenone. PH. Norasne eum
      prius?

DOR. Non; nec, quis esset, unquam audieram dicier.

PH. Unde igitur fratrem meum esse scibas? DOR. Parmeno

dicebat eum esse. Is mihi hanc dedit. PH. Occidi. (700)

DOR. Meam ipse induit: post una ambo abierunt foras. 35

PY. Iam satis credis sobriam esse me, et nil mentitam tibi?

Iam satis certumst virginem vitiatam esse? PH. Age nunc,
      belua,

credis huic quod dicat? PY. Quid isti credam? Res ipsa
      indicat.

PH. Concede istuc paululum. Audin'? Etiam nunc paulum:
      sat est.

Dicdum hoc rursum, Chaerea tuam vestem detraxit tibi? 40

---

and he quotes Lucretius, *vietam vestem* (III. 385), of the spider's "flimsy
web," i. e. "putri mollitia praedi-
tam." A "thin" dried-up look is
probably implied.

22 colore mustelino] Menander αὐτὸς ἐστὶ γαλεώτης γέρων, which,
Donatus argues, must have been
misunderstood by Terence, who
should have translated γαλεώτης by
stellio, "a lizard." MSS. unanimous-
ly give *mustelino*. Bentley alters
to *stelionino*.

23 egerim] MSS. Bentley *eme-
rim* from the supposed imitation by
Cicero (*Att.* I. 19. 4), *ille alter ita
nihil est, ut plane quid emerit, nesciat.*
For the sense, *egerim* is preferable.
"You will actually make me forget
what I have done," i.e. about send-
ing this eunuch.

27 Agedum] cf. *dicdum*, inf. v.
40. *adesdum, And.* I. 1. 2.

Dor. Factum. Ph. Et eam est indutus? Dor. Factum.
  Ph. Et pro te huc deductust? Dor. Ita.

Ph. Iuppiter magne, o scelestum atque audacem hominem.
  Py. Vae mihi:

etiam nunc credis indignis nos esse inrisas modis?

Ph. Mirum ni tu credas, quod iste dicat. Quid agam nescio.

Heus negato rursus. Possumne ego hodie ex te exsculpere

verum? Vidistine fratrem Chaeream? Dor. Non. Ph. Non
  potest   46

sine malo fateri, video: sequere hac: modo ait, modo negat.

Ora me. Dor. Obsecro te vero, Phaedria. Ph. I intro
  nunc iam !

Dor. Oi ei. Ph. Alio pacto honeste quomodo hinc abeam
  nescio;

actumst siquidem. Tu me hic etiam, nebulo, ludificabere?

Py. Parmenonis tam scio esse hanc technam, quam me
  vivere.   51

Do. Sic est. Py. Inveniam pol hodie, parem ubi referam
  gratiam.

Sed nunc quid faciendum censes, Dorias? Do. De istac
  rogas

virgine? Py. Ita, utrum taceamne an praedicem? Do. Pol,
  si sapis,   (720)

---

45 **Heus negato rursus**] "Mind you say no this time:" an aside to Dorus.

54 **utrum taceamne an**] The apparent redundancy of interrogatives utrum ne is not sufficiently explained by reference to the form utrumne, in which the interrogative particle ne is added to utrum, as to other interrogative words (e.g. quone? Hor. S. II. 3. 295, uterne? II. 2. 107, quantane? II. 3. 317). Parry's explanation that "utrum is here used as a pronoun followed by a disjunctive question," indicates the truth; the fact being that we have here the origin of the familiar use of utrum as an interrogative adverb. Utrum faciam? taceamne, an praedicem? is the full construction; this in ordinary usage becomes compressed, first by omission of faciam (as in the passage before us), secondly, (the original construction of utrum being then forgotten) by regarding utrum ne as two interrogative adverbs one of which is superfluous, and making utrum an the ordinary form of a disjunctive interrogation. The form utrumne must have come into use after this recognition of utrum as an adverb,

quod scis, nescis, neque de eunucho, neque de vitio virginis.
Hac re et te omni turba evolves, et illi gratum feceris.
Id modo dic, abisse Dorum.   Py. Ita faciam.   Do. Sed
    videon' Chremen?
Thais iam aderit.   Py. Quid ita?   Do. Quia, quum inde
    abeo, iam tum inceperat
turba inter eos.   Py. Tu aufer aurum hoc: ego scibo ex
    hoc, quid siet.   59

ACTUS IV.   SCENA V.

Chremes. Pythias.

Ch. Attat data hercle verba mihi sunt: vicit vinum quod
    bibi.
Ac dum accubabam, quam videbar mihi esse pulchre so-
    brius!
Postquam surrexi, neque pes neque mens satis suum officium
    facit.
Py. Chreme.   Ch. Quis est?   Ehem Pythias: vah, quanto
    nunc formosior
videre mihi, quam dudum!   Py. Certe tu quidem pol multo
    hilarior.   (730) 5
Ch. Verbum hercle hoc verum erit, Sine Cerere et Libero
    friget Venus.

---

and cannot therefore be referred to in explanation of the idiom before us. A majority of passages which illustrate the use of *utrum* followed by *ne—an* are from Plautus and Terence, which seem to bear out the view that this is the earliest idiom; and Greek πότερον is in many ways analogous.

Sc. v.] Enter Chremes, some-what the worse for his convivial party, and tells them that Thais is coming. Metre: iambic trimeter.

1 **data verba**] cf. *And.* I. 3. 6; *Eun.* Prol. 24. "Oh dear, I *have* been taken in: the wine I drank has been too much for me. Yet while I was at supper, how beauti-fully sober I thought I was."

5 **dudum**] cf. III. 1. 58, note.

Sed Thais multo [me] antevenit? Py. Anne abiit iam a
    milite?

Ch. Iamdudum: aetatem. Lites factae sunt inter eos max-
    umae.

Py. Nihil dixit, ut sequerere sese? Ch. Nihil, nisi abiens
    mi innuit.

Py. Eho, nonne id sat erat? Ch. At nescibam id dicere
    illam, nisi quia   10

correxit miles, quod intellexi minus: nam me extrusit foras.

Sed eccam ipsam: miror ubi ego huic antevorterim.

ACTUS IV. SCENA VI.

Thais. Chremes. Pythias.

Th. Credo equidem illum iam adfuturum esse, ut illam a me
    eripiat; sine veniat.

Atqui si illam digito attigerit uno, oculi illico effodientur.

Usque adeo ego illius ferre possum ineptiam et magnifica
    verba,   (740)

verba dum sint: verum enim si ad rem conferentur, vapu-
    labit.

Ch. Thais, ego iam dudum hic adsum. Th. O mi Chremes,
    te ipsum expectabam.   5

Scin' tu, turbam hanc propter te esse factam? et adeo ad te
    adtinere hanc

---

8 **Iamdudum**] here in its ordinary sense of "long ago," not as
III. 1. 58.

aetatem] a conversational idiom,
similar to our "an age," common
in Plaut. and Ter. (cf. *Hec.* V. 1. 19);
cf. Lucr. VI. 236, *quod solis vapor
aetatem non posse videtur.*

Sc. VI.] Thais returns from
Thraso's house expecting him to
come and carry off Pamphila by

force; and telling Chremes that
Pamphila is his sister, asks him to
help her to resist Thraso. He is
sorely tempted to run away, but
agrees to stay.

Metre: 1—8, 10, trochaic tetrameter: 11, 13, 14, 17—32, trochaic tetram. catalectic: 9, troch.
dimeter catalectic: 12, iamb. tetram.: 13, 16, iamb. tetram. catal.

omnem rem? Сн. Ad me? qui quæso istuc? Тн. Quia,
'　　　dum tibi sororem studeo
reddere ac restituere, haec atque huiusmodi sum multa passa.
Сн. Ubi east? Тн. Domi apud me. Сн. Hem. Тн. Quid
　　　est?　　　　　　　　　　　　.
Educta ita, uti teque illaque dignumst. Сн. Quid ais? Тн.
　　　Id quod res est.　　.　　　　　　　　10
Hanc tibi dono do, neque repeto pro illa quicquam abs te
　　　preti.
Сн. Et habetur et referetur, Thais, ita uti merita es, gratia.
Тн. At enim cave, ne prius, quam hanc a me accipias, amittas,
　　　Chreme:　　　　　　　　　　　(750)
nam haec east, quam miles a me vi nunc ereptum venit
Abi tu, cistellam, Pythias, domo effer cum monumentis. 15
Сн. Viden' tu illum, Thais? Py. Ubi sitast? Тн. In risco:
　　　Odiosa, cessas?
Сн. Militem secum ad te quantas copias adducere?
Attat. Тн. Num formidulosus obsecro es, mi homo? Сн.
　　　Apage sis.
Egon' formidulosus? Nemost hominum, qui vivat, minus.
Тн. Atque ita opust. Сн. Ah metuo, qualem tu me esse
　　　hominem existumes.　　　　　　　　20
Тн. Immo hoc cogitato: quicum res tibi est, peregrinus est:
minus potens, quam tu, minus notus, minus amicorum hic
　　　habens.
Сн. Scio istuc. Sed, tu quod cavere possis, stultum admit-
　　　terest.　　　　　　　　　　　(760)

15 cistellam] a small casket or trinket box. The "Cistellaria" of Plautus derives its name from, the "Rudens" turns upon the discovery of, a similar casket. *monumenta* need not be only "trinkets," which were often placed on children when they were exposed (*crepundia*), but any token that might lead to recognition, dress or ornaments (*signa* below, v. 19). Pamphila, indeed, had not been exposed as an infant, but kidnapped by robbers.

16] Chremes becomes very nervous at the approach of Thraso. Pythias puts in a blundering question about the *cistella*.

21 peregrinus] As a foreigner, Thraso will be at disadvantage if they go to law.

Malo ego nos prospicere, quam hunc ulcisci accepta iniuria.

Tu abi: atque obsera ostium intus, dum ego hinc transcurro
    ad forum: 25

volo ego adesse hic advocatos nobis in turba hac. TH.
    Mane.

CH. Melius est. TH. Mane. CH. Omitte, iam adero. TH.
    Nil opus est istis, Chreme.

Hoc modo dic, sororem illam tuam esse: et te parvam
    virginem

amisisse: nunc cognosse. Signa ostende. PY. Adsunt. TH.
    Cape.

Si vim faciet, in ius ducito hominem: intellextin'? CH. Probe.

TH. Fac animo haec praesenti dicas. CH. Faciam. TH.
    Attolle pallium.   31

Perii, huic ipsi est opus patrono, quem defensorem paro.

ACTUS IV. SCENA VII.

THRASO. GNATHO. SANGA. CHREMES. THAIS.

THR. Hancine ego ut contumeliam tam insignem in me ac-
    cipiam, Gnatho?   (770)

Mori me satiust. Simalio, Donax, Syrisce, sequimini.

Primum aedes expugnabo. GN. Recte. THR. Virginem
    eripiam. GN. Probe.

THR. Male mulcabo ipsam. GN. Pulchre. THR. In medium
    huc agmen cum vecti, Donax;

26 **advocatos**] cf. II. 3. 48, note.
31 **Attolle pallium**] "Tuck up your cloak."
32 "The champion I have got wants help himself."
Sc. VII.] Thraso appears with his followers to besiege the house of Thais in military fashion. At a parley he demands Pamphila, whom

Chremes claims as his sister and an Athenian citizen. Thraso holds a council of war and retires, expecting Thais to capitulate.
Metre: 1—17, iambic tetrameter; 18—46, trochaic tetram. catalectic.
1 **Hancine ut accipiam**] an elliptical expression = *suadesne ut accipiam?*

tu, Simalio, in sinistrum cornu; tu, Syrisce, in dexterum.   5
Cedo alios : ubi centuriost Sanga, et manipulus furum? SA.
    Eccum adest.
THR. Quid, ignave? peniculon' pugnare, qui istum huc portes,
    cogitas?
SA. Egone? Imperatoris virtutem noveram, et vim militum :
sine sanguine hoc fieri non posse : qui abstergerem voinera.
THR. Ubi alii? SA. Qui, malum, alii? Solus Sannio servat
    domi.   10
THR. Tu hosce instrue : ego ero post principia : inde omni-
    bus signum dabo.   (780)
GN. Illuc est sapere : ut hosce instruxit, ipsus sibi cavit
    loco.
THR. Idem hoc iam Pyrrhus factitavit. CH. Viden' tu, Thais,
    quam hic rem agit?
Nimirum consilium illud rectumst de occludendis aedibus.
TH. Sane, qui tibi nunc vir videtur esse, hic nebulo mag-
    nus est :   15
ne metuas. THR. Quid videtur? GN. Fundam tibi nunc
    nimis vellem dari,
ut tu illos procul hinc ex occulto caederes : facerent fugam.
THR. Sed eccam Thaidem ipsam video. GN. Quam mox
    inruimus? THR. Mane ;
omnia prius experiri quam armis sapientem decet.

9 qui] ablat. "I brought it to wipe our wounds with."

10 malum] an interjection. "What the plague do you mean by '*others*'?"

servat] "keeps at home." The use of *servare* = "keep close to," and so "inhabit" is familiar in Vergil, G. IV. 383, Aen. II. 579, &c., and Plautus uses it, as here, without case : *servare apud me, Cist.* I. I. 107.

11 post principia] i.e. in the rearmost line, that of the Triarii, behind the Principes: see Smith, *Dict. Ant.* "Army." This position was naturally most convenient for running away; and as such is chosen by Thraso.

16] Gnatho suggests that it would be safer to sling the enemy than attack at close quarters.

18 Quam mox inruimus?] "How soon are we to rush in?" Cf. III. 2. 39, note.

19 armis] the reading of all MSS. except one (Codex Academicus, from whose *armis sapientem* Bentley corrects *arma*), is strictly "ablativus instrumenti" = to make trial by

Qui scis an, quae iubeam, sine vi faciat? GN. Di vostram
    fidem,   20

quanti est sapere! Numquam accedo, quin abs te abeam
    doctior.   (790)

THR. Thais, primum hoc mihi responde: quum tibi do istam
    virginem,

dixtin' hos mihi dies soli dare te? TH. Quid tum postea?

THR. Rogitas? quae mi ante oculos coram amatorem ad-
    duxti tuum:

quid cum illoc agas? et cum eo clam te subduxti mihi. 25

TH. Lubuit. THR. Pamphilam ergo huc redde, nisi si mavis
    eripi.

CH. Tibi illam reddat, aut tu illam tangas? omnium! GN.
    Ah quid agis? Tace.

THR. Quid tu tibi vis? Ego non tangam meam? CH. Tuam
    autem, furcifer?

GN. Cave sis: nescis cui maledicas nunc viro. CH. Non tu
    hinc abis?

Scin' tu ut tibi res se habeat? Si quicquam hodie hic turbae
    coeperis,   30

faciam ut huius loci dieique meique semper memineris.

GN. Miseret tui me, qui hunc tantum hominem facias inimi-
    cum tibi.   (801)

means of arms, as in phrase *legibus experiri*.

22 quum do] "On my giving you that maiden." The object is merely to allude to the actual moment of giving as connected with the promise (dixti, &c.) not to bring out the fact of its having taken place in past time; and it is accordingly represented more vividly by the use of the present tense. Cf. Verg. *Aen.* II. 275, *Quantum mutatus ab illo Hectore qui redit exuvias indutus Achilli,* i.e. *redeunte;* IX. 266, *cratera antiquum, quem dat Sidonia Dido*="the gift of." Cf. Gossrau to *Aen.* IV.

228.

23 dare] "that you would give;" cf. *And.* II. 3. 5, *Si tu negaris ducere.* After *spero, promitto,* &c., the present (or in this case imperf.) infin. is sometimes used where the future is more usual. Similar Greek verbs are followed by fut. or aor. infin.: and so in English, "I hope to do:" "I promise to do."

27 omnium] cf. *And.* V. 3. 1.

31] This line occurs almost verbatim, Plaut. *Capt.* IV. 2. 21—probably as a common form of threat, like "I'll make him rue the day," &c.

CH. Diminuam ego caput tuum hodie, nisi abis.   GN. Ain'
    vero, canis?
Sicine agis?   THR. Quis tu homo es? quid tibi vis? quid
    . cum illa rei tibi est?
CH. Scibis: principio . eam esse dico liberam.   THR. Hem.
    CH. Civem Atticam.   THR. Hui.   35
CH. Meam sororem.   THR. Os durum.   CH. Miles, nunc
    adeo edico tibi,
ne vim facias ullam in illam.   Thais, ego eo ad Sophronam
nutricem, ut·eam adducam, et signa ostendam haec.   THR.
    Tun' me prohibeas,
meam ne tangam?   CH. Prohibebo inquam.   GN. Audin' tu?
    hic furti se adligat:
satis hoc tibi est?   THR. Idem hoc tu ais?   TH. Quaere qui
    respondeat.   40
THR. Quid nunc agimus?   GN. Quin redimus: iam haec tibi
    aderit supplicans   (810)
ultro.   THR. Credin'?   GN. Immo certe: novi ingenium
    mulierum:
nolunt ubi velis: ubi nolis, cupiunt ultro.   THR. Bene putas.
GN. Iam dimitto exercitum?   THR. Ubi vis.   GN. Sanga, ita
    ut fortis decet
milites, domi focique fac vicissim ut memineris.   45
SA. Iamdudum animus est in patinis.   GN. Frugi es.   THR.
    Vos me hac sequimini.

<hr>

39 **furti se adligat**] convicts himself of theft. The genitive case as
in *reus criminis, damnatus voti,* &c.:
cf. Plaut. *Poen.* III. 4. 27, *homo
furti se adstringet.*

41 **Quin redimus**] cf. *And.* II. 2.
9, note.

43 **cupiunt ultro**] "They per-
versely desire;" cf. *And.* I. 1. 73,
note.

45 **domi focique**] *Domi* at first
sight, in this connection, appears to
be a genitive case, and is so explained by most commentators. If
so it would support the view that
the forms *domi, humi,* &c., are examples of the genitive which, according to old grammarians, was employed in words of first and second
declension only to express locality
("place at which"), expressed in all
other words by the ablative. This
grammatical absurdity is, however,
rejected by modern scholars (see.

ACTUS V. SCENA I.

THAIS. PYTHIAS.

TH. Pergin', scelesta, mecum perplexe loqui?
Scio, nescio, abiit, audivi, ego non adfui.
Non tu istuc mihi dictura aperte es, quicquid est?
Virgo conscissa veste lacrumans obticet;
eunuchus abiit: quamobrem? quid factumst? Taces?   5
PY. Quid tibi ego dicam misera? Illum eunuchum ne-
    gant   (821)
fuisse. TH. Quis fuit igitur? PY. Iste Chaerea.
TH. Qui Chaerea? PY. Iste ephebus, frater Phaedriae.
TH. Quid ais, venefica? PY. Atqui certo comperi.
TH. Quid is obsecro ad nos? quamobrem adductust? PY.
    Nescio: 10
nisi amasse credo Pamphilam. TH. Hem, misera occidi,
infelix, si quidem tu istaec vera praedicas.

Max Müller, Lect. on Science of Language, 1st Ser. VI. p. 207). *Domi, humi, Romae, Tarenti* are classed with *ruri* and *noctu* (which exclude the supposition of a genitive case), either (1) as remnants of an obsolete *locative* case, or (2) as *datives* (cf. the pronominal adverbs *ibi, ubi*—unquestionably the early dative form preserved in *sibi, tibi,* and dat. plural *-bus* of 3, 4, and 5 decl.). The functions of the Sanskrit *locative* were in Latin originally (as in Greek) discharged by the *dative* case: the *ablative* however (resembling it in form, and undistinguishable in plural) gradually encroached upon this usage, till in Classical Latin it was the regular case of "locality."
What then of *domi focique* in this passage? *Domi bellique, domi et*

militiae (all locative datives) were common phrases = "at home and abroad." In rapid conversation it might easily be, and no doubt often was, forgotten that these words were not genitive cases: so Gnatho here treats them as such, substituting the genitive case *foci* and making both depend on *memineris.* To insist that *domi* here must be a genitive case, is to force unduly upon easy conversational idiom the canons of strict grammatical accuracy.
Act V. Scene 1.] Thais attacks Pythias about what has happened at her house, and learns that Chaerea was the pseudo-eunuch. He is now seen coming, still in the eunuch's clothes.
Metre: iambic trimeter.

Num id lacrumat virgo? Py. Id opinor. Th. Quid ais,
    sacrilega?
Istucine interminata sum hinc abiens tibi?
Py. Quid facerem? Ita ut tu iusti soli creditast. (830) 15
Th. Scelesta ovem lupo commisisti. Dispudet,
sic mihi data esse verba. Quid illuc hominis est?
Py. Hera mea, tace, tace obsecro, salvae sumus:
habemus hominem ipsum. Th. Ubi is est? Py. Hem ad
    sinisteram.
Viden'? Th. Video. Py. Comprendi iube, quantum potest.
Th. Quid illo faciemus, stulta? Py. Quid facias, rogas? 21
Vide amabo, si non, quum aspicias, os impudens
videtur. Th. Non est. Py. Tum quae eius confidentiast!

ACTUS V. SCENA II.

CHAEREA. THAIS. PYTHIAS.

Ch. Apud Antiphonem uterque, mater et pater,
quasi dedita opera, domi erant, ut nullo modo   (840)
introire possem, quin viderent me. Interim
dum ante ostium sto, notus mihi quidam obviam
venit. Ubi vidi, ego me in pedes quantum queo   5

---

14 **interminata sum**] "I strictly charged."

16 **ovem lupo**] a common proverb. καταλείπειν ὄιν ἐν λύκοισι,
Hdt. IV. 149. *Ut mavelis lupos apud
oves linquere quam hos domi cus-
todes*, Plaut. *Pseud.* I. 2. 8. *O prae-
clarum custodem ovium, ut aiunt,
lupum*, Cic. *Phil.* II. 11. 27. "A
wolf in sheep's clothing," "a wolf
in the fold," are similar proverbial
expressions; and the idea is expanded in the familiar story of "Little
Red Riding-hood."

17 **data verba**] cf. *And.* I. 3. 6

note.
Quid hominis] cf. supra III. 4. 8.
21 **illo**] "with him;" cf. *And.*
III. 5. 8.
22 **amabo**] cf. I. 2. 50 note.
Sc. II.] Chaerea excuses himself
to Thais, and on hearing her
schemes about Pamphila engages
to put all right by marrying the
girl.
Metre: iambic trimeter.
2 **dedita opera**] "on purpose,"
ἐκ προνοίας.
5 **ego me in pedes**] sc. "do"
or *conicio, Phorm.* I. 4. 13.

in angiportum quoddam desertum ; inde item

in aliud, inde in aliud : ita miserrumus

fui fugitando, ne quis me cognosceret.

Sed estne haec Thais, quam video? Ipsast.   Haereo.

Quid faciam?   Quid mea autem?   Quid faciet mihi?   10

TH. Adeamus.   Bone vir Dore, salve : dic mihi,

aufugistin'?   CH. Hera, factum.   TH. Satin' id tibi placet?

CH. Non.   TH. Credin' te inpune habiturum?   CH. Unam

          hanc noxiam   (851)

amitte : si aliam admisero unquam, occidito.

TH. Num meam saevitiam veritus es?   CH. Non.   TH. Quid

          igitur?   15

CH. Hanc metui, ne me criminaretur tibi.

TH. Quid feceras?   CH. Paulum quiddam.   PY. Eho pau-

          lum, inpudens !

an paulum hoc esse tibi videtur, virginem

vitiare civem?   CH. Conservam esse credidi.

PY. Conservam?   Vix me contineo, quin involem in   20

capillum.   Monstrum etiam ultro derisum advenit.

TH. Abin' hinc, insana?   PY. Quid ita vero? debeam,

credo, isti quicquam furcifero, si id fecerim :   (861)

praesertim quom se servum fateatur tuum?

TH. Missa haec faciamus.   Non te dignum, Chaerea,   25

---

6 **angiportum**] "an alley," in
Ad. IV. 2. 39, of a "cul-de-sac."
   9 **Haereo**] "I am in a fix."
   11] Thais pretends to take Chaerea for her slave, Dorus.
   13 **inpune habiturum**] so *male
bene habere*, like Greek εὖ, κακῶς
ἔχειν.
   21 **ultro**] here=*insuper*, over
and above (see note to *And.* I. I.
73). The wretch comes to insult
us over and above what he has
done, "adds insult to injury."
   22 **Quid ita vero**] sc. abeam.
"And why so, pray! It's little
I should have to answer for, to that

gallows bird, supposing me to have
done it," i.e. whatever I did to him,
he did more to answer for to us.
"*debere* paenas dicimus ei cui iniuriam fecerimus," Donatus: so
Verg. *Aen.* XI. 51, *nil iam caelesti-
bus ullis Debentem*, of a dead man,
whose account with heaven is thereby closed; Soph. *Ajax*, 589, 590,
and Jebb's note ad loc.
   23 **quicquam**] "anything at all."
The ironical tone of the words
makes it practically = "nothing ;"
cf. *And.* II. 6. 3.
   si id fecerim] *si involaverim in
capillum*, v. 20.

fecisti: nam si ego digna hac contumelia
sum maxume, at tu indignus qui faceres tamen.
Neque edepol, quid nunc consili capiam scio
de virgine istac: ita conturbasti mihi
rationes omnes, ut eam non possim suis,   30
ita ut aequum fuerat atque ut studui, tradere:
ut solidum parerem hoc mihi beneficium, Chaerea.   (870)
CH. At nunc dehinc spero aeternam inter nos gratiam
fore, Thais. Saepe ex huiusmodi re quapiam et
malo principio magna familiaritas   35
conflatast. Quid si hoc quispiam voluit deus?
TH. Equidem pol in eam partem accipioque et volo.
CH. Immo ita quaeso. Unum hoc scito: contumeliae
non me fecisse causa, sed amoris. TH. Scio.
Et pol propterea magis nunc ignosco tibi.   40
Non adeo inhumano ingenio sum, Chaerea,
neque ita inperita, ut, quid amor valeat, nesciam.   (880)
CH. Te quoque iam, Thais, ita me di bene ament, amo.
PY. Tum pol tibi ab istoc, hera, cavendum intellego.
CH. Non ausim. PY. Nil tibi quicquam credo. TH. Desinas.
CH. Nunc ego te in hac re mi oro ut adiutrix sies;   46
ego me tuae commendo et committo fidei:
te mihi patronam capio, Thais: te obsecro:
emoriar, si non hanc uxorem duxero.
TH. Tamen si pater quid... CH. Ah volet, certo scio: 50
civis modo haec sit. TH. Paululum opperirier
si vis, iam frater ipse hic aderit virginis;   (890)
nutricem arcessitum iit, quae illam aluit parvolam:

---

29 **conturbasti rationes**] "You
have thrown all my plans into confusion." There is no allusion to
the technical phrase *conturbare rationes* of bankrupts.

32 **solidum**] real, substantial;

cf. *And.* IV. I. 23, *solidum gaudium,*
and note.

41 **inhumano**] "unfeeling," so
humani ingeni, And. I. I. 86; and
homo inhumanissumus, Phorm. III.
2. 34.

in cognoscendo tute ipse aderis, Chaerea.

Сн. Ego vero maneo.   Тн. Visne interea, dum venit,   55
domi opperiamur potius, quam hic ante ostium?

Сн. Immo percupio.   Py. Quam tu rem actura, obsecro, es?

Тн. Nam quid ita?   Py. Rogitas?   Hunc tu in aedes co-
          gitas

recipere posthac?   Тн. Cur non?   Py. Crede hoc meae
          fidei,

dabit hic pugnam aliquam denuo.   Тн. Au, tace obsecro.

Py. Parum perspexisse eius videre audaciam.   61

Сн. Non faciam, Pythias.   Py. Non pol credo, Chaerea,

nisi si commissum non erit.   Сн. Quin, Pythias,   (901)

tu me servato.   Py. Neque pol servandum tibi

quicquam dare ausim, neque te servare.   Apage te.   65

Тн. Adest optume ipse frater.   Сн. Perii hercle! obsecro

abeamus intro, Thais : nolo me in via

cum hac veste videat.   Тн. Quamobrem tandem? an quia
          pudet?

Сн. Id ipsum.   Py. Id ipsum?   Virgo vero.   Тн. I prae,
          sequor.

Tu istic mane, ut Chremem introducas, Pythias.   70

54 in cognoscendo] at the recognition.

57 Immo percupio] "Amatorie:
non *volo* sed *percupio*," Donatus.
Immo as usual corrects a previous

statement ; and so expresses generally either denial, or substitution of
a different expression.

63 Quin servato] cf. *And.* I. I.
18 note.

ACTUS V. SCENA III.

PYTHIAS. CHREMES. SOPHRONA.

Py. Quid? quid venire in mentem nunc possit mihi?

quidnam, qui referam sacrilego illi gratiam,　　　　(910)

qui hunc supposuit nobis? CH. Move vero ocius

te, nutrix. So. Moveo. CH. Video, sed nihil promoves.

Py. Iamne ostendisti signa nutrici? CH. Omnia.　　　5

Py. Amabo, quid ait? cognoscitne? CH. Ac memoriter.

Py. Bene edepol narras: nam illi faveo virgini.

Ite intro; iamdudum hera vos exspectat domi.

Virum bonum eccum Parmenonem incedere

video: vide ut otiosus it, si dis placet.　　　　　10

Spero me habere, qui hunc meo excruciem modo.

Ibo intro, de cognitione ut certum sciam:　　　　(920)

post exibo, atque hunc perterrebo sacrilegum.

Sc. III.] Chremes and Sophrona come with the news that Pamphila has been recognised as Chremes' sister. Pythias shews them in, intending to come out again and have it out with Parmeno.

Metre: iambic trimeter.

2 qui] is ablative = *quo*. What can I think of, to pay off...; cf. *And.* Prol. 6.

3 supposuit] The MS. reading makes the scansion difficult: we must then admit the hiatus *qui hûnc*. Bentley's correction *supposivit* certainly removes this difficulty, and is perhaps justified by *deposivit exposivit* in Plautus, *deposivit* Catull. 34. 8.

9 incedere] of an easy, dignified walk, Verg. *Aen.* I. 46.

10 vide ut otiosus it] "See how leisurely he's coming." *Vide* (or *viden'*) *ut, aspice ut* &c., are often used with indicative, where Latin usage would seem to demand sub-

junctive mood. They become stereotyped rhetorical expressions, not necessarily appealing to the intelligence of any second person; cf. Verg. *Ecl.* IV. 52, *Aspice venturo laetantur ut omnia saeclo:* and Conington's note; *G.* I. 57: *Aen.* VI. 780: Ov. *Her.* IX. 9. 86. *Quis scit an* (= *fortasse*) *haec saevas tigridas insula habet?*

si dis placet] An indignant, ironical expression; cf. *Ad.* III. 4. 30. We use "if you please," "as you please," in much the same way; cf. Thackeray's Ballads,

"They carried the news to King Louis;

He heard it as calm as you please,

And like a majestical monarch

Sat filing his locks and his keys."

11 meo modo] "after my own fashion," i.e. as much as I please; cf. *And.* I. 1. 129.

12 cognitione] in this passage, and

ACTUS V. SCENA IV.

Parmeno. Pythias.

PA. Reviso, quidnam Chaerea hic rerum gerat.
Quod si astu rem tractavit, di vostram fidem,
quantam et quam veram laudem capiet Parmeno!
Nam ut mittam, quod ei amorem difficillumum et
carissumum, a meretrice avara virginem   5
quam amabat, eam confeci sine molestia,
sine sumptu, sine dispendio: tum hoc alterum,
id verost quod ego mihi puto palmarium
me reperisse, quomodo adulescentulus   (930)

Eun. v. 3. 12, is used for the more common *agnitio*, i.e. the recognition of the true relations of characters in a drama in which the denouement so often consists. Aristotle (*De Poet.* 11.) employs the corresponding Greek term ἀναγνώρισις for the denouement of a story: it is, he says, ἐξ ἀγνοίας εἰς γνῶσιν μεταβολὴ ἢ εἰς φιλίαν ἢ εἰς ἔχθραν. He instances the mutual recognition of Iphigenia and Orestes in Euripides' *Iphigenia in Tauris.*

Sc. IV.] Parmeno congratulates himself on the double service he has rendered to Chaerea in enabling him to attain the object of his love and to see these meretrices in their true and less attractive light. He is interrupted by Pythias, lamenting Chaerea's fate, viz. the punishment for outrage on an Athenian citizen. Parmeno sees no help for it, but to tell his old master Laches, the father of Chaerea and Phaedria.

Metre: 1—20, iamb. trim.; 21—48, troch. tetram. catalectic.

4—6] The words *a meretrice avara virginem, quam amabat*, are thrown in as an explanation of

amorem diff. et car., and the sentence finishes upon this new tack, *virginem* being resumed in *eam* and *confeci*, which refers properly to *amorem*, being transferred less appropriately to what has been inserted in explanation. Translate: "To say nothing of this, that I accomplished for him a love affair of great difficulty and expense, viz. getting a maiden whom he loved out of the clutches of an avaricious courtesan—without trouble, loss or expense."

5 carissumum] might = "which he had most at heart," in which case it would be explained by *quam amabat.*

Various emendations have been proposed : *in amorem—conieci*, Klette: *carissimum a meretrice avara virginem quo amabat eum confeci*, Bentley: *amore difficillimo carissimo*, Wagner, with more probability, for AMORE DIFFICILLVMO (abl.) and AMORĒ DIFFICILLVMŌ (acc.) might easily be confused in copying. But let us retain MS. reading, so long as sense can be extracted from it.

meretricum ingenia et mores posset noscere,   10
mature ut quum cognorit, perpetuo oderit.
Quae dum foris sunt, nihil videtur mundius,
nec magis compositum quicquam, nec magis elegans,
quae, cum amatore suo quum cenant, ligurriunt.
Harum videre inluviem, sordes, inopiam,   15
quam inhonestae solae sint domi atque avidae cibi,
quo pacto ex iure hesterno panem atrum vorent,
nosse omnia haec saluti est adulescentulis.

Py. Ego pol te pro istis dictis et factis, scelus,   (940)
ulciscar; ut ne impune in nos inluseris.   20
Pro deum fidem, facinus foedum! o infelicem adulescentulum!
o scelestum Parmenonem, qui istum huc adduxit. Pa. Quid
      est?

Py. Miseret me: itaque ut ne viderem, misera huc effugi foras,
quae futura exempla dicunt in eum indigna. Pa. O Iuppiter
quae illaec turbast? Numnam ego perii? Adibo. Quid
      istuc, Pythias?   25
Quid ais? in quem exempla fient? Py. Rogitas, audacissume?
Perdidisti istum quem adduxti pro eunucho adulescentulum,
dum studes dare verba nobis. Pa. Quid ita? aut quid fac-
      tumst? cedo.

Py. Dicam: virginem istam, Thaidi hodie quae dono datast,
scis eam hinc civem esse? et fratrem eius esse adprime
      nobilem?   (951) 30
Pa. Nescio. Py. Atqui sic inventast: eam iste vitiavit miser.
Ille ubi rescivit factum frater violentissumus, . . .
Pa. Quidnam fecit? Py. Conligavit primum eum miseris modis.
Pa. Conligavit? Py. Atque equidem orante, ut ne id faceret,
      Thaide.

14] Bentley pronounces this v.
spurious, unmetrical, and interrupt-
ing the construction. Weisse's text
omits *suo*, which removes the metrical difficulty.
20 ut ne] cf. *And.* I. I. 34 note.
34 **equidem orante**] The common derivation of *equidem* = *ego*

Pᴀ. Quid ais? Pʏ. Nunc minatur porro sese id quod moe-
  chis solet: 35
quod ego nunquam vidi fieri, neque velim. Pᴀ. Qua audacia
tantum facinus audet? Pʏ. Quid ita tantum? Pᴀ. An non
  hoc maxumumst?
Quis homo pro moecho umquam vidit in domo meretricia
prendi quemquam? Pʏ. Nescio. Pᴀ. At ne hoc nesciatis,
  Pythias,   (960)
dico, edico vobis, nostrum esse illum herilem filium. Pʏ.
  Hem,   40
obsecro an is est? Pᴀ. Ne quam in illum Thais vim fieri sinat.
Atque adeo autem cur non egomet intro eo? Pʏ. Vide,
  Parmeno,
quid agas, ne neque illi prosis, et tu pereas: nam hoc putant,
quicquid factumst, a te esse ortum. Pᴀ. Quid igitur faciam
  miser?   44
quidve incipiam? Ecce autem video rure redeuntem senem:
dicam huic, an non dicam? Dicam hercle: etsi mihi magnum malum
scio paratum: sed necesse est, huic ut subveniat. Pʏ. Sapis.
Ego abeo intro: tu isti narra omne ordine, ut factum siet.

---

quidem (the 1st syllable becoming shortened by usage as in *ěcastor= per aedem Castoris*) is disproved by this and other passages where the word could not stand for *ego quidem*, e.g. Persius I. 110, *Per me equidem sint omnia protinus alba;* V. 45, Non *equidem hoc dubites;* and Prop. III. 23. 5, Hic *equidem Phoebo visus mihi pulcrior ipso. Equidem=quidem;* cf. *enim, nam,* and in Greek

ἐκεῖνος, κεῖνος, ἐθέλω, θέλω. The prefix of an initial short vowel is also seen in such words as ὀμφα-λος = o-ϝδφαλος, Sanskrit "*nâbhi,*" our "navel:" ὄ-νομα, Skt. *nâman,* Lat. *nomen:* and in the Homeric ἐέρση, ἐείκοσι, κ.τ.λ.

43 **neque prosis et**] Lest instead of (or "so far from") doing him good, you come to harm yourself; cf. the similar force of οὔτε—τε in Greek.

ACTUS V.   SCENA V.

LACHES.   PARMENO.

LA. Ex meo propinquo rure hoc capio commodi: (970)
neque agri neque urbis odium me umquam percipit.
Ubi satias coepit fieri, commuto locum.
Sed estne ille noster Parmeno?   Et certe ipsus est.
Quem praestolare, Parmeno, hic ante ostium?   5
PA. Quis homost?   Ehem, salvom te advenire, here, gaudeo.
LA. Quem praestolare?   PA. Perii: lingua haeret metu.
      LA. Hem,
quid est quod trepidas?   Satin' salve?   dic mihi.
PA. Here, primum te arbitrari, quod res est, velim:
quicquid huius factumst, culpa non factumst mea.   10
LA. Quid?   PA. Recte sane interrogasti.   Oportuit   (980)
rem praenarrasse me.   Emit quendam Phaedria
eunuchum, quem dono huic daret.   LA. Cui?   PA. Thaidi.
LA. Emit? perii hercle.   Quanti?   PA. Viginti minis.
LA. Actumst.   PA. Tum quandam fidicinam amat hinc
      Chaerea.   15
LA. Hem, quid?   amat?   An iam scit ille, quid meretrix siet?
an in astu venit?   Aliud ex alio malum.

Sc. V.] Laches, as Parmeno in the preceding scene, is introduced in a state of tranquillity, that the sudden revulsion of feeling may be more entertaining; one of the minor περιπέτειαι (Arist. *Poet.* II.) which give additional life to the representation. Parmeno, frightened at what Pythias has said, tells him the whole story, and off he goes to Chaerea's rescue.

Metre: iambic trimeter.

2 **percipit**]="seizes"—its original sense; cf. Lucr. III. 80, *vitae Percipit humanos odium lucisque videndae*"—a passage which also illus-trates *odium*="weariness;" cf. III. 1.4.

3 **satias**]=satietas; cf. *Hec.* IV. 2. 18, Lucr. V. 1391, "*Cum satiate cibi.*"

8 **Satine salve?**] sc. est. *salve* adverb: so Donatus explains it by *integre*. Lindemann on Plaut. *Trin.* V. 3. 2, would read *satin' salvae*, sc. *res*: but *salva res est* is the common usage, *Ad.* IV. 5. 9: Plaut. *Capt.* II. 2. 34.

10 **huius**] cf. I. 2. 122 suprm.

17 **in astu**] to the city, i.e. to Athens, from Piraeus. The Athenians commonly spoke of their city as τὸ ἄστυ.

PA. Here, ne me spectes: me inpulsore haec non facit.
LA. Omitte de te dicere. Ego te, furcifer,
si vivo. Sed istuc quicquid est, primum expedi.   20
PA. Is pro illo eunucho ad Thaidem deductus est.   (990)
LA. Pro eunuchon'? PA. Sic est. Hunc pro moecho postea
comprehendere intus et constrinxere. LA. Occidi.
PA. Audaciam meretricum specta. LA. Numquid est
aliud mali damnive, quod non dixeris,   25
reliquom? PA. Tantum est. LA. Cesso huc introrumpere?
PA. Non dubium est quin mihi magnum ex hac re sit malum:
nisi quia necessus fuit hoc facere. Id gaudeo,
propter me hisce aliquid esse eventurum mali:
nam iamdiu aliquam causam quaerebat senex,   30
quamobrem insigne aliquid faceret iis: nunc repperit.

ACTUS V. SCENA VI.

PYTHIAS. PARMENO.

PY. Numquam edepol quicquam iamdiu quod magis vellem
        evenire   (1001)
mi evenit, quam quod modo senex intro ad nos venit errans.

---

26 **Tantum est**] "That's all."
Tantus, like τοσοῦτος, has this "li-
miting" sense, "just so much," and so
almost = "too little." Caes. *B. G.* VI.
35.9, *praesidii tantum est, ut ne murus
quidem cingi, possit.* Cf. the favourite
exp. of Herodotus, τοσαῦτα περὶ τού-
του εἰρήσθω.
28 **necessus**] Bembine MS. so in
Heaut. II. 3. 119. Donatus in his
note recognises the form *necessus* as
parallel to *necesse* and *necessum:* and
Plautus has *necessust, necessumst, necesse est.* The form *necesus* occurs
in the decree concerning the Bac-
chanalia, *sei ques esent quei sibei dei-
cerent necesus ese bacanal habere,* and
we find *vis magna necessis* in Lucr.

VI. 815. The latter is of course
a genitive; and Lachmann would
make *necesus* also the same case,
comparing the forms *nominus La-
tini* and *senatuos (o for u* because of
previous *u)* in the same decree. But
necessis may well be from a nominative *necessis.* parallel to *necessus* and
necessum, as *exanimis* to *exanimus,* of
which *necesse* will be the neuter. See
Corssen, *Krit. Nachträge,* p. 272.
Sc. VI.] Pythias tells Parmeno
what a fool she has made of him,
and that Laches and Chaerea are
vowing vengeance on him. He
blusters, but with an uneasy presen-
timent that he will get into trouble.
Metre: iambic tetram. catal.

Mihi 'solae ridiculo fuit, quae quid timeret scibam.

PA. Quid hoc autemst? PY. Nunc id prodeo ut conveniam
    Parmenonem.

Sed ubi obsecro est? PA. Me quaerit haec. PY. Atque
    eccum video: adibo.   5

PA. Quid est, inepta? Quid tibi vis? quid rides? Pergin'?
    PY. Perii:

defessa iam sum misera te ridendo. PA. Quid ita? PY.
    Rogitas?

Numquam pol hominem stultiorem vidi, nec videbo. Ah,

non possum satis narrare quos ludos praebueris intus.

At etiam primo callidum et disertum credidi hominem.   10

Quid? illicone credere ea quae dixi, oportuit te?   (1011)

An poenitebat flagitii, te auctore quod fecisset

adulescens, ni miserum insuper etiam patri indicares?

Nam quid illi credis animi tum fuisse, ubi vestem vidit

illam esse eum indutum pater? Quid? iam scis te perisse?

PA. Hem quid dixisti, pessuma? An mentita es? Etiam
    rides?   16

Itan' lepidum tibi visum est, scelus, nos inridere? PY.
    Nimium.

PA. Siquidem istuc inpune habueris. PY. Verum. PA. Red-
    dam hercle. PY. Credo.

Sed in diem istuc, Parmeno, est fortasse, quod minare.

---

3 solae] dat. fem. of *solus;* cf. *alterae, Heaut.* II. 3. 30; *Phorm.* v. 8. 35, and frequent in Plautus. In later classical Latin such variations from the gen. and dat. in *ius* and *i, solus, ille, alius,* &c., are very rare. Madvig (37. obs. 2) quotes alii generis (Varro), *aliae pecudis* (Cicero), *nullo usui* (Caesar).

4 id] adverbial accus. "on that account."

9 ludos praebueris] cf. *And.* III. 1. 21 n.

10 disertum] seems to mean "shrewd," "cunning;" though not elsewhere in this sense.

11 illico] "then and there;" cf. *Ad.* II. 1. 2 note.

12 An poenitebat] "Were you *not content* with"—a meaning found only in Plautus and Terence, and in Cicero's letters; whence we may infer it was a conversational idiom. Cic. *Ep. ad Fam.* I. 7, *Meae fortunae ne nimium poeniteret, tuâ virtute perfectum est.* Parry quotes from *Att.* I. 20. 2.

19] "But that threat of yours is

Tu iam pendebis, qui stultum adulescentulum nobilitas   20
flagitiis, et patri indicas : uterque exempla in te edent. (1021)
PA. Nullus sum. PY. Hic pro illo munere tibi honos est
      habitus : abeo.
PA. Egomet meo indicio miser, quasi sorex, hodie perii.

.

ACTUS V. SCENA VII.

GNATHO. THRASO.

GN. Quid nunc?   qua spe, aut quo consilio huc imus?
      Quid coeptas, Thraso?
TH. Egone?   ut Thaidi me dedam, et faciam quod iubeat.
      GN. Quid est?
TH. Qui minus quam Hercules servivit Omphalae?   GN.
      Exemplum placet.
Utinam tibi commitigari videam sandalio caput.
Sed fores crepuerunt ab ea. TH. Perii. Quid hoc autemst
      mali?   5
Hunc ego numquam videram etiam : quidnam hic properans
      prosilit?

adjourned for some time."   *In diem*
=to some day or other; cf. *Phorm.*
v. 2. 16, not as in the phrase *in diem
vivere*, to live from day to day, i.e.
for each particular day only, careless
of the future.

   20 **iam pendebis**] "You'll be
strung up at once," i.e. to a post for
whipping: cf. *Phorm.* I. 4. 43.
   23] "I have been a fool indeed;
      and, like a rat,
Betrayed myself to-day by my own
      sqneaking."—COLMAN.
   Sc. VII.] Thraso comes to sur-
render to Thais as a second Hercules

to Omphale.
   Metre: trochaic tetrameter catalectic.
   4] "O that I might see your head
well pounded with a slipper.". Plautus, *M. G.* v. 5. 31, *mitis sum fusti-
bus.* Lucian speaks of Hercules as
παιόμενος ὑπὸ τῆι Ὀμφάλης τῷ σαν-
δαλίῳ: and there may have been
some comedy at Athens, familiar to
readers of Menander, in which some
such scene was represented.   One
commentator remarks, *Erant usita-
ta mulierum arma ungues et sandalia.*
   6 **etiam**] "as yet."

ACTUS V. SCENA VIII.

CHAEREA. PARMENO. PHAEDRIA. GNATHO. THRASO.

CH. O populares, ecquis me vivit hodie fortunatior? (1030)
Nemo hercle quisquam: nam in me plane di potestatem
    suam
omnem ostendere: cui tam subito tot congruerint commoda.
PA. Quid hic laetus est? CH. O Parmeno mi, o mearum
    voluptatum omnium   4
inventor, inceptor, perfector, scin' me in quibus sim gaudiis?
Scis Pamphilam meam inventam civem? PA. Audivi. CH.
    Scis sponsam mihi?
PA. Bene, ita me di ament, factum. GN. Audin' tu, hic quid
    ait? CH. Tum autem Phaedriae
meo fratri gaudeo esse amorem omnem in tranquillo: unast
    domus.
Thais patri se commendavit: in clientelam et fidem   9
nobis dedit se. PA. Fratris igitur Thais totast. CH. Scilicet.
PA. Iam hoc aliud est, quod gaudeamus: miles pelletur foras.

Sc. VIII.] Chaerea comes from Thais' house in great joy, and thanks Parmeno (to P.'s great astonishment) for the cause of his and Phaedria's happiness, telling how everything is settled with regard to Pamphila and Thais. Thraso, in despair, asks Gnatho to get him one more chance of seeing Thais, which Gnatho undertakes on condition of perpetual dinners; at the same time persuading the young man to remain friends with Thraso, who gives good dinners and is quite harmless.

Metre: 1, 20—64, troch. tetram. catal.: 2—19, iamb. tetram.

1 **me vivit hodie**] Bentley, on authority of English MSS., transposes thus, *me hodie vivit.* The line (troch. tetram. catal.) then runs, *O*

popu\lares | ecquis | me hodie | vivit | fortu\nati\or. With the order of the text *me vivit* must stand for a trochee, *vivit* being pronounced monosyll.—a harsh contraction, but cf. *And.* I. 1. 25.

8 **in tranquillo**] *tranquillum* = "a calm" in Cicero and best writers, and often used metaphorically as here: cf. Livy, III. 14, *nec cetera modo tribuni tranquillo peregere.* Cf. *in vado, And.* V. 2. 24.

9 **in clientelam et fidem**] She has put herself under our patronage and protection; cf. *And.* V. 4. 21, *clientela* the relation of client to patronus; cf. *Dict. Ant.* s. v. *cliens.* Tacitus uses it = a body of dependents: so modern French *clientèle.*

Cн. Tu frater ubi ubi est fac quam primum haec audiat.
Pa. Visam domum.   (1041)

Tн. Numquid, Gnatho, tu dubitas quin ego nunc perpetuo
perierim?

Gn. Sine dubio opinor.   Cн. Quid commemorem primum,
aut laudem maxume?

illumne qui mihi dedit concilium ut facerem, an me, qui
ausus siem   15

incipere; an fortunam conlaudem, quae gubernatrix fuit;

quae tot res, tantas, tam opportune in unam conclusit diem:

an mei patris festivitatem et facilitatem? O Iuppiter,

serva obsecro haec bona nobis.   Pн. Di vostram fidem, in-
credibilia

Parmeno modo quae narravit. Sed ubi est frater? Cн.
Praesto adest.   20

Pн. Gaudeo.   Cн. Satis credo. Nihil est Thaide hac, frater, tua   (1050)

dignius quod ametur: ita nostrae omni est fautrix familiae.

Pн. mihi illam laudas?   Tн. Perii, quanto minus spei est,
tanto magis amo.

Obsecro, Gnatho, in te spes est.   Gn. Quid vis faciam?
Tн. Perfice hoc

precibus, pretio, ut haeream in parte aliqua tandem apud
Thaidem.   25

Gn. Difficile est.   Tн. Si quid conlibuit, novi te. Hoc si
effeceris,

quodvis donum praemio a me optato, id optatum feres.

---

13 tu] only occurs in Bembine MSS.; but it is necessary for metre.

23 mihi] is emphatic: no need to praise her to *me*, who know her so well.

25 precibus pretio] "by hook or by crook;" cf. II. 3. 28. Wagner instances German *für Geld und gute Worte*.

in parte] this use of *pars=locus* apparently comes from its sense in the phrase *partes agere* or *suscipere*; cf. *supra*, I. 2. 71.

tandem]="after all;" cf. *Phormio*, IV. 4. 20: and Lucr. III. 793, *ipsa animi vis...soleret tandem in eodem homine atque in eodem vase manere*.

Gn. Itane? Th. Sic erit. Gn. Si efficio hoc, postulo ut
mihi tua domus
te praesente absente pateat; invocato ut sit locus
semper. Th. Do fidem futurum. Gn. Accingar. Ph. Quem
ego hic audio?   30
O Thraso. Th. Salvete. Ph. Tu fortasse quae facta hic sient
nescis. Th. Scio. Ph. Cur te ergo in his ego conspicor
regionibus?   (1061)
Th. Vobis fretus. Ph. Scin' quam fretus? Miles, edico tibi,
si te in platea offendero hac post umquam: quod dicas mihi:
alium quaerebam, iter hac habui: periisti. Gn. Heia, haud
sic decet.   35
Ph. Dictumst. Gn. Non cognosco vostrum tam superbum.
Ph. Sic erit.
Gn. Prius audite paucis: quod quum dixero, si placuerit,
facitote. Ph. Audiamus. Gn. Tu concede paulum istuc,
Thraso.
Principio ego vos credere ambos hoc mi vehementer velim
me huius quicquid facio, id facere maxume causa mea: 40
verum si idem vobis prodest, vos non facere inscitiast.
Ph. Quid id est? Gn. Militem ego rivalem recipiundum
censeo. Ph. Hem.   (1071)

29 **invocato, &c.**] "that there
may always be a place for me (at
your table) whether I'm asked or
not." Cf. the opening scene of
Plaut. *Captivi*, where Ergasilus the
parasite explains his nickname.

34 **quod dicas**] although you say;
cf. *Ad.* II. 1. 8.

35 **periisti**] "It's all up with you."
Perii! "I am undone," has practically
the force of a present tense: used
here in preference to the future, it
expresses the certainty of the consequence. Cf. the Greek use of *pro-
phetic present*.

36] I don't recognise these haughty
manners as yours—*morem* is understood; cf. *And.* IV. 5. 22.

37 **audite paucis**] see *And.* III.
3. 4.

40 **huius**] cf. I. 2. 122.

42] "I think you should admit the
Captain as your rival." *Rivalis* is
only found in this place of Terence
(cf. II. 2. 37; II. 3. 62). Its derivation is familiar.

42—46] "Nay, consider: you are
living freely with her, Phaedria;
feasting, I may say, to your heart's
content. You have little to give:
and Thais ought to get a great deal,
to be able to devote herself to you
without causing you expense."

In v. 44 the first *et* seems unnecessary. Bentley conj. *ut*, [*et enim—
victitas* a parenthesis] "As you

Cн. Recipiundum? Gn. Cogita modo: tu hercle cum illa,
          Phaedria,

et libenter vivis, et enim bene libenter victitas.   44

Quod des paullumst; et necesse est multum accipere Thaidem,

ut tuo amori suppeditare possit, sine sumptu tuo.

Ad omnia haec magis opportunus, nec magis ex usu tuo

nemo est. Principio et habet quod det, et dat nemo largius.

Fatuus est, insulsus, tardus, stertit noctes et dies.

Neque istum metuas ne amet mulier : facile pellas ubi velis.

Cн. Quid agimus? Gn. Praeterea hoc etiam, quod ego vel
          primum puto,   (1080) 51

accipit homo nemo melius prorsus neque prolixius.

Cн. Mirum ni illoc homine quoquo pacto opust. Pн. Idem
          ego arbitror.

Gn. Recte facitis. Unum etiam hoc vos oro, ut me in vos-
          trum gregem

live extravagantly, she ought to receive more, &c." But we may suppose that Gnatho begins what is intended to be two alternatives ("You both live expensively, and —"), but then he can only repeat the first a little more strongly. Can there be a play upon the double meaning of *libenter?*—"You would freely (i.e. gladly) live with her, but you always live very freely." (*Libenter* "at your will" and so "extravagantly.") I cannot find this explanation hinted at, and therefore confine myself to suggesting it.

46 **suppeditare**] is neuter = "to be sufficient for." Some make *supped. possit* impersonal—"that there may be an abundant supply for your love."

49] "A fool, a dolt, a block, that snores out night and day." Colman. Munro on *Lucr.* III. 1048, *et vigilans stertis*, quotes this passage, which he regards as one among many indications that Lucretius was familiar with this play ; cf. v. 1. 28: I. 2. 95 : v. 5. 2 and notes.

52 **accipit**] "entertains," receives as a guest, frequent in Plautus; cf. Hor. *Sat.* II. 8. 67, *Tene ego ut accipias laute torquerier omni Sollicitudine districtum;* Verg. *Aen.* VIII. 75. Ov. *Fast.* II. 725, *Socios dapibusque meroque Accipit;* Cic. *Att.* XVI. 7, *nec potui accipi, illo praesertim absente, liberalius.* Cf. also *Ad.* II. I. 12, *indignis acceptus modis,* where it appears in an ironical sense like our "treat."

prolixius] "more liberally, abundantly:" *prolixus* is probably connected with *laxus, lassus* (though Varro gives *prolicere = proliquere,* "to flow forth," as the derivation), participial forms whose fundamental notion is "stretched out" (cf. *lentus*), and which root is the same as that of *langueo, longus,* Greek λαγαρός, λάγγος. Hence it = literally "stretched out far" (cf. *Heaut.* II. 3. 49, *capillus prolixus*), and so "distant," *prolixo ictu,* Lucr. IV. 1248. Other meanings "favourable," "obliging," are found in Cicero: our "prolix" and "comprehensive"

recipiatis : satis diu iam hoc saxum volvo. PH. Recipimus.

CH. Ac libenter.   GN. At ego pro isto, Phaedria,. et tu

Chaerea,   56

hunc comedendum et deridendum vobis propino. CH. Placet.

PH. Dignus est.   GN. Thraso, ubi vis accede. TH. Obsecro

te, quid agimus?

GN. Quid? isti te ignorabant : postquam eis mores ostendi

tuos,

et conlaudavi secundum facta et virtutes tuas,   60

impetravi. TH. Bene fecisti. Gratiam habeo maxumam.

Nunquam etiam fui usquam, quin me omnes amarent plu-

rumum.   (1091)

GN. Dixin' ego in hoc esse vobis Atticam elegentiam?

PH. Nil praeter promissum est. Ite hac. Ω vos valete, et

plaudite.

only in later writers, e.g. Gellius and Macrobius.

55 saxum volvo] Greek λίθον κυλινδεῖν = "to labour in vain," a proverb, borrowed from the fable of Sisyphus, Hom. *Od.* XI. 595, ἤτοι ὁ μὲν σκηριπτόμενος χερσίν τε ποσίν τε λᾶαν ἄνω ὤθεσκε ποτὶ λόφον· ἀλλ' ὅτε μέλλοι Ἄκρον ὑπερβαλέειν, τότ' ἀποστρέψασκε κραταιΐς. Αὖτις ἔπειτα πέδονδε κυλίνδετο λᾶας ἀναιδής.

57] "I hand him on to you to be eaten out of house and home, and made your butt."

propinare poculum] Greek προπίνειν φιάλαν = to taste a cup and pass it on to another, to drink a cup to his health, as e.g. Dido at the feast. *Dixit et in mensam laticum libavit honorem, Primaque, libato, summo tenus attigit ore: Tum Bitiae dedit,* Verg. *Aen.* I. 736. This custom, familiar to the days of mediaeval chivalry, survives in the "grace-cup" of city and collegiate entertainments. From this *propino*, like προπίνω (vid. Liddell and Scott, s.v.) passed into the sense of "give away"

—so Ennius apud Non., *Enni poeta salve, qui mortalibus Versus propinas flammeos medullitus.*

deridendum] Bentley reads *ebibendum,* quoting Nonius s.v. *propinare;* Terentius, *Eunuch., Hunc vobis comedendum et bibendum et deridendum propino.* Bentley asks "Qualis propinatio ubi nulla *potus* est mentio?" but the secondary senses of *propino* are well established: for example see Forcellini. *Qualis utilitas in stulto homine deridendo?* he also asks : but to laugh at a fool like Thraso, however unprofitable, is surely most natural. *Comedendum atque ebibendum* would no doubt make very good sense : but there is no sufficient reason for deserting MS. authority in this case.

63 Atticam elegantiam] "True Attic taste ;" cf. III. I. 18 note.

64 Ω plaudite] *And.* v. 6. 17 note.

With the close of the *Eunuchus* a critic, quoted by Colman, remarks : "I cannot think that this play concludes consistently with the manners of gentlemen : there is a meanness in

TER.   II

Phaedria and Chaerea consenting to take Thraso into their society with a view of fleecing him, which the poet should have avoided." This criticism, to be worth anything, should be extended to the beginning, middle, and end of this and every other play borrowed from the later Athenian comedy; the whole moral tone of which, and of the degenerate and corrupt civilization reflected by it, is inconsistent "with the manners of gentlemen," in any true sense of that word. The "meanness" here complained of is only too well in keeping with the tissue of triumphant cunning, fraud, and immorality, which renders this and other plays of Terence, however valuable for the artistic skill of the "situations" and their treasures of pure Latinity, valueless for moral ends and barren of ennobling principle.

CAMBRIDGE: PRINTED BY C. J. CLAY, M.A. AT THE UNIVERSITY PRESS.

CATENA CLASSICORUM,

A SERIES OF CLASSICAL AUTHORS,

EDITED BY MEMBERS OF BOTH UNIVERSITIES UNDER
THE DIRECTION OF

THE REV. ARTHUR HOLMES, M.A.

FELLOW OF CLARE COLLEGE, CAMBRIDGE, AND LATE FELLOW OF ST JOHN'S COLLEGE,
PREACHER AT THE CHAPEL ROYAL, WHITEHALL.

AND

THE REV. CHARLES BIGG, M.A.

LATE SENIOR STUDENT AND TUTOR OF CHRIST CHURCH, OXFORD,
SECOND CLASSICAL MASTER OF CHELTENHAM COLLEGE.

The following Parts have been already published:—

SOPHOCLIS TRAGOEDIAE,

Edited by R. C. JEBB, M.A. Fellow and Assistant Tutor of Trinity College,
Cambridge, and Public Orator of the University.
[Part I. The Electra. 3s. 6d.   Part II. The Ajax. 3s. 6d.

JUVENALIS SATIRAE,

Edited by G. A. SIMCOX, M.A. Fellow and Classical Lecturer of Queen's
College, Oxford.   [Thirteen Satires. 3s. 6d.

THUCYDIDIS HISTORIA,

Edited by CHARLES BIGG, M.A. late Senior Student and Tutor of Christ
Church, Oxford. Second Classical Master of Cheltenham College.
[Vol. I. Books I. and II. with Introductions. 6s.

DEMOSTHENIS ORATIONES PUBLICAE,

Edited by G. H. HESLOP, M.A. late Fellow and Assistant Tutor of Queen's
College, Oxford. Head Master of St Bees.
[Parts I. & II. The Olynthiacs and the Philippics. 4s. 6d.

ARISTOPHANIS COMOEDIAE,

Edited by W. C. GREEN, M.A. late Fellow of King's College, Cambridge.
Classical Lecturer at Queens' College.
[Part I. The Acharnians and the Knights. 4s.
[Part II. The Clouds. 3s. 6d.
[Part III. The Wasps. 3s. 6d.

ISOCRATIS ORATIONES,

Edited by JOHN EDWIN SANDYS, B.A. Fellow and Tutor of St John's
College.
[Part I. Ad Demonicum et Panegyricus. 4s. 6d.

CATENA CLASSICORUM—(Continued).

A. PERSII FLACCI SATIRARUM LIBER,

Edited by A. Pretor, M.A. of Trinity College, Cambridge, Classical Lecturer of Trinity Hall. 3s. 6d.

HOMERI ILIAS,

Edited by S. H. Reynolds, M.A. Fellow and Tutor of Brasenose College, Oxford. [Vol. I. Books I. to XII. 6s.

TERENTI COMOEDIAE,

Edited by T. L. Papillon, M.A. Fellow of New College, Oxford, late Fellow and Tutor of Merton. [Part I. Andria et Eunuchus.

The following Parts are in course of Preparation:—

PLATONIS PHAEDO,

Edited by Alfred Barry, D.D. late Fellow of Trinity College, Cambridge; Principal of King's College, London.

DEMOSTHENIS ORATIONES PUBLICAE,

Edited by G. H. Heslop, M.A. late Fellow and Assistant Tutor of Queen's College, Oxford; Head Master of St Bees.
[Part III. De Falsâ Legatione.

MARTIALIS EPIGRAMMATA,

Edited by George Butler, M.A. Principal of Liverpool College; late Fellow of Exeter College, Oxford.

DEMOSTHENIS ORATIONES PRIVATAE,

Edited by Arthur Holmes, M.A. Fellow and Lecturer of Clare College, Cambridge. [Part I. De Coronâ.

HORATI OPERA,

Edited by J. M. Marshall, M.A. Fellow and late Lecturer of Brasenose College, Oxford; one of the Masters in Clifton College.

HERODOTI HISTORIA,

Edited by H. G. Woods, M.A. Fellow and Tutor of Trinity College, Oxford.

TACITI HISTORIAE,

Edited by W. H. Simcox, M.A. Fellow and Lecturer of Queen's College, Oxford.

OVIDI TRISTIA,

Edited by Oscar Browning, M.A. Fellow of King's College, Cambridge; and Assistant Master at Eton College.

CICERONIS ORATIONES,

Edited by Charles Edward Graves, M.A. Classical Lecturer and late Fellow of St John's College, Cambridge.
[Part I. Pro P. Sextio.

RIVINGTONS: LONDON, OXFORD, AND CAMBRIDGE.

3, WATERLOO PLACE, PALL MALL,
July, 1872.

𝔅ooks for 𝔖chools and ℭolleges

PUBLISHED BY

MESSRS. RIVINGTON

LATIN

Henry's First Latin Book.

By Thomas Kerohever Arnold, M.A.
Twenty-first Edition. 12mo. 3*s*. Tutor's Key, 1*s*.

A Second Latin Book, and Practical

Grammar ; intended as a Sequel to Henry's First Latin Book.
By Thomas Kerohever Arnold, M.A.
Tenth Edition. 12mo. 4*s*. Tutor's Key, 2*s*.

A Practical Introduction to Latin

Prose Composition. Part I.
By Thomas Kerchever Arnold, M.A.
Sixteenth Edition. 8vo. 6*s*. 6*d*. Tutor's Key, 1*s*. 6*d*.

Historiæ Antiquæ Epitome.

From Cornelius Nepos, Justin, &c. With English Notes, Rules
for Construing, Questions, and Geographical Lists.
By Thomas Kerchever Arnold, M.A.
Eighth Edition. 12mo. 4*s*.

LONDON, OXFORD, AND CAMBRIDGE

B

Cornelius Nepos.

Part I. With Critical Questions and Answers, and an Imitative Exercise on each Chapter.

By **Thomas Kerchever Arnold**, M.A.

Fifth Edition. 12mo. 4*s.*

Latin Prose Exercises.

Being easy graduated English Sentences for translation into Latin, with Rules, Vocabulary, &c. For the use of Beginners and Junior Forms of Schools.

By **R. Prowde Smith**, B.A., Assistant Master at the Grammar School, Henley-on-Thames.

Crown 8vo. 2*s.* 6*d.*

This book can be used with or without the Public Schools Latin Primer.

(See Specimen Page No. 1.)

" Most teachers will admit that boys experience difficulty in elementary Latin composition in a great measure from not understanding the structure of their own language. They commence Latin at an early age, without any knowledge of English Grammar, for it is assumed that this will grow upon them during their study of Latin, and yet no elementary exercise book at present in use seems to recognize this deficiency. . . . Now it appears that a great deal of trouble and vexation might be saved even to a clever boy, if his observation were directed aright from the beginning. If he be made to parse his English sentences before turning them into Latin, he will soon perceive that certain fixed principles pervade both languages, and he will be pleased to find that, in his practical knowledge of his mother tongue, he already possesses an unsuspected fund of information, which will enable him to master any language to which he turns his attention. . . . . . The object, then, of this book is to teach Latin composition and English Grammar simultaneously, and it is believed that the beginner will find the acquisition of the former much easier, when he finds he is approaching it through routes which turn out on inspection to be already familiar to him. The system indicated above has been tested for several years, and has always been found to work successfully."—*From the Preface.*

A First Verse Book.

Being an Easy Introduction to the Mechanism of the Latin Hexameter and Pentameter.

By **Thomas Kerchever Arnold**, M.A.

Ninth Edition. 12mo. 2*s.* Tutor's Key, 1*s.*

Progressive Exercises in Latin Elegiac Verse.

By **C. G. Gepp**, B.A., late Junior Student of Christ Church, Oxford ; Assistant Master at Tonbridge School.

Second Edition.   Crown 8vo.   3s. 6d.   Tutor's Key, 5s.

(*See Specimen Page No.* 2.)

" Mr. Gepp has brought together two hundred passages from English Poets as a series of ' Progressive Exercises in Latin Elegiac Verse,' supplementing each passage with so many hints as a school-boy will be the better for having, and adding copious instructions and Indices. The selection is well made, and the Notes appear to be judicious."—*Examiner.*

" A very carefully prepared book, and will be useful to those who still find that time devoted to the making of Latin Verse is not time wasted. A lad of taste, with an average Latin Vocabulary at command, and with an average reading of the poets, should, after a course of these Exercises, occupying but a moderate time, become a respectable writer of Elegiacs."—*Standard.*

" Now that the absurdity of making all boys, however unfitted by nature, write Latin Verses is universally admitted, there is a danger of falling into the opposite error of supposing that the exercise can be of no use to any. The comparatively few who, besides being able to read Latin poetry intelligently, have a taste for versification, may derive both advantage and pleasure from it, and could not have a better guide to direct them than Mr. Gepp, who cautions them against the faults to which they are liable, and furnishes them with such aids as will prevent them from being baffled by the difficulties of the task, without, however, relieving them from the necessity of mental exertion. The English poetry to be turned into Latin Verse is accompanied by a Prose Paraphrase as a stepping-stone, with suggestive Notes and References. After having gone through such a judicious preparation as this, the student may fairly calculate on success."—*Athenæum.*

" A well planned and skilfully worked out little book, giving many choice passages from our familiar English poetry, with a Prose version cast into a mould suggestive to the versemaker."—*Daily Telegraph.*

" There would probably be a less fierce set against a study, which is simply delightful to those who have mastered it, had reformers and reviewers had so pleasant a manual as Mr. Gepp's to begin with. Fearful to discourage pupils on the threshold, he has contrived to get all the cautions, hints on poetic ornament and licence, and preliminary aids to versification into about a dozen pages, and then divided the body of his book into two parts ; the first consisting of pieces of English Verse and song for translation into Latin Verse, the task being simplified by the addition of a Prose paraphrase of each passage, and by collateral hints and references ; the second composed of more difficult pieces, to the mastery of which gradually less help is vouchsafed, to the intent that the versifier may by degrees learn to run alone. . . . . We shall be glad if our brief notice of this book leads to its introduction into Preparatory Schools." — *Illustrated Review.*

Classical Examination Papers.

Edited, with Notes and References, by **P. J. F. Gantillon**, M.A., sometime Scholar of St. John's College, Cambridge ; Classical Master in Cheltenham College.

Crown 8vo. 7s. 6d.
Or interleaved with writing-paper, half-bound, 10s. 6d.

(*See Specimen Page No. 3.*)

" If any of our readers have classical pupils they will find this a most serviceable volume, alike for their own and for their pupils' use. The papers are mostly Cambridge or Oxford scholarship papers, and they are most carefully edited and annotated, so as to make their use as easy and as profitable as possible. The papers chosen are of the very highest order, and we can only say that such a help would have been invaluable to ourselves when engaged in such work as to require it."—*Literary Churchman.*

" 'The papers are well selected, and are fairly representative of the principal classical examinations of the present day."—*Athenæum.*

" All who have had anything to do with examinations, especially as examinees, will recognize the utility of a well-selected and well-edited collection of examination papers. It is a sort of scholastic chart, and marks the rocks and quicksands on which carelessness or ignorance may suffer shipwreck. Mr. Gantillon's book is a judicious collection of papers. His notes convey information in cases where it is not easily accessible, and where it is, mention the sources at which it may be found. In the notes to the philosophical papers, he takes frequent opportunities of stating concisely the opinions of the ancient philosophers, and of referring to the writings of their more modern successors."—*Scotsman.*

Eclogæ Ovidianæ.

With English Notes. Part I. ; from the Elegiac Poems.
By **Thomas Kerchever Arnold**, M.A.

Twelfth Edition. 12mo. 2s. 6d.

M. T. Ciceronis de Officiis Libri Tres.

With Introduction, Analysis, and Commentary.

Edited for the Syndics of the University Press, Cambridge. By the Rev. **Hubert Holden**, LL.D., Head Master of Ipswich School, late Fellow and Classical Lecturer of Trinity College, Cambridge, Classical Examiner to the University of London.

Second Edition. Crown 8vo. 7s. 6d.

Materials and Models for Greek and
Latin Prose Composition.

Selected and arranged by **J. Y. Sargent, M.A.,** Tutor, late
Fellow of Magdalen College, Oxford ; and **T. F. Dallin, M.A.,**
Fellow and Tutor of Queen's College, Oxford.

Crown 8vo.   7s. 6d.

(*See Specimen Page No. 4.*)

"The idea on which this volume is constructed is a very good one. Passages from English authors have been put together (taken for the most part from Oxford examination papers). At the end of each, reference is made to one or more passages of the great Greek and Latin prose writers, in which there is some similarity of thought or subject. . . . There could not be a better conception of what is intended by good composition in the classical language, and the authors have given both teachers and learners a most excellent help for realizing it in this volume."—*Spectator.*

"A manual certainly differing both in design and execution from Holden's 'Foliorum Centuriæ,' or Mr. Frost's 'Selections,' and is noticeable because it proceeds upon the system and the principles which can alone be successful in the teaching of classical composition. Every scholar has found by experience how useful it is before beginning to translate into Latin or Greek to read over some original passage of a classical author containing an analogy, however slight, to the version to be rendered, in order rather

to impregnate himself with the general atmosphere and spirit, to get his thoughts to run in the proper classical groove, than to crib any particular words or phrases. The difficulty that the tyro has to surmount with his limited stock of reading, is to lay his hand upon these passages ; and it is this difficulty which Mr. Sargent now removes."—*Globe.*

"This is certainly the most systematic and useful work of its kind that has yet appeared in this country."—*Standard.*

"This book may be recommended as a useful help to the acquisition of the power of writing Latin and Greek prose. The pieces are well arranged and of convenient length, and the references to passages in classical authors form a valuable feature of the book."—*Athenæum.*

"It is a happy notion to adapt, for the purpose of being translated into Latin or Greek, passages from the best English writers, as near as possible representing the style and subject, of the best classical examples. This is efficiently done by Mr. Sargent and Mr. Dallin."—*Westminster Review.*

M. Minucii Felicis Octavius.

The Text newly revised from the Original MS., with an English Commentary, Analysis, Introduction, and Copious Indices. Edited by **H. A. Holden, LL.D.,** Head Master of Ipswich School, late Fellow and Assistant Tutor of Trinity College, Cambridge.

Crown 8vo.   9s. 6d.

AND AT OXFORD AND CAMBRIDGE

Cicero.

With English Notes from the best and most recent sources.
Edited by **Thomas Kerchever Arnold**, M.A.

12mo.

SELECTED ORATIONS. *Third Edition.* 4s.

SELECTED EPISTLES. 5s.

THE TUSCULAN DISPUTATIONS. *Second Edition.* 5s. 6d.

DE FINIBUS MALORUM ET BONORUM. (On the Supreme
Good.) 5s. 6d.

CATO MAJOR, SIVE DE SENECTUTE DIALOGUS. 2s. 6d.

The Commentaries of Gaius.

Translated, with Notes, by **J. T. Abdy**, LL.D., Regius Professor of Laws in the University of Cambridge, and Barrister-at-Law of the Norfolk Circuit; formerly Fellow of Trinity Hall; and **Bryan Walker**, M.A., M.L., Fellow and Lecturer of Corpus Christi College, and Law Lecturer of St. John's College, Cambridge; formerly Law Student of Trinity Hall and Chancellor's Legal Medallist.

Crown 8vo. 12s. 6d.

Juvenalis Satirae.

Edited by **G. A. Simcox**, M.A., Fellow and Classical Lecturer of Queen's College, Oxford. Crown 8vo.

THIRTEEN SATIRES. 3s. 6d.

Forming a Part of the " Catena Classicorum."

" Of Mr. Simcox's 'Juvenal' we can only speak in terms of the highest commendation, as a simple, unpretending work, admirably adapted to the wants of the school-boy or of a college passman. It is clear, concise, and scrupulously honest in shirking no real difficulty. The pointed epigrammatic hits of the satirist are everywhere well brought out, and the notes really are what they profess to be, explanatory in the best sense of the term."—*London Review.*

" This is a link in the *Catena Classicorum*, to which the attention of our readers has been more than once directed as a good Series of Classical Works for School and College purposes. The introduction is a very comprehensive and able account of Juvenal, his Satires, and the Manuscripts."—*Athenæum.*

" This is a very original and enjoyable edition of one of our favourite classics."—*Spectator.*

WATERLOO PLACE, PALL MALL, LONDON

Persii Satirae.

Edited by A. Pretor, M.A., of Trinity College, Cambridge,
Classical Lecturer of Trinity Hall, Composition Lecturer of
the Perse Grammar School, Cambridge.

Crown 8vo. 3s. 6d.

Forming a Part of the " Catena Classicorum."

"Mr. Pretor has adopted in his edition a plan which he defends on a general principle, but which has really its true defence in the special peculiarities of his author. Mr. Pretor has given his readers translations of almost all the difficult passages. We think he has done so wisely in this case : for the allusions and constructions are so obscure that help is absolutely necessary. He has also been particularly full in his notes. He has thought and written with great independence. He has used every means to get at the meaning of his author. He has gone to many sources for illustration. And altogether he has produced what we may fairly regard as the best edition of Persius in English."—*Museum.*

"In undertaking to edit for the *Catena Classicorum* an author so obscure as Persius confessedly is, Mr. Pretor has boldly grappled with a most difficult task. He has, however, performed it very well, because he has begun, as his Introduction shows, by making himself thoroughly acquainted with the mind and temper—a sufficiently cynical one—of the poet, and thus laying a good basis for his judgment on the conflicting opinions and varying interpretations of previous editors. The bulk of his commentary is from Jahn ; and if we were disposed to object, we should say that some portion of the matter he has transferred to his pages might as well have been omitted. To explain Persius satisfactorily, *i.e.* to make him really intelligible, it is necessary rather to keep before the reader the thread of the story, and to point out the less obvious, because purposely obscured, allusions and the sudden changes of the characters in the dialogues, than to dwell too much on the explanation of the words. If the satires of Persius are difficult, they are also very short ; and the more a commentary can be kept within reasonable limits, the more willing students will try to master the matter. All that can be required by the students of Persius, including an elaborate introduction, a preliminary exposition of each satire, and a very copious index verborum, is now compressed in a volume of less than 150 pages. It is a most useful book, and will be welcome in proportion as such an edition was really very much wanted."—*Cambridge Univ. Gazette.*

Liber Precum Publicarum Ecclesiæ
Anglicanæ.

A Gulielmo Bright, A.M., et Petro Goldsmith Medd,
A.M., Presbyteris, Collegii Universitatis in Acad. Oxon. Sociis,
Latine redditus.

With all the Rubrics in red.

New Edition. Small 8vo. 6s.

AND AT OXFORD AND CAMBRIDGE

Terenti Comoediae.

Edited by **T. L. Papillon**, M.A., Fellow of New College, and late Fellow of Merton, Oxford.

Crown 8vo.

ANDRIA ET EUNUCHUS.   4*s.* 6*d.*

Forming a Part of the "*Catena Classicorum.*"

"An excellent and supremely useful edition of the well known plays of Terence. It makes no pretension to ordinary critical research, and yet perhaps, within the limits, it is all that could be desired. Its aim being merely 'to assist the ordinary students in the higher forms of schools and at the Universities,' numerous, and upon the whole, very scholarly notes and references have been given at the bottom of each page of the text."— *Westminster Review.*

"Mr. Papillon's labours . . . exhibit a fair promise of usefulness as a school and college edition. The foot notes are, in the main, helpful and appropriate." — *Contemporary Review.*

"We must admit that Mr. Papillon has succeeded admirably in producing a thoroughly useful and reliable edition of two of Terence's most popular comedies. We find not only an introduction devoted to the life and writings, the style and literary merits, of the great Roman comic poet, but also a complete account and analysis of each of the plays here printed. Altogether we can pronounce this volume one admirably suited to the wants of students at school and college, and forming a useful introduction to the works of Terence."—*Examiner.*

A Copious and Critical English-Latin Lexicon.

By **T. K. Arnold**, M.A., and **J. E. Riddle**, M.A.

New Edition. 8vo.   21*s.*

Riddle and Arnold's English-Latin

Dictionary, *for the use of Schools ;* being an Abridgment of Riddle and Arnold's Copious and Critical English-Latin Lexicon.

By the Rev. **J. C. Ebden**, late Fellow and Tutor of Trinity Hall, Cambridge.

Post 8vo.   7*s.* 6*d.*

WATERLOO PLACE, PALL MALL, LONDON

GREEK

The First Greek Book.

On the plan of "Henry's First Latin Book."
By **Thomas Keroheyer Arnold**, M.A.
Sixth Edition. 12mo. 5*s*. Tutor's Key, 1*s*. 6*d*.

A Practical Introduction to Greek

Accidence. With Easy Exercises and Vocabulary.
By **Thomas Keroheyer Arnold**, M.A.
Eighth Edition. 8vo. 5*s*. 6*d*.

A Practical Introduction to Greek

Prose Composition. Part I.
By **Thomas Keroheyer Arnold**, M.A.
Eleventh Edition. 8vo. 5*s*. 6*d*. Tutor's Key, 1*s*. 6*d*.

Homer for Beginners.

ILIAD, Books I.—III. With English Notes. By **Thomas Keroheyer Arnold**, M.A.
Third Edition. 12mo. 3*s*. 6*d*.

AND AT OXFORD AND CAMBRIDGE

The Iliad of Homer.

From the Text of Dindorf. With Preface and Notes.
By **S. H. Reynolds**, M.A., Fellow and Tutor of Brasenose
College, Oxford.   Crown 8vo.
Books I.—XII.   6s.
Forming a Part of the " Catena Classicorum."

The Iliad of Homer.

With English Notes and Grammatical References.
By **Thomas Kerchever Arnold**, M.A.
Fourth Edition. 12mo. Half-bound, 12s.

A Complete Greek and English

Lexicon for the Poems of Homer and the Homeridæ; illustrating
the Domestic, Religious, Political, and Military Condition of
the Heroic Age, and explaining the most Difficult Passages.
By **G. Ch. Crusius.**   Translated from the German by
Henry Smith, Professor of Languages in Marietta College.
Edited by **Thomas Kerchever Arnold**, M.A.
New Edition. 12mo. 9s.

Materials and Models for Greek and

Latin Prose Composition.
Selected and arranged by **J. Y. Sargent**, M.A., Tutor, late
Fellow of Magdalen College, Oxford ; and **T. F. Dallin**,
M.A., Fellow and Tutor of Queen's College, Oxford.
Crown 8vo. 7s. 6d.
(See Page 5 and Specimen Page No. 4.)

Classical Examination Papers.

Edited, with Notes and References, by **P. J. F. Gantillon**,
M.A., sometime Scholar of St. John's College, Cambridge ;
Classical Master in Cheltenham College.
Crown 8vo. 7s. 6d.
Or interleaved with writing-paper for Notes, half-bound, 10s. 6d.
(See Page 4 and Specimen Page No. 3.)

Demosthenes.

Edited, with English Notes and Grammatical References, by **Thomas Kerchever Arnold**, M.A. 12mo.

THE OLYNTHIAC ORATIONS. *Third Edition.* 3s.
THE PHILIPPIC ORATIONS. *Third Edition.* 4s.
THE ORATION ON THE CROWN. *Second Edition.* 4s. 6d.

Demosthenis Orationes Privatae.

Edited by **Arthur Holmes**, M.A., Senior Fellow and Lecturer of Clare College, Cambridge, and Preacher at the Chapel Royal, Whitehall. Crown 8vo.

DE CORONA. 5s.

Forming a Part of the "Catena Classicorum."

Demosthenis Orationes Publicae.

Edited by **G. H. Heslop**, M.A., late Fellow and Assistant Tutor of Queen's College, Oxford; Head Master of St. Bees.

Crown 8vo.

THE OLYNTHIACS, 2s. 6d. }
THE PHILIPPICS, 3s. } or, in One Volume, 4s. 6d.
DE FALSA LEGATIONE, 6s.

Forming Parts of the "Catena Classicorum."

"The annotations are scarcely less to be commended for the exclusion of superfluous matter than for the excellence of what is supplied. Well known works are not quoted, but simply referred to, and information which ought to have been previously acquired is omitted."—*Athenæum*.

"Mr. Heslop's critical scholarship is of an accurate and enlarged order. His reading of the chief authorities, historical, critical, explanatory, and technical, has been commendably thorough; and it would be impossible to go through either the Olynthiacs, or Philippics, with his aid, and not to have picked up many pieces of information to add to one's stock of knowledge of the Greek language and its use among the orators who rendered its latter day famous. He is moreover an independent editor, and we are glad to find holds his own views as to readings and interpretations, undismayed by the formidable names that occasionally meet him in his way."—*Contemporary Review*.

"Mr. Heslop has carefully digested the best foreign commentaries, and his notes are for the most part judicious extracts from them."—*Museum*.

Scenes from Greek Plays.   Rugby

Editions.   Abridged and adapted for the use of Schools.

By **Arthur Sidgwick**, M.A., Assistant Master at Rugby School, and formerly Fellow of Trinity College, Cambridge.

Small 8vo.   1s. 6d.; or in Paper Cover, 1s. each.

Aristophanes.

    THE CLOUDS.   THE FROGS.   THE KNIGHTS.   PLUTUS.

Euripides.

    IPHIGENIA IN TAURIS.   THE CYCLOPS.

(See Specimen Page No. 5.)

The object of these editions is to remove some of the obstacles which young boys find in the earlier stages of learning Greek.

The beginner can only do a short piece at a stretch, makes it out very slowly, and, in the process of looking out the words, undergoes a great deal of bewilderment and some unproductive labour. The result is, that he misses the spirit of the book, and wastes a good deal of time.

In the notes to these Plays an attempt has been made to save the labour of the lexicon in those nume-rous cases where such saving involved no loss to the learner. Explanations have been given of all the grammatical usages which offer any difficulty; and an index has been added at the end to assist the classification and illustration of these usages.

The stage directions have been inserted, to make the action of the Play more lively and intelligible. It is hoped that the liberty thus taken with the text will be pardoned, as its sole object is to interest the learner, which is the first condition of successful teaching.

Sophocles.

With English Notes from SCHNEIDEWIN.

    Edited by **T. K. Arnold**, M.A., the Ven. **Archdeacon Paul**, and the Rev. **Henry Browne**, M.A.

12mo.

AJAX. 3s. PHILOCTETES. 3s. ŒDIPUS TYRANNUS. 4s. ŒDIPUS COLONEUS. 4s. ANTIGONE. 4s.

Sophoclis Tragoediae.

Edited by R. C. Jebb, M.A., Fellow and Assistant Tutor of Trinity College, Cambridge, and Public Orator of the University.

Crown 8vo.

The Electra. *Second Edition, revised.* 3s. 6d.

The Ajax. 3s. 6d.

Forming Parts of the " Catena Classicorum."

(*See Specimen Page No.* 6.)

" The Introduction proves that Mr. Jebb is something more than a mere scholar,—a man of real taste and feeling. His criticisms upon Schlegel's remarks on the Electra are, we believe, new, and certainly just. As we have often had occasion to say in this Review, it is impossible to pass any reliable criticism upon school-books until they have been tested by experience. The notes, however, in this case appear to be clear and sensible, and direct attention to the points where attention is most needed."—*Westminster Review.*

" We have no hesitation in saying that in style and manner Mr. Jebb's notes are admirably suited for their purpose. The explanations of grammatical points are singularly lucid, the parallel passages generally well chosen, the translations bright and graceful, the analysis of arguments terse and luminous. Mr. Jebb has clearly shown that he possesses some of the qualities most essential for a commentator."—*Spectator.*

" The Notes appear to us exactly suited to assist boys of the Upper Forms at Schools, and University Students: they give sufficient help without overdoing explanations. . . His critical remarks show acute and exact scholarship, and a very useful addition to ordinary notes is the scheme of metres in the choruses."—*Guardian.*

" We have seen it suggested that it is unsafe to pronounce on the merits of a Greek Play edited for educational purposes until it has been tested in the hands of pupils and tutors. But our examination of the instalment of, we hope, a complete 'Sophocles,' which Mr. Jebb has put forth, has assured us that this is a needless suspension of judgment, and prompted us to commit the justifiable rashness of pronouncing upon its contents, and of asserting after due perusal that it is calculated to be admirably serviceable to every class of scholars and learners."—*Contemporary Review.*

" We do not know whether the matter or the manner of this excellent commentary is deserving of the higher praise : the skill with which Mr. Jebb has avoided, on the one hand, the wearisome prolixity of the Germans, and on the other the jejune brevity of the Porsonian critics, or the versatility which has enabled him in turn to elucidate the plots, to explain the verbal difficulties, and to illustrate the idioms of his author. All this, by a studious economy of space and a remarkable precision of expression, he has done for the 'Ajax' in a volume of some 200 pages."—*Athenæum.*

" An accidental tardiness in noticing these instalments of a Sophocles which promises to be one of the ablest and most useful editions published in this country must not be construed into any lack of due appreciation of their value. It seemed best to wait till more than one play had issued from the press ; but it is not too late to express the favourable impression which we have formed, from the two samples before us, of Mr. Jebb's eminent qualifications for the task of interpreting Sophocles."—*Saturday Review.*

AND AT OXFORD AND CAMBRIDGE

Isocratis Orationes.

Edited by **John Edwin Sandys**, M.A., Fellow and Tutor
of St. John's College, Cambridge.

Crown 8vo.

AD DEMONICUM ET PANEGYRICUS.   4s. 6d.

Forming a Part of the " Catena Classicorum."

"This is one of the most excellent works of that excellent series, the 'Catena Classicorum.' Isocrates has not received the attention to which the simplicity of his style and the purity of his Attic language entitled him as a means of education. Now that we have so admirable an edition of two of his works best adapted for such a purpose, there will no longer be any excuse for this neglect. For carefulness and thoroughness of editing. it will bear comparison with the best, whether English or foreign. Besides an ample supply of exhaustive notes of rare excellence, we find in it valuable remarks on the style of Isocrates and the state of the text, a table of various readings, a list of editions, and a special introduction to each piece. As in other editions of this series, short summaries of the argument are inserted in suitable places, and will be found of great service to the student. The commentary embraces explanations of difficult passages, with instructive remarks on grammatical usages, and the derivation and meanings of words illustrated by quotations and references. Occasionally the student's attention is called to the moral sentiment expressed or implied in the text. With all this abundance of annotation, founded on a diligent study of the best and latest authorities, there is no excess of matter and no waste of words. The elegance of the exterior is in harmony with the intrinsic worth of the volume."—*Athenæum.*

"This work deserves the warmest welcome, for several reasons. In the first place, it is an attempt to introduce Isocrates into our schools, and this attempt deserves encouragement. The *Ad Demonicum* is very easy Greek. It is good Greek. And it is reading of a healthy nature for boys. . . . . Then the editor has done everything that an editor should do. We have a series of short introductory essays ; on the style of Isocrates, on the text, on the *Ad Demonicum*, and on the *Panegyricus.* These *are characterized by sound sense, wide and thorough learning, and the capability of presenting thoughts clearly and well."—*Museum.*

"By editing Isocrates Mr. Sandys does good service to students and teachers of Greek Prose. He places in our hands in a convenient form an author who will be found of great use in public schools, where he has been hitherto almost unknown." — *Cambridge University Gazette.*

"The feeling uppermost in our minds, after a careful and interesting study of this edition, is one of satisfaction and admiration : satisfaction that a somewhat unfamiliar author has been made so thoroughly readable, and admiration of the comparatively young scholar who has brought about this result by combining in the task such industry, research, and acumen, as are not always found united in editors who have had decads upon decads of mature experience."—*Saturday Review.*

"The style of Isocrates is discussed in a separate essay, remarkable for sense, clearness of expression, and aptness of illustration. In the introductions to the two orations, and in the notes, abundant attention is given to questions of authenticity and historical allusions."—*Pall Mall Gazette.*

Aristophanis Comoediae.

Edited by **W. C. Green**, M.A., late Fellow of King's College, Cambridge ; Assistant Master at Rugby School.

Crown 8vo.

THE ACHARNIANS and THE KNIGHTS. 4*s.*
THE CLOUDS. 3*s. 6d.*
THE WASPS. 3*s. 6d.*

An Edition of "THE ACHARNIANS and THE KNIGHTS," revised and especially prepared for Schools. 4*s.*

Forming Parts of the " Catena Classicorum."

"The utmost care has been taken with this edition of the most sarcastic and clever of the old Greek dramatists, facilitating the means of understanding both the text and intention of that biting sarcasm which will never lose either point or interest, and is as well adapted to the present age as it was to the times when first put forward." —*Bell's Weekly Messenger.*

Herodoti Historia.

Edited by **H. G. Woods**, M.A., Fellow and Tutor of Trinity College, Oxford.

Crown 8vo.   [*In the Press.*

Forming a Part of the " Catena Classicorum."

A Copious Phraseological English-

Greek Lexicon; founded on a work prepared by **J. W. Frädersdorff**, Ph. Dr., late Professor of Modern Languages, Queen's College, Belfast.

Revised, Enlarged, and Improved by the late **Thomas Kerchever Arnold**, M.A., and **Henry Browne**, M.A., Vicar of Pevensey, and Prebendary of Chichester.

Fourth Edition. 8vo. 21*s.*

AND AT OXFORD AND CAMBRIDGE

Thucydidis Historia.

Edited by **Charles Bigg**, M.A., late Senior Student and Tutor of Christ Church, Oxford; Principal of Brighton College.   Crown 8vo.

BOOKS I. AND II.   6s.

Forming a Part of the " Catena Classicorum."

" Mr. Bigg, in his ' Thucydides,' prefixes an analysis to each book, and an admirable introduction to the whole work, containing full information as to all that is known or related of Thucydides, and the date at which he wrote, followed by a very masterly critique on some of his characteristics as a writer."—*Athenæum.*

" While disclaiming absolute originality in his book, Mr. Bigg has so thoroughly digested the works of so many eminent predecessors in the same field, and is evidently on terms of such intimacy with his author, as perforce to inspire confidence. A well pondered and well written introduction has formed a part of each link in the 'Catena' hitherto published, and Mr. Bigg, in addition to a general introduction, has given us an essay on 'Some Characteristics of Thucydides,' which no one can read without

being impressed with the learning and judgment brought to bear on the subject."—*Standard.*

" We need hardly say that these books are carefully edited; the reputation of the editor is an assurance on this point. If the rest of the history is edited with equal care, it must become the standard book for school and college purposes."—*John Bull.*

" Mr. Bigg first discusses the facts of the life of Thucydides, then passes to an examination into the date at which Thucydides wrote; and in the third section expatiates on some characteristics of Thucydides. These essays are remarkably well written, are judicious in their opinions, and are calculated to give the student much insight into the work of Thucydides, and its relation to his own times, and to the works of subsequent historians."—*Museum.*

Dean Alford's Greek Testament.

With English Notes, intended for the Upper Forms of Schools, and for Pass-men at the Universities.

Abridged by **Bradley H. Alford**, M.A., late Scholar of Trinity College, Cambridge.

Crown 8vo.   10s. 6d.

The volume consists of the revised text, printed from the latest editions of the larger work. In cases where two readings seem of equal authority, the alternative text is presented beneath. The notes are faithful abridgments of those in the larger edition, presenting the results there arrived at, and supporting them by short proofs. Especial care has been taken to mark the sequence of thought from chapter to

chapter, and in the more closely reasoned portions from verse to verse. Additional grammatical notes will be found, adapted to the use of younger Students, and accompanied by references to the usages of the Septuagint version and the rules of Donaldson's Greek Grammar.

The whole is prefaced by concise notices of the authorship, object, and date of each book.

WATERLOO PLACE, PALL MALL, LONDON

The Greek Testament.

With a Critically Revised Text ; a Digest of Various Readings ;
Marginal References to Verbal and Idiomatic Usage ; Prolego-
mena ; and a Critical and Exegetical Commentary. For the
use of Theological Students and Ministers.

By **Henry Alford**, D.D., late Dean of Canterbury.
New Edition. 4 Vols. 8vo. 102*s.*

The Volumes are sold Separately, as follows :—

Vol. I.—The Four Gospels. 28*s.*
Vol. II.—Acts to II. Corinthians. 24*s.*
Vol. III.—Galatians to Philemon. 18*s.*
Vol. IV.—Hebrews to Revelation. 32*s.*

The Greek Testament.

With Notes, Introductions, and Index.

By **Chr. Wordsworth**, D.D., Bishop of Lincoln ; formerly
Canon of Westminster, and Archdeacon.
New Edition. 2 Vols. Impl. 8vo. 60*s.*

The Parts may be had Separately, as follows :—

The Gospels. 16*s.*
The Acts. 8*s.*
St. Paul's Epistles. 23*s.*
General Epistles, Revelation, and Index. 16*s.*

The Cambridge Greek and English

Testament, in Parallel Columns on the same page.

Edited by **J. Scholefield**, M.A., late Regius Professor of
Greek in the University.
New Edition. Small 8vo. 7*s.* 6*d.*

The Cambridge Greek Testament.

Ex editione Stephani tertia, 1550.
Small 8vo. 3*s.* 6*d.*

An Introduction to Aristotle's Ethics.

Books I.—IV. (Book X., c. vi.—ix. in an Appendix.)   With a Continuous Analysis and Notes.   Intended for the Use of Beginners and Junior Students.

By the Rev. **Edward Moore**, B.D., Principal of S. Edmund Hall, and late Fellow and Tutor of Queen's College, Oxford.

Crown 8vo.   10*s.* 6*d.*

" For the purpose for which it is designed to provide, namely, a simple Introduction to the Ethics for beginners generally, and especially for those who are commencing it with a view to the Oxford Final Examinations, this is a most excellent edition of the Nicomachean Ethics. . . . Not only is it suited for the classes already named, and for students in the public schools ; it will also be found very serviceable to those whose Greek has been permitted to grow rusty by disuse, and who, for philosophical or linguistic purposes, may desire to revive it.   We can fully credit the statement of the accomplished editor, that clearness and simplicity have been the qualities most aimed at, and can testify that he has fully succeeded in his intention." — *Edinburgh Courant.*

Aristotelis Ethica Nicomachea.

Edidit, emendavit, crebrisque locis parallelis e libro ipso, aliisque ejusdem Auctoris scriptis, illustravit **Jacobus E. T. Rogers**, A.M.

Small 8vo.   4*s.* 6*d.*   Interleaved with writing-paper, half-bound.   6*s.*

WATERLOO PLACE, PALL MALL, LONDON

CATENA CLASSICORUM

A Series of Classical Authors

Edited by Members of both Universities, under the direction
of the Rev. **Arthur Holmes**, M.A., Cambridge, and
the Rev. **Charles Bigg**, M.A., Oxford.

Crown 8vo.

(See Specimen Page No. 6.)

Sophoclis Tragoediae. By R. C. Jebb, M.A.
   THE ELECTRA. 3s. 6d.   THE AJAX. 3s. 6d.

Juvenalis Satirae. By G. A. Simcox, M.A. 3s. 6d.

Thucydidis Historia. By Charles Bigg, M.A. Books I. and
   II. 6s.

Demosthenis Orationes Publicae. By G. H. Heslop, M.A.
   THE OLYNTHIACS. 2s. 6d. ⎫
   THE PHILIPPICS. 3s. ⎬ or, in One Volume, 4s. 6d.
   DE FALSA LEGATIONE. 6s. ⎭

Demosthenis Orationes Privatae. By Arthur Holmes, M.A.
   DE CORONA, 5s.

Aristophanis Comoediae. By W. C. Green, M.A.
   THE ACHARNIANS AND THE KNIGHTS. 4s.
   THE CLOUDS. 3s. 6d.   THE WASPS. 3s. 6d.

   An Edition of THE ACHARNIANS AND THE KNIGHTS,
   Revised and especially adapted for Use in Schools. 4s.

Isocratis Orationes. By John Edwin Sandys, M.A.
   AD DEMONICUM ET PANEGYRICUS. 4s. 6d.

Persii Satirae. By A. Pretor, M.A. 3s. 6d.

Homeri Ilias. By S. H. Reynolds, M.A. Books I. to XII. 6s.

Terenti Comoediae. By T. L. Papillon, M.A.
   ANDRIA ET EUNUCHUS. 4s. 6d.

      Other Works are in preparation.

AND AT OXFORD AND CAMBRIDGE

MATHEMATICS

RIVINGTON'S MATHEMATICAL SERIES

Algebra. Part I.

By **J. Hamblin Smith**, M. A., of Gonville and Caius College,
and late Lecturer at St. Peter's College, Cambridge.

12mo. 2*s.* 6*d.* With Answers, 3*s.*

(See Specimen Page No. 7.)

"The design of this treatise is to explain all that is commonly included in a First Part of Algebra. In the arrangement of the chapters, I have followed the advice of experienced teachers. I have carefully abstained from making extracts from books in common use. The only work to which I am indebted for any material assistance is the Algebra of the late Dean Peacock, which I took as the model for the commencement of my treatise. The Examples, progressive and easy, have been selected from university and college examination papers, and from old English, French, and German works."—*From the Preface.*

"It is evident that Mr. Hamblin Smith is a teacher, and has written to meet the special wants of students. He does not carry the student out of his depth by sudden plunges, but leads him gradually onward, never beyond his depth from any desire to hurry forward. The examples appear to be particularly well arranged, so as to afford a means of steady progress. With such books the judicious teacher will have abundant supply of examples and problems for those who need to have each step ensured by familiarity, and he will be able to allow the more rapid learner to travel onward with ease and swiftness. We can confidently recommend Mr. Hamblin Smith's books. Candidates preparing for Civil Service examinations under the new system of open competition will find these works to be of great value."—*Civil Service Gazette.*

WATERLOO PLACE, PALL MALL, LONDON

RIVINGTON'S MATHEMATICAL SERIES *(continued).*

Exercises on Algebra. Part I.

By J. Hamblin Smith, M.A. 12mo. 2s. 6d.

Copies may be had without the Answers.

"I have arranged in this book a series of examples in Elementary Algebra, co-extensive with my treatise on that subject. The Examples are progressive and easy. They have been selected chiefly from papers set during the last three years in university and college examinations. The exercises are arranged on the following plan:—Part I. conducts the student by gradual steps as far as Geometrical Progression, each exercise having the limit of its extent specified in the heading by a reference to the chapters of my Elementary Algebra. Part II. contains papers of greater length and somewhat more difficulty than those in Part I. No question in these papers implies a knowledge of any part of Algebra beyond Geometrical Progression, but at the end of each exercise one piece of bookwork is given. Part III. takes in the whole of the subject, so far as I have written on it in my treatise, especial prominence being given to that portion of the work which follows the chapter on Geometrical Progression. The questions in bookwork in Parts II. and III. follow the order in which the matters to which they refer are given in my treatise."—*From the Preface.*

Trigonometry.

By J. Hamblin Smith, M.A. 12mo. 4s. 6d.

(*See Specimen Page No. 8.*)

"I have attempted in this work to explain and illustrate the principles of that portion of Plane Trigonometry which precedes De Moivre's Theorem. The method of explanation is similar to that adopted in my Elementary Algebra. The examples, progressive and easy, have been selected chiefly from College and University Examination Papers; but I am indebted for many to the works of several German writers, especially those of Dienger, Meyer, Weiss, and Weigand. I have carried on the subject somewhat beyond the limits set by the Regulations for the Examination of Candidates for Honours in the Previous Examination, for two reasons: first, because I hope to see those limits extended; secondly, that my work may be more useful to those who are reading the subject in schools, and to candidates in the Local Examinations."—*From the Preface.*

Elementary Hydrostatics.

By J. Hamblin Smith, M.A. 12mo. 3s.

"The elements of Hydrostatics seem capable of being presented in a simpler form than that in which they appear in all the works on the subject with which I am acquainted. I have therefore attempted to give a simple explanation of the Mathematical Theory of Hydrostatics and the practical application of it. Prior to the publication of this work, some copies were privately circulated, with a view to obtain opinions from teachers of experience as to the sufficiency and accuracy of the information contained in it. A few suggestions received in consequence of this arrangement will be found in the Notes at the end of the volume."—*From the Preface.*

AND AT OXFORD AND CAMBRIDGE

RIVINGTON'S MATHEMATICAL SERIES *(continued).*

Elements of Geometry.

By J. Hamblin Smith, M.A. Part I., containing the First Two Books of Euclid, with Exercises and Notes, arranged with the Abbreviations admitted in the Cambridge Examinations. 12mo, 2s. ; limp cloth, 1s. 6d.

Part II., containing the Third and Fourth Books of Euclid, with Exercises, &c.   12mo, 2s. ; limp cloth, 1s. 6d.

Parts I. and II. bound together, 3s.

Part III., to Complete the Volume, is in the Press.

(See Specimen Page No. 9.)

"To preserve Euclid's order, to supply omissions, to remove defects, to give brief notes of explanation and simpler methods of proof in cases of acknowledged difficulty—such are the main objects of this edition of the Elements. The work is based on the Greek text, as it is given in the editions of August and Peyrard. To the suggestions of the late Professor De Morgan, published in the Companion to the British Almanack for 1849, I have paid constant deference. A limited use of symbolic representation, wherein the symbols stand for words and not for operations, is generally regarded as desirable, and I have been assured, by the highest authorities on this point, that the symbols employed in this book are admissible in the Examinations at Oxford and Cambridge. I have generally followed Euclid's method of proof, but not to the exclusion of other methods recommended by their simplicity, such as the demonstrations by which I propose to replace (at least for a first reading) the difficult Theorems 5 and 7 in the First Book. I have also attempted to render many of the proofs, as, for instance, Propositions 2, 13, and 35 in Book I., and Proposition 13 in Book II., less confusing to the learner. In Propositions 4, 5, 6, 7, and 8 of the Second Book, I have ventured to make an important change in Euclid's mode of exposition, by omitting the diagonals from the diagrams and the gnomons from the text. In the Third Book I have deviated with even greater boldness from the precise line of Euclid's method. For it is in treating of the properties of the circle that the importance of certain matters, to which reference is made in the Notes of the present volume, is fully brought out. I allude especially to the application of Superposition as a test of equality, to the conception of an Angle as a magnitude capable of unlimited increase, and to the development of the methods connected with Loci and Symmetry."—*From the Preface.*

Elementary Statics.

By J. Hamblin Smith, M.A. 12mo, 3s.

" This book is now published in such a form that it may meet the requirements of Students in Schools, especially those who are preparing for the Local Examinations. . . . . . . The Examples have been selected from Papers set in Cambridge University Examinations. The propositions requiring a knowledge of Trigonometry are marked with *Roman* numerals."—*From the Preface.*

RIVINGTON'S MATHEMATICAL SERIES *(continued).*

Algebra. Part II.

By E. J. Gross, M.A., Fellow of Gonville and Caius College, Cambridge. [*Preparing.*

Geometrical Conic Sections.

By G. Richardson, M.A., Assistant Master at Winchester College, and late Fellow of St. John's College, Cambridge.
[*Preparing.*

Analytical Geometry of Two Dimensions.

By H. E. Oakeley, M.A., late Fellow and Senior Mathematical Lecturer of Jesus College, Cambridge, H.M. Inspector of Schools. [*Preparing.*

Other Works are in Preparation.

The Properties of Triangles and their Circles treated Geometrically.

By C. W. Bourne, M.A., Assistant Mathematical Master at Marlborough College.

Fcap. 4to. 2s. 6d.

Arithmetic for the Use of Schools.

With a numerous Collection of Examples.

By R. D. Beasley, M.A., Head Master of Grantham Grammar School.

12mo. 3s.

The Examples separately :—Part I. 8d. Part II. 1s. 6d.

AND AT OXFORD AND CAMBRIDGE

Arithmetic, Theoretical and Practical.

By W. H. Girdlestone, M.A., of Christ's College, Cambridge, Principal of the Theological College, Gloucester.

New Edition.   Crown 8vo, 6*s.* 6*d.*

Also a School Edition.   Small 8vo.   3*s.* 6*d.*

(See Specimen Page No. 10.)

"We may congratulate Mr. Girdlestone on having produced a thoroughly philosophical book on this most useful subject. It appears to be especially suited for older students, who, having been taught imperfectly and irrationally in the earlier part of their school career, desire to go over the whole ground again from the beginning; but in the hands of an intelligent and discriminating teacher it may also be perfectly adapted to the comprehension of young boys."—*Times.*

"We consider this work one of the highest order of its kind, far, very far, superior to those of former days. Assuredly, if brevity (as it is considered) be the soul of wit, so must it be that of Arithmetic, when its object is equally attained by it, as by a roundabout method; and on this account alone it commends itself to the attention of the rising generation, who might go to work with it in self-instruction without the superintendence of a teacher. But with or without such assistance, the *élève* who masters the contents of the work before us in all its parts may well be considered a finished accountant."—*Nautical Magazine.*

"This work belongs to a department of science to which we do not often refer; but so decided is its superiority to ordinary arithmetical treatises, and, while adapting itself to the humblest capacity, so comprehensive is the view it affords of the laws of number, not unfrequently neglected by many who devote serious thought to the higher branches of mathematics,

that it seems entitled to exceptional notice. . . . . Let us add that the practical is quite equal to the theoretical value of his performance. He (Mr. Girdlestone) never misses an opportunity of showing how arithmetical labour may be conveniently shortened, and not only is every one of his rules followed by abundant exercises, but he gives by way of appendix a series of examination papers set at different institutions, ascending from the humblest requisitions to the University papers of Oxford and Cambridge. To all the questions answers are given at the end."—*Saturday Review.*

From the Very Reverend the Dean of Ely (now Bishop of Carlisle):—"Mr. Girdlestone's book on arithmetic seems very complete and good, with plenty of examples, which is a valuable feature.—H. GOODWIN, Deanery, Ely."

From the late Professor De Morgan:—" Mr. Girdlestone's is an intellectual book."—A. DE MORGAN.

From the Rev. W. W. Griffin, late Fellow and Tutor of St. John's College, Cambridge, and Senior Wrangler :—" Mr. Girdlestone's book on arithmetic appears to me to be the work of one who in actual teaching has found out the impediments which pupils have in gaining scientific views of arithmetic. His explanations seem to be clear, examples in sufficient number are worked as models, and a good collection given besides for practice.— W. W. GRIFFIN, Ospringe Vicarage, Faversham."

WATERLOO PLACE, PALL MALL, LONDON

DIVINITY

A Manual of Confirmation.

With a Pastoral Letter instructing Catechumens how to prepare themselves for their First Communion.

By **Edward Meyrick Goulburn**, D.D., Dean of Norwich.
Eighth Edition. Small 8vo. 1s. 6d.

The Treasury of Devotion.

A Manual of Prayers for General and Daily Use.

Compiled by a Priest. Edited by the Rev. **T. T. Carter**, M.A., Rector of Clewer, Berks.

Fourth Edition. 16mo, limp cloth, 2s. ; cloth extra, 2s. 6d.
Bound with the Book of Common Prayer, 3s. 6d.

The Way of Life.

A Book of Prayers and Instruction for the Young at School.

With Special Devotions for Confirmation. Compiled by a Priest. Edited by the Rev. **T. T. Carter**, M.A., Rector of Clewer, Berks.

16mo, cloth extra, 1s. 6d.

AND AT OXFORD AND CAMBRIDGE

Prayers and Meditations for the Holy
Communion.

With a Preface by C. J. Ellicott, D.D., Lord Bishop of Gloucester and Bristol.

With rubrics and borders in red.   Royal 32mo.   2s. 6d.

"The present Manual of Prayers came by accident under my notice. Having long felt the want of such a manual for the use of those who had been recently confirmed, and observing that the present work went far to supply the need, I suggested to the writer of the volume the desirableness of publication. The manuscript was in consequence submitted to me for perusal, and is now presented to those recently confirmed, with the full persuasion that the warmth of the prayers, the deep spirit of devotion that pervades them, and the freshness that especially marks the volume, will appeal to young and warm hearts, and, with the blessing of the Holy Ghost, will be helpful to them in the after-confirmation life." — *From the Preface.*

"Devout beauty is the special character of this new manual, and it ought to be a favourite. Rarely has it happened to us to meet with so remarkable a combination of thorough practicalness with that almost poetic warmth which is the highest flower of genuine devotion. It deserves to be placed along with the manual edited by Mr. Keble so shortly before his decease, not as superseding it, for the scope of the two is different, but to be taken along with it. Nothing can exceed the beauty and fulness of the devotions before communion in Mr. Keble's book, but we think that in some points the devotions here given after Holy Communion are even superior to it."—*Literary Churchman.*

"We know of no more suitable manual for the newly confirmed, and nothing more likely to engage the sympathies of youthful hearts."—*Church Review.*

"A manual for the recently confirmed, nicely printed, and theologically sound."—*Church Times.*

"In freshness and fervour of devotion, few modern manuals of prayer are to be compared with it."—*Church Herald.*

"Merits the Bishop of Gloucester's epithets of 'warm, devout, and fresh.' And it is thoroughly English Church besides."—*Guardian.*

"The devotion which it breathes is truly fervent, and the language attractive, and as proceeding from a young person the work is altogether not a little striking."—*Record.*

A Short and Plain Instruction for the

Better Understanding of the Lord's Supper; to which is annexed the Office of the Holy Communion, with Proper Helps and Directions. By **Thomas Wilson**, D.D., late Lord Bishop of Sodor and Man.

Large Type.   *Complete Edition*, with red borders, 16mo.   2s. 6d.

Also a Cheap Edition, without red borders, 1s.; or in paper cover, 6d.

(See Specimen Page No. 11.)

KEYS TO CHRISTIAN KNOWLEDGE.

Small 8vo. 2s. 6d. each.

A Key to the Knowledge and Use of
the Holy Bible.
By the Rev. J. H. Blunt, M.A.

"Another of Mr. Blunt's useful and workmanlike compilations, which will be most acceptable as a household book, or in schools and colleges. It is a capital book too for schoolmasters and pupil teachers." — *Literary Churchman.*

"As a popular hand-book, setting forth a selection of facts of which everybody ought to be cognizant, and as an exposition of the claims of the Bible to be received as of superhuman origin, Mr. Blunt's 'Key' will be useful."—*Churchman.*

"A great deal of useful information is comprised in these pages, and the book will no doubt be extensively circulated in Church families."—*Clerical Journal.*

"We have much pleasure in recommending a capital hand-book by the learned Editor of 'The Annotated Book of Common Prayer.'"—*Church Times.*

"Merits commendation for the lucid and orderly arrangement in which it presents a considerable amount of valuable and interesting matter."—*Record.*

A Key to the Knowledge and Use of
the Book of Common Prayer.
By the Rev. J. H. Blunt, M.A.
(*See Specimen Page No.* 12.)

"A very valuable and practical manual, full of information, which is admirably calculated to instruct and interest those for whom it was evidently specially intended—the laity of the Church of England. It deserves high commendation."—*Churchman.*

"A thoroughly sound and valuable manual."—*Church Times.*

"To us it appears that Mr. Blunt has succeeded very well. All necessary information seems to be included, and the arrangement is excellent."—*Literary Churchman.*

"It is the best short explanation of our offices that we know of, and would be invaluable for the use of candidates for confirmation in the higher classes."—*John Bull.*

A Key to the Knowledge of Church
History (Ancient).
Edited by the Rev. J. H. Blunt, M.A.

"It contains some concise notes on Church History, compressed into a small compass, and we think it is likely to be useful as a book of reference."—*John Bull.*

"A very terse and reliable collection of the main facts and incidents connected with Church History."—*Rock.*

"It is both well arranged and well written."—*Literary Churchman.*

AND AT OXFORD AND CAMBRIDGE

KEYS TO CHRISTIAN KNOWLEDGE *(continued)*.

A Key to the Knowledge of Church
History *(Modern)*.

Edited by the Rev. J. H. Blunt, M.A.

A Key to Christian Doctrine and Prac-
tice, founded on the Church Catechism.

By the Rev. J. H. Blunt, M. A.

" Of cheap and reliable text-books of this nature there has hitherto been a great want. We are often asked to recommend books for use in Church Sunday schools, and we therefore take this opportunity of saying that we know of none more likely to be of service both to teachers and scholars than these ' Keys.' "—*Churchman's Shilling Magazine.*

" This is another of Mr. Blunt's most useful manuals, with all the precision of a school book, yet diverging into matters of practical application so freely as to make it most serviceable, either as a teacher's suggestion book, or as an intelligent pupil's reading book."—*Literary Churchman.*

" Will be very useful for the higher classes in Sunday schools, or rather for the fuller instruction of the Sunday school teachers themselves, where the parish Priest is wise enough to devote a certain time regularly to their preparation for their voluntary task."—*Union Review.*

A Key to the Narrative of the Four
Gospels.

By the Rev. John Pilkington Norris, M.A., Canon of Bristol, formerly one of Her Majesty's Inspectors of Schools.

" This is very much the best book of its kind we have seen." — *Literary Churchman.*

" This is a golden little volume. . . . . . Canon Norris's book supplies a real want, and ought to be welcomed by all earnest and devout students of the Holy Gospels."—*London Quarterly Review.*

" We hope that this little book will have a very wide circulation, and that it will be studied ; and we can promise that those who take it up will not readily put it down again."—*Record.*

A Key to the Narrative of the Acts
of the Apostles.

By the Rev. John Pilkington Norris, M. A.

" The book is one which we can heartily recommend."—*Spectator.*

" Few books have ever given us more unmixed pleasure than this."—*Literary Churchman.*

" This is a sequel to Canon Norris's ' Key to the Gospels,' which was published two years ago, and which has become a general favourite with those who wish to grasp the leading features of the life and work of Christ. The sketch of the Acts of the Apostles is done in the same style ; there is the same reverent spirit and quiet enthusiasm running through it, and the same instinct for seizing the leading points in the narrative."—*Record.*

Household Theology : A Handbook of

Religious Information respecting the Holy Bible, the Prayer Book, the Church, the Ministry, Divine Worship, the Creeds, &c., &c.

By the Rev. J. H. Blunt, M.A.

New Edition. Small 8vo. 3*s.* 6*d.*

(*See Specimen Page No.* 13.)

"At the very outset we are well inclined towards this little volume : for the author tells us plainly that he hopes ' some Dissenters may be found who will care enough about historical truth and sound reasoning to follow the writer through statements and arguments in which they will meet with a fair representation of the conclusions arrived at by the learned men who are his authorities ; and that, by doing so, they will find themselves disabused of many mistakes and prejudices, and prepared to look more respectfully and more lovingly upon the Church and her principles.' In the 270 pages of clear, bold type there is compressed a complete summary of information upon the subjects indicated by the title, given in such simple language that every one can understand it, and without the slightest approach to controversial bitterness. There is presented to the reader an impartial epitome of the several matters treated, which will soon remove from biassed and prejudiced minds doubts and misgivings touching principles and practices of the English Church. Indeed, we have seldom had the pleasure of meeting with a text-book of religious information which said so much in so few and intelligible words. A very useful plan is adopted by the author to enable those who may be interested in the study of special subjects to carry on their inquiries without trouble to their friends. At the end of every chapter is given a list of the standard books from which more complete information can be obtained."—*Church Bells.*

"It is recommended by the Bishop of Central New York and most of our other Bishops to whose notice it has been brought. It ought to be made a text-book in all our parishes."—*Gospel Messenger, Utica, U.S.*

Sermons for Children.

Being Thirty-three short Readings, addressed to the Children of St. Margaret's Home, East Grinstead.

By the late Rev. J. M. Neale, D.D.

Second Edition. Small 8vo. 3*s.* 6*d.*

The Holy Catholic Church ; its Divine

Ideal, Ministry, and Institutions. With a Catechism on each Chapter, forming a Course of Methodical Instruction on the subject.

By Edward Meyrick Goulburn, D.D., Dean of Norwich.

Crown 8vo. [*Nearly Ready.*

AND AT OXFORD AND CAMBRIDGE

MODERN LANGUAGES, &c.

A Plain and Short History of England
for Children: in Letters from a Father to his Son. With a Set of Questions at the end of each Letter.

By **George Davys**, D.D., formerly Bishop of Peterborough.

New Edition. 18mo. 1s. 6d.

Also, an Edition with Twelve Coloured Illustrations.
Square crown 8vo. 3s. 6d.

A Practical Introduction to English
Prose Composition : an English Grammar for Classical Schools, with Questions, and a Course of Exercises.

By **Thomas Kerchever Arnold**, M.A.

Ninth Edition. 12mo. 4s. 6d.

The First French Book.
On the plan of "Henry's First Latin Book."

By **Thomas Kerchever Arnold**, M.A.

Sixth Edition. 12mo. 5s. 6d. Key, 2s. 6d.

(*See Specimen Page No.* 14.)

WATERLOO PLACE, PALL MALL, LONDON

Select Plays of Shakspere. Rugby

Editions. With Notes adapted for the Use of Schools.

By **Charles E. Moberly**, M.A., Assistant Master at Rugby School. [*Ready.*

AS YOU LIKE IT.

Small 8vo. 2*s.* ; or in Paper Cover, 1*s.* 6*d.* each.

THE TEMPEST.	MUCH ADO ABOUT NOTHING.
MACBETH.	HAMLET.
KING LEAR.	CORIOLANUS. [*Preparing.*

Selections from Modern French Authors.

Edited, with English Notes and Introductory Notice, by **Henri Van Laun**, Master of the French Language and Literature at the Edinburgh Academy.

Crown 8vo. 3*s.* 6*d.* each.

I. HONORÉ DE BALZAC.   II. H. A. TAINE.

(*See Specimen Page No.* 15.)

The First German Book.

On the plan of " Henry's First Latin Book," and the " First French Book."

By **Thomas Kerchever Arnold**, M.A., and **J. W. Frädersdorff**, Ph.D. of the Taylor Institution, Oxford.

Sixth Edition. 12mo. 5*s.* 6*d.* Key, 2*s.* 6*d.*

The First Hebrew Book.

On the plan of "Henry's First Latin Book."

By **Thomas Kerchever Arnold**, M.A.

Third Edition. 12mo. 7*s.* 6*d.* Key, 3*s.* 6*d.*

AND AT OXFORD AND CAMBRIDGE

A Theory of Harmony.

Founded on the Tempered Scale. With Questions and Exercises for the Use of Students.

By **John Stainer**, Mus. Doc., M.A., Magd. Coll., Oxon, Organist to St. Paul's Cathedral.

Second Edition, Royal 8vo.   7s. 6d.

OPINIONS OF THE PRESS.

"There is much ingenuity in Dr. Stainer's method, and he has the gift of conveying his ideas in concise terms."—*Athenæum.*

"A work of this kind from the pen of so sound and liberal-minded a musician as Dr. Stainer must be valuable and interesting . . . . To the student perplexed and chained down by the multitudinous rules of the old theorists, we cannot give better comfort than to advise him to read forthwith Dr. Stainer's ingenious and thoughtful book."—*Choir.*

"With such works as Dr. Stainer's at command, cheap, concise, and comparatively simple, a knowledge of the theory of music, or 'thorough bass,' ought to be insisted on by every conscientious professor of the art."—*John Bull.*

"It is, moreover, the first work of its class that needs no apology for its introduction, as it is really much needed, especially by teachers, who would fail without the aid of its principles to account for many of the effects in modern music, used in direct opposition to the teaching of the schools. It is difficult, if not impossible, to give a more elaborate description of a book destined to effect an entire change in musical teaching without entering into details that could not but prove uninteresting to the general reader, while to the musician and amateur the possession of the book itself is recommended as a valuable confirmation of ideas that exist to a large extent in the minds of every one who has ever thought about music, and who desires to see established a more uniform basis of study. The great and leading characteristic of the work is its logical reasoning and definitions, a character not possessed by any previous book on the subject, and for this Dr. Stainer's theory is certain to gain ground, and be the means of opening an easy and pleasant path in a road hitherto beset with the thorns and briars of perplexing technicalities."—*Morning Post.*

" . . . Passing on through the explanation of the various discords, the derivation and treatment of which spring logically from his premises, Dr. Stainer gives us some very able remarks upon pedal points (a subject but imperfectly handled in most theoretical works), and expresses himself with remarkable clearness in describing modulation. We can scarcely doubt that even those who dissent from many of the author's views will read his treatise both with pleasure and profit."—*Musical Times.*

www.ingramcontent.com/pod-product-compliance
Lightning Source LLC
Chambersburg PA
CBHW030824270326
41928CB00007B/882